THE SCIENTIFIC STUDY OF THE OLD TESTAMENT

ITS PRINCIPAL RESULTS, AND THEIR BEARING UPON RELIGIOUS INSTRUCTION

BY

Dr RUDOLF KITTEL

PROFESSOR AT THE UNIVERSITY OF LEIPZIG, GERMANY

TRANSLATED BY

J. CALEB HUGHES, M.A., Ph.D.

With Eleven Plates and Sketches in the Text

WILLIAMS & NORGATE
14 HENRIETTA STREET, COVENT GARDEN, LONDON
NEW YORK: G. P. PUTNAM'S SONS
1910

In the interest of creating a more extensive selection of rare historical book reprints, we have chosen to reproduce this title even though it may possibly have occasional imperfections such as missing and blurred pages, missing text, poor pictures, markings, dark backgrounds and other reproduction issues beyond our control. Because this work is culturally important, we have made it available as a part of our commitment to protecting, preserving and promoting the world's literature. Thank you for your understanding.

PREFACE

WHEN I was asked some months ago by the Ministry of Public Worship and Education for the Kingdom of Saxony whether I was willing to deliver a course of six lectures to elementary school teachers on the subject of the authentic results of Old Testament research, congratulating the authorities upon their readiness to arrange educational courses dealing with the results of theological science, I assured them that I regarded it as my obvious duty, in so important a matter, to place all my knowledge and experience at their disposal.

The reasons which induced the Government to make such a proposal need hardly be explained. The question of religious instruction in the schools, particularly in the elementary schools, had become a burning one all over Germany. We, in the Kingdom of Saxony, are reorganising our elementary school system. The almost unanimous demand of the teaching profession for some time past has been, that religious instruction should "harmonise with

the *authentic results* of scientific research."
The Government, to meet this demand, could
not do better than to invite the recognised
advocates of the scientific research in question
to declare the existence and extent of such
results. On account of its importance to
religious instruction in the elementary schools,
Biblical research naturally claimed the first
consideration.

Since the elementary school teachers are, in
virtue of their profession, religious instructors
also, it was but natural that the Government
should wish our lectures to be delivered to them.
As long as the elementary school authorities
regard the religious instruction of youth as
their most important task, and particularly
while they entrust this instruction throughout
the school to the teachers—as is done in Saxony,
differing in this respect from the other German
states,—it is certainly their duty to take care
that the teachers keep abreast with the advance
of religious thought. Religious knowledge, like
every other knowledge, in so far as it is related
to the exact sciences (like historical research,
natural science, etc.) is progressive. It is
subject to continual changes in its positive
conceptions, in its more perfect expressions or
its more suitable formulations. To observe this

progress and to keep in touch with it is the principal task of those whose vocation it is to instruct youth in the knowledge of religious matters.

These lectures are easily understood and do not require a knowledge of the Hebrew language. Originally they were not intended for publication, but merely to be delivered to about seventy teachers, successful as religious instructors in elementary schools (among them being three female teachers), who were summoned by the Government for this purpose. Whilst delivering them, at the local University College, towards the close of September 1909, my audience expressed a wish—which was repeated at the end of the course—to have the lectures published, and thus enable them to study them further, and at the same time give an opportunity to those teachers who were either unable to be present or had not been summoned, who nevertheless had evinced a keen interest in them, to read the lectures.

My chief objection against doing this was that I had not confined myself to notes, for the "discourses," although carefully prepared, are, strictly speaking, not "lectures." When, however, through the kindness of a few zealous hearers, a written report of each lecture was placed at my disposal, in response to this friendly participation I could not but feel that it was my duty to reconstruct the lectures for publication.

Naturally, these reports required a thorough revision, as well as to be supplemented from my own memory. It is to be hoped that those who heard the lectures will find them essentially reproduced in this book. I have arranged them in exactly the same form as they would be, if I had to deliver them again.

At the close of each lecture questions bearing on the subject were asked by those present. The answers to these often gave opportunities to further elucidate what had been said in the lecture. Thinking that they might occur to the reader, I have included in this book my answers to some of those questions which seem to be of special interest. Some of the sketches shown during the lectures are also included, and will probably be welcomed by the reader, as they were by the hearer.

May these lectures be found a useful contribution to the solution of the great and important problems which confront our state schools —and with them the German and Christian schools generally.

KITTEL.

LEIPZIG, *November* 1909.

CONTENTS

	PAGE
PREFACE	vii

I. RESULTS BASED UPON THE EXCAVATIONS

Introduction: What do we mean by authentic results?	1
Degrees of certainty	2
1. Assyrian-Babylonian parallels to the Biblical stories of antediluvian times . . .	9
(a) Creation and Fall	10
(b) The Deluge	16
(c) The antediluvian patriarchs . .	19
2. The Code of Hammurabi and the Mosaic law	25
(a) Significance of the Hammurabi Code	25
(b) Compared with that of Moses . .	28
(c) The formation of the Mosaic law (cf. II. 1)	37
3. Tell Amarna, Gezer, Taanach, Megiddo, and the ancient Canaanitish civilisation and religion	40
(a) The Amarna discovery and its significance	41
(b) The excavations in Palestine . .	43
(c) The civilisation and religion of ancient Canaan	50

CONTENTS

II. RESULTS BASED UPON LITERARY CRITICISM

	PAGE
1. The legal literature (*cf.* I. 2)	60
(*a*) Nature and importance of Pentateuch criticism	61
(*b*) A summary of its history; its principal schools	71
(*c*) Its abiding results and its future problems (the Deuteronomist, the Priestly Code, the Jahwist and the Elohist)	76
2. Nature and method of Hebrew historical writings	93
(*a*) The older form of the so-called historical books	94
(*b*) Their present form	99
(*c*) Their historical value	112
3. The peculiarity of the prophetical books	115
(*a*) The prophets as orators, poets, and writers (*cf.* III. 4)	116
(*b*) The present form of the prophetical books	121
4. The ancient Hebrew lyric, especially psalmody	125
(*a*) Profane and religious lyrics	125
(*b*) Age and formation of the latter (David, composer of psalms?)	128
(*c*) Exilic and post-exilic period: individual or community	139
(*d*) Religious significance: universal character	142

III. RESULTS BASED UPON HISTORICAL (RELIGIOUS AND GENERAL) RESEARCH

		PAGE
1. The so-called patriarchs	. . . .	149
(a) Various interpretations of their history		149
(b) The historical facts	. . .	157
2. Moses and the Israelites in Egypt	. .	164
(a) The desert tribes and the migration		164
(b) The figure of Moses	. . .	170
3. Idea of God, religion, and morality among the early Israelites	. . . .	176
(a) Israel's relation to the Canaanites and its significance	. . .	176
(b) The popular religion (influenced by Canaanitish customs)	. . .	179
(c) The true religion	. . . .	187
(d) The moral standpoint of this period		193
4. The great prophets of Israel (cf. II. 3)	.	200
(a) The moral and religious condition of Israel and its political relation to Assyria at the time of their appearance	. . . . .	202
(b) The ethical monotheism and its consequences	. . . .	214
(c) The peculiarity of prophetic thought		221
(d) The ecstasy of the prophet and his relation to the object	. . .	225
5. Israel's hope for the future	. . .	235
(a) Its contents (the idea of a Messiah)		239
(b) Its age and historical development	.	242

CONTENTS

APPENDIX: SOME OF THE DISCUSSIONS AT THE CLOSE OF THE LECTURES

		PAGE
On I. 1.	(1) "Sacred legends"?	256
	(2) The story of the Creation and natural science	262
	(3) Application in the schools	269
On I. 2.	Hammurabi and Moses	274
On II. 1–4.	(1) Babylonian and Biblical penitential psalms	277
	(2) Literary criticism and revelation	281
On III. 1–3.	Application in the schools	283
	(*a*) Imperfect moral conceptions	284
	(*b*) Subject-matter of uncertain historical value	289
INDEX		294

LIST OF ILLUSTRATIONS

Hammurabi and the Sun-God . . . *Frontispiece*	
	PAGE
Massebahs at Gezer	32
Sacred Tree in Modern Palestine	40
A Section through the Hill of the Town of Lachis, in Palestine	44
The Great Rock Altar of Zorah (Ṣa'ra) . . .	48
Section of the Town Wall of Megiddo . . .	49
Small Images of Astarte from Gezer . . .	52
Image of Astarte recovered from the Ruins of Gezer	53
Urn containing the Corpse of a Child immured in the Wall of the Northern Citadel of Megiddo .	55
Child's Grave in the Town Wall of Megiddo . .	56
The Great Rock Altar of Zorah (Ṣa'ra) . . .	56
Rock Altar at Megiddo with Cup-marks . . .	57
The Stone of Marmita, showing the Cup-marks .	58
Astarte from Taanach	64

LIST OF ILLUSTRATIONS

	PAGE
Letter of King Abdichiba of Jerusalem to Amenophis IV.	64
Clay Tablet from Taanach	72
Small Bēs Idol from Taanach	72
A Specimen from the St Petersburg Manuscript of the Prophets, A.D. 916 (Hosea iii. 4)	77
The Great Altar of Baalbek	80
The Northern Block of the Rock Altar of Megiddo	88
Dolmen from the country east of the Jordan	96
Image of the God Ramman (Hadad) from er-Rummāne	96
The Royal Seal of King Jeroboam of Israel	104

The Scientific Study of the Old Testament

I

RESULTS BASED UPON THE EXCAVATIONS

BEFORE we begin to discuss the most important authentic results of modern Old Testa-

ERRATA.

Page 22, line 6 from bottom, *for* Enmiduranki *read* Enmeduranki.

Page 22, line 5 from bottom, *for* Mehushael *read* Methushael.

Page 47, line 4 from top, *read* Plate VII., page 72.

Page 49, line 5 from bottom, and page 76 Note, *for* Plate IX. *read* Plate XI.

Page 52, fig. 3, *for* or perhaps *read* scarcely.

Page 160, *for* 1430 *read* 1450.

LIST OF ILLUSTRATIONS

	PAGE
Letter of King Abdichiba of Jerusalem to Amenophis IV.	64
Clay Tablet from Taanach	72
Small Bēs Idol from Taanach	72
A Specimen from the St Petersburg Manuscript of the Prophets, A.D. 916 (Hosea iii. 4)	77
The Great Altar of Baalbek	80
The Northern Block of the Rock Altar of Megiddo	88
Dolmen from the country east of the Jordan	96
Image of the God Ramman (Hadad) from er-Rummāne	96
The Royal Seal of King Jeroboam of Israel	104

The Scientific Study of the Old Testament

I

RESULTS BASED UPON THE EXCAVATIONS

BEFORE we begin to discuss the most important authentic results of modern Old Testament research, it is perhaps advisable to consider a not unimportant question, the significance of which, I fear, is not fully apprehended by many people who are interested in the advance of thought in the fields of Old Testament study. The question is: *What exactly do we mean by authentic results?* What idea does this expression convey to our minds?

The question is not concerned with concrete facts, such as the historicity of this or that event. We shall consider those matters later. Here we confine ourselves to the abstract question of scientific method, viz. in what sense may we expect authentic results in Biblical, particularly Old Testament, research? Do these results possess absolute or only relative certainty? Are all those results which we ourselves are convinced to be, in a general sense, authentic, to be regarded as absolutely certain; or are there degrees of certainty which we, to be strict, must carefully distinguish between?

The latter proposition is certainly the correct one to make.

A certainty of the *first degree* is based upon documentary evidence, in so far as it deserves this name in its strictest meaning, whether found in the Bible or in inscriptions, clay tablets and papyri, etc., and in so far as they themselves give irrefutable information (I make this restriction because even an excellent and, taken generally, a thoroughly credible record can contain information and expressions which are not clear, at least are no longer intelligible to us to-day).

From a document of this kind we can obtain a certainty of the first degree, assured facts and abiding results in the general historical sense.

Besides this certainty we also have one of

the *second* degree. There are documents which, although otherwise excellent, are not entirely free from ambiguity, or have come down to us in fragments, essential parts having been lost. When we have such a document, the need for the interpretation of doubtful passages and the completing of the whole, supplementing the missing fragments from other sources, and thus connecting it with what is already known, compels us to introduce some element of subjectivity and to rely upon our own individual consideration of what we regard as probabilities.

Obviously, results obtained in this way cannot be so trustworthy as in the first case. Instead of real historical truth we possess now but a likely probability, a probability which to the compiler, and perhaps to competent critics as well, may be deemed equivalent to a certainty. So that the critics feel justified in speaking of it as an "authentic result," though, strictly speaking, it is only a likely probability, which has the support of well-known scholars, but is liable to be overthrown by further research. It is therefore a certainty of the second degree.

The example cited is only one of many. If the document itself is not of the first kind, but only of the second, *e.g.* is not the work of the principal characters mentioned in it or of their contemporaries, but is the product of a later period than that reflected in the document, then it obviously can give us only a certainty of the second degree. Or, if the document itself is of the first kind, but is used to explain earlier events than those mentioned in it, we can describe such inferences as absolute certainties only when their conclusions, as such, are legitimate and decisive. In every other case they are but certainties of the second or even of the third degree.

There is also a certainty of the *third* degree. Besides documents of the first and second classes, we find records of the third class which belong, relatively speaking, to a period far remote from the events which they describe, but which are, on the whole, well informed thereof and contain valuable matter for consideration. And in addition to conclusive inferences, or such as may be regarded as very probable, which are inferred from facts, there are others of a higher degree of probability, of a very high degree of probability down to degrees of more or less reliable possibility. Much of what belongs to this classification bears the stamp of subjectivity and depends largely upon the individual convictions of the investigator himself. It is here that the indispensable *hypothesis, i.e.* a presupposition based upon something that is already known, has its place, which is used in all scientific research (Biblical and otherwise) when a certainty of the first degree is not at our disposal.

In the use and exploitation of the documents, the power of discrimination, imagination, and intuition naturally plays a leading part. In this way the hypothesis is formed. To condemn this practice would be folly; it is indispensable, and is everywhere, if kept within certain limits, a valuable scientific expedient. But it obviously can only give us a certainty of the third degree, or, under favourable conditions, of the second. However, by means of it we can, under certain circumstances, attain an assured result in the wider sense of the term. There are hypotheses—the Copernican theory is only a hypothesis!—which, in the course of time, have attained so high a degree of probability that they are regarded as absolute facts, and are applied by science as though they were axioms. This is a shortened form of procedure, a simplified use of language which is perfectly intelligible to the initiated, but rather dangerous when used by the masses. Notwithstanding this fact, public speakers and writers make use of it even when addressing popular assemblies, although it would be more correct to differentiate between what is really authentic and what is based upon hypotheses, because every hypothesis has not attained the rank of the Copernican. In Biblical science there are, besides those which are universally accepted, assumptions which are confidently upheld only by their proposer and his narrow circle of followers, and, in addition to those which are the abiding property of the science, there are others which have had or will have but a short existence.

It will be seen, therefore, how essential it is, when the authentic results of Old Testament criticism are under consideration, to consider first of all the question as to what is the nature of the scientific certainty in this particular connection. It is only when this question has been satisfactorily answered that the ground is sufficiently prepared for further advance. It shows also how easy it is in this as in every other branch of science, when addressing the public, to speak generally of "authentic results" when really the certainty is not always of the same degree. When an investigator infers likely probabilities from what is already known, he himself may be convinced that he is dealing with genuine conclusions, whilst others may hesitate to accept them as such. When such is really the case, the hypothetical character of the conclusions ought to be emphasised. But even when such is not the case, the difference between real certainty and merely subjective certainty of conclusions must not be overlooked.

In these lectures I shall regard it as my special task to distinguish between abiding facts and the conclusions and suppositions deduced from them; also between what is accepted by the majority of scholars and my own personal opinions.

It would be quite interesting here to discuss the question of educational method and to consider how far (the condition of affairs being as described) the results of Biblical—more particularly of Old Testament — research may be regarded as subjects of religious instruction in the elementary schools. I must here, however, confine myself to my special subject and communicate to you the results themselves, limiting myself to the remark that certainties of the first degree (in so far as the subject in question may be said to possess them) must, of necessity, be the implicit property of the schools; however, certainties of the second and even of the third degree cannot be wholly excluded, if the teacher is able to distinguish between the different degrees. Quite a different question, and belonging more to that of specific class subjects, is: Under what circumstances, and particularly at what age, have the pupils a right to results of this kind?

Proceeding now to give an account of the latest results of Old Testament research, I intend to limit myself to the principal facts, classifying the subject-matter under three main divisions, and selecting therefrom what seems to be of special importance. Of course this classification does not exhaust all the subject-matter at our disposal, but it will not be difficult for anyone to proceed by analogy to conclusions on allied subjects, or, with the aid of the list of literature found at the end of this book, to attain further knowledge upon the subject. The three divisions referred to are results based upon *the excavations*, upon *literary criticism*, and upon *general and religious historical investigations*.

Results based upon the Excavations

In this field of research several late discoveries have been made which have marvellously helped us to a clearer understanding of the Old Testament.

1. *Assyrian-Babylonian Parallels to the Biblical Stories of the Antediluvian Period*

We shall first of all make a few general remarks upon these parallels and their importance in the understanding of the Biblical stories. Much of what I shall say is probably already known to you. The questions at issue have for many years past been widely discussed, public interest having been aroused by the so-called Bible-Babel controversy which followed the publication of Professor Delitzsch's book. For all that, we cannot omit my remarks from these lectures, but I shall confine myself to the principal facts, more especially to those of fundamental importance. I shall not consider the numerous corroborations, elucidations, additions, and interpolations to the Biblical narratives of the period of the Kings, which are to be found in the Assyrian cuneiform inscriptions. These are of little importance for our purpose.

We shall begin with the narratives of the Creation and the Fall. As you probably all know, we find narratives describing the creation of the world not only in the Bible but in the records of a number of other ancient civilised nations. These of necessity demand a comparison with the Biblical. But, with the exception of the Babylonian narrative, not one of them deserves to be called a parallel. The Babylonian is found in several redactions, which we shall consider together.

The essence of the narrative is that, at the beginning, there were no deities, but only a liquid mass. This mass or chaos is mythically represented as being composed of Ocean (Apsu) and Sea (Tiâmat). From these two the gods were formed. The gods decide to bring order into the disordered mass, *i.e.* to create a world. The representatives of Chaos try to prevent this and rebel. Thus the creation resolves itself into a mighty *combat* between the gods and the elements and forces in the world, more particularly between Marduk, the god of the rising sun and of creation, and Tiâmat, which is represented as a mighty dragon. Marduk overcomes the dragon and cleaves it in half; from one half he makes the firmament, and from the other the earth. Afterwards he created the heavenly bodies and caused the sun and the moon to shine. Then came the plants and animals, and lastly, man.

When we compare this Babylonian myth with the Biblical narrative, we find unmistakable *points of resemblance.* The point of departure in both is Chaos ("The earth," *i.e.* the world, "was waste and void"; see Gen. i. 2). In both it is said that the original flood (Tiamât, Hebrew *tehôm*) was divided into the upper and lower waters. In both we find the same sequence of events—first the creation of the heavenly bodies, then of the plants and animals, and, lastly, of man; in both, the formula, "He saw that it was good," seems to play a definite rôle.

But along with these similarities we find essential *differences.* In the Biblical account, God Himself, the Unique and Spiritual, stands at the beginning of all things, exalted far above them all, and His first act is to create light. In the Babylonian narrative, which is throughout pantheistic in spirit, Chaos is the beginning of everything, out of which the gods were the first to be created. In the former narrative, God is before all else; in the latter, the deity must first come into being. The pagan pantheistic character of the Babylonian narrative becomes especially clear when we consider the position of Tiâmat. The ocean is thought to be animated; the dread of the sea and its opposition to earth are pictured as a dragon, and the whole creation of the world is thought of as a terrible combat between the deity and nature. By dint of great exertion only is the deity able to bring about the creation of eternal nature. The account of the creation of man also shows the antithesis. In the Biblical narrative man is created in the image of God, and He breathes into him the breath of life; in the Babylonian narrative one of the gods is decapitated, and from his blood, mixed with earth, man is fashioned. In short, in the latter we have polytheism, paganism, and natural religion; in the former, monotheism and a spiritual religion, which reaches its climax when it declares that God creates by merely giving expression to His will.

Although the differences are so great and far-reaching as to place the Biblical narrative in its spirit and contents far above the other, yet the *relation* between the two is so close that it needs some explanation. It is not enough to say that the coincidences are accidental. In some way or other, we must

ASSYRIAN-BABYLONIAN PARALLELS 13

assume that there was an original source, either an oral or a written one, from which both have been derived. More will be said upon this point later when we are discussing the narrative of the Deluge.

Here I shall only point out the abiding *religious superiority* of the Biblical story of the Creation. If it was desired to examine this narrative from every possible point of view, it would perhaps be necessary to take into account its relation to the conclusions of the natural sciences. But if we did that, we should go beyond the limits of our theme; all that we really require will be found in what follows.[1] The superiority of the Biblical narrative is seen in the following facts:— *First*, God Himself is the Creator; nature does not beget itself. The narrative protests in the most definite fashion against all manner of pantheism. *Secondly*, God creates without difficulty, without struggle. God and the universe are not antitheses. Thus the Bible strongly opposes dualism. *Thirdly*, God creates by the mere word of command. The process of creating and the Creator are represented as purely spiritual. *Fourthly*, in the Creation, especially that of man, God reveals His

[1] See further on p. 262.

nature as power, wisdom, and love. Man is His image.

We have no Babylonian parallel to the Biblical narrative of the *Fall*. We need hardly consider the cylinder-seal which, for some time past, has been erroneously interpreted as representing the Fall. We can only say that the idea of man's original state of blissful felicity, often described as the Golden Age, is common to many nations of antiquity. Similarly the thought that man forfeited this happiness through his own fault. The idea that the serpent, represented as a power inimical to man and thoroughly evil, had a share in effecting this, is also to be found; also the conception of the tree of life and many others. But all these are isolated fragments; a connected narrative which we could call a parallel to the Biblical story, has not yet been discovered.

The best example for the purpose of comparison is the Babylonian Adapa myth. But this story deals with only one item in the Biblical narrative, and that in a somewhat peculiar manner. A god-created man, Adapa (= Adam ?), lost the immortality destined for him, because he refused (p. 15) to partake of the bread and water of life which one deity intended for him, that he might thereby become immortal (at the instigation of another god). For this reason Adapa was not permitted to remain in Heaven, but was compelled to return to the earth.

At one point a decided resemblance to the Biblical narrative is undeniable, *i.e.* where the attempt is made to explain man's mortality. Both narratives strike the same keynote: man was originally intended to be immortal. This was to be effected by eating the food of life. But he forfeited this privilege, and henceforth must dwell upon the earth as a mortal, afflicted with every evil. But the resemblance between them is a very remote one, which simply proves that they have been derived from a common tradition, nothing more. The very great difference between the two is far more striking than the resemblance, and with it the strength of the moral and monotheistic disposition of Israel over and above the polytheistic mythology of Babylon.

So much may be said upon this subject as the result of the excavations. But what we have said does not exhaust all the problems relating to this narrative and that of the Creation. The solution of the other problems cannot, however, be regarded as authenticated conclusions, certainly not among those based upon the results of excavation, and their popularity depends largely upon the position of their proposer—without accusing the latter of being arbitrary and careless. My own opinion will be found briefly expressed at the end of this chapter.[1]

Much clearer is the parallel to the narrative of the *Deluge*. The Biblical account is well known to all. The Babylonian version is found in the famous epic of Gilgamesh. The epic is written upon twelve tablets, and narrates the adventures of King Gilgamesh and his efforts to obtain eternal life. One episode of this ancient poem, which takes us back to a period prior to 2000 B.C., found on the eleventh tablet, describes the Deluge. This, like the Biblical narrative, tells of a pious man, here called Utnapishtin (also Xisuthros), whom the deity intends to save, and who, for that purpose, is commanded to build a ship, into which he takes all kinds of animals. After the waters of the flood have receded, he sends forth first a dove, then a swallow, and lastly a raven.

One cannot fail to note the wonderful harmony which exists between the two narratives. But here again the differences are at once obvious, and are greater and far more

[1] See further pp. 89, 256 ff., 289 ff.

significant than the coincidences. The narrators take totally different points of view: one reflects an exalted monotheism; the other, polytheism with all its weaknesses and shortcomings. In the Babylonian narrative the gods themselves are terrified at the flood and flee to heaven, and there cower like whipped "dogs"; and when Noah offers the sacrifice, they collect around it "like flies." These examples offer sufficient proofs that even here, where the points of resemblance are prominent, we find in one a refining and recasting of the most exalted kind, but in the other confusion.

But how is the parallel to be explained? This question brings us back once more to the narrative of the Creation. It has often been maintained that the Jews became acquainted with Babylonian myths for the first time during the Exile, and that a Jewish priest appropriated them and remodelled them after his own fashion. Whatever may be said in other respects concerning the latest recension (the Priestly) of certain Old Testament narratives, it is highly improbable that Israel did not become acquainted with these myths prior to the Exile. One seizes, therefore, upon the possible alternative explanation, and assumes that they became known to Israel in the days of Omri and Ahab—at which time the political relations of Israel with Assyria were very close, and when Israel's conceptions were influenced by Babylonian thought. As long as the Amarna tablets were unknown, such a theory was quite feasible. But since we have become acquainted with these, and have learnt that even at the time of their composition—the fifteenth century B.C.—Babylonian mythology was read and studied in Canaan, this theory may also be regarded as superseded. Since the early Canaanites knew some of these myths before Israel became a people — how they became acquainted with them we shall explain later,—everything points to the fact that the Babylonian version of the Creation and the Deluge' became known to the Israelites, at the latest, soon after their settlement in Canaan, *i.e.* in the period of the Judges.

It is quite possible that Israel became acquainted with these myths in this manner, and that, under the influence of prophetical ideals, they were remodelled and gradually attained the form in which we now find them. This view has the support of many scholars, but personally I am unwilling to accept it, at least as far as the narrative of the Deluge is concerned. We can hardly gainsay the

Biblical tradition according to which many of the later Israelites derive their origin from the Far East. If this tradition is true, and if even in antiquity these narratives of the Creation and the Deluge were current among the nations of the East, it is highly probable that the nomad tribes from whom the Israelites were descended possessed a knowledge of these traditions in remote times, before they ever came into contact with the Canaanites.

If we accept the view—and it is favoured by the majority of scholars—that the tradition of the Deluge is founded upon some great historical flood which inundated large tracts of country, we can quite easily conceive that both the Biblical and Babylonian narratives rest upon common reminiscences—not confined to these two peoples—which at an early period were augmented by legendary matter, after which each was developed independently. The similarity between the two is too great to deny that they existed together for some time, but the difference between them is also too great to deny that they afterwards developed independently of one another.

Finally, a few words concerning the *antediluvian patriarchs*. In Gen. v. we find a list of ten patriarchs from Adam to Noah.

20 SCIENCE AND THE OLD TESTAMENT

The list belongs to the Priestly code (P)—a designation which we will explain later.[1] In another place, namely, in the Jahwistic (J) version of the antediluvian history, we find fragments of two other genealogical tables—a short one from Adam to Enosh, and a longer one from Adam through Cain to Lamech (the father of Noah). Examining these fragments closely, we find that they are related and are really *one list*, and are the Jahwistic parallel to the Priestly table.

A further examination of these parallels, due regard being paid to the meanings of the Hebrew names in both, as well as to certain slight variations in their form, gives us convincing proofs that the two tables, the Priestly and the Jahwistic, are based upon *one and the same* original. To understand how this is possible, we must, for the present, assume that (No. 4) Cain and Kenan are but variants of the same name, likewise (No. 6) Irad and Jared, and (No. 8) Methushael and Methuselah. There remains only one difference, viz. that Enoch is the fifth in the one list, but seventh in the other, whilst Mahalalel of P (No. 5) appears in J as Mehujael (No. 7). Compare the two lists.

[1] For this sign, as well as J, see p. 73.

The meanings of Nos. 1–3 are identical in both tables. Adam and Enosh both mean "man," Seth probably means "sprout." If, therefore, Cain is in the one list referred to as the son of Enosh (= man), and in the other as the son of Adam (= man), he is in both cases distinguished as the son of the first man, which further supports the fundamental unity of the tables.

The fact that the Babylonians also possess a tradition of ten antediluvian men, who are called by them kings, further supports the assumption of a common tradition.

It is true that we know of the Babylonian tradition only on the authority of Berosus,[1] but since he has been proved reliable in other cases, we can safely accept his authority here as well. I shall only cite three of the names which he mentions:—No. 3, Amēlu, which in English means "man"; No. 7, Evedoranchusor, to give the Babylonian form of the word Enmiduranki, is the name of a favourite of the deity, who enjoyed special intercourse with the gods. There is therefore no doubt but that he is, if not in name, the Enoch of the Bible. The same can be said of Xisuthros, the Babylonian Noah.

[1] Strictly speaking, this is not a result of "excavation"; but it is better referred to here than anywhere else.

So that in Babylon we find an ancient genealogical table which, despite differences in details, furnishes a distinct parallel to that found in the Bible. I think we can claim this to be an authentic conclusion, although opinions differ in the interpretation of details. We may at least maintain the following conclusions: *first*, that the names and tables in Genesis have not been invented arbitrarily, as has sometimes been thought, but are based upon very ancient traditions, which were current in the Orient; *secondly*, that the Biblical lists, differing as they do from one another in details, cannot, without further proofs, be regarded as records which give a true historical account.

The relation between the three lists can be seen at a glance from the following tables:—

	Gen. v. (P).	Gen. iv. 25 f. (J).	Gen. iv. 17 f. (J).	Babylonian.
1.	Adam	Adam	Adam	
2.	Seth	Seth		
3.	Enosh	Enosh		Amēlu
4.	Kenan		Cain	
5.	Mahalalel		Enoch	
6.	Jared		Irad	
7.	Enoch		Mehujael	Enmiduranki
8.	Methuselah		Mehushael	
9.	Lamech		Lamech	
10.	Noah			Xisuthros

Let us *summarise* our results. We are able to prove beyond dispute that parallels

ASSYRIAN-BABYLONIAN PARALLELS

to important narratives of antediluvian times exist outside the Bible. These parallels present a remarkable agreement, even in details, with the Biblical version, even though the latter shows signs of an independent development. This fact, along with the other characteristics [1] of the Biblical stories of primitive times—concerning which but little can be said whilst we are discussing the results of the excavations,—leads us to conclude that the narratives in their present form *cannot* be regarded as *records* in the strictest meaning of the term. Nor are they legends or myths in the usual sense of the words. Rather are they partly the product of a childlike, naïve age, partly the result of the meditations of great thinkers deeply imbued with the spirit of prophetic religious ideas. Thus the most important of these stories, without being historical on all points, but rather adorned in many parts with legends and myths, appear — not in their details but in their great principles—as true facts of the most exalted and permanent worth.

The story of the *Deluge* tells of a great flood in primitive times which sorely afflicted man; the story of the *Creation* bears witness

[1] See p. 260.

to the eternally true fact that the wise creative will of the one spiritual God called the world into being; whilst the story of the *Fall* tells us that once, in the far-off past, when created beings became conscious for the first time that they were men, and afterwards that they were sinners, the soul passed through the same experiences as those reflected in the narrative; it tells us in poetic language that the first revolt of the human will against the Divine caused an irreparable *flaw* in our nature, and that there was a moment in the life of men when they became aware of sin and the consequent fearful estrangement from God. Everywhere where men are conscious of the seriousness of sin and of evil, it must also be clear to them that primitive men—however else they were constituted and whatever their further past may have been—did not pass dreaming and playing into a consciousness of sin, but that the transition was accompanied by a severe shock and a deep fall. That in the widest sense is the historical value of the narrative, although it is blended with legendary details and myths.

2. *The Code of Hammurabi and the Mosaic Law*

I presume that you all know that in the year 1901-2, during the French excavations on the site of the ancient Persian capital, Susa, a large diorite block, inscribed with cuneiform characters, was brought to light. The inscription proved to be a copy of the laws issued by the Babylonian king Hammurabi, about 2000 B.C. How this Babylonian record found its way into ancient Persia is of minor interest to us. It is enough to say that the site of the discovery was at one time a part of the ancient Elamite empire, and that the block, which no doubt was looked upon as a valuable sacred relic—in form it resembles a stone pillar, a kind of massebah, and on the upper part has a picture of the sun-god, who apparently is dictating the code to the king —was stolen on the occasion of a raid and removed to this place (see frontispiece, Plate I.).

More important to us is the question of the *significance* of this remarkable monument to Babylonian and particularly to Biblical research. Its importance in this respect cannot be too highly estimated. There were laws in Babylonia before the time of Hammurabi.

But the manner in which this king promulgated a code which embraces almost every phase of life, and so made it possible for his empire to attain the highest possible degree of fairness in deciding almost every important affair, may be regarded as the work of a genius. This respect is in no way minimised because of the imperfections found in the laws—for what code is without its imperfections? Without doubt, this code, like every other which strives to attain fairness, was of incalculable benefit to Hammurabi's empire. It was, as we can prove to be the case, copied over and over again, and in this way was disseminated among the various provinces of the empire.

Now Palestine, especially the northern part, was from the earliest times subject to Babylonian rule. Whether this overlordship was exercised in the days of Hammurabi or not, we cannot say, but that it was is quite probable, considering the great significance and power of this king. We can declare with certainty that Palestine was under the influence of Babylonian civilisation, and that this influence continued for centuries later throughout the whole of Syria, especially in the north. It is therefore by no means improbable that in the time of Hammurabi justice was administered in Syria (which was part of the Babylonian empire) in accordance with this code. It is no less probable that, after the political severance of Syria from Babylon, the former adopted this code and made it the basis of its own legislation. Just as, several centuries later, when Palestine and Syria were in name and reality subject to Egypt, we find Babylonian writings and myths current in these countries, so also, we may presume, was the Babylonian code—whether preserved in writing or only orally—known and practised in these countries during the Amarna period and earlier. For the direct practical necessity, intensified by the extensive commerce with the East, would have compelled them to adopt these laws and to put them into practice.

To what extent they were adopted can be estimated from the Biblical narratives, apart from the Law as such. Compare the well-known excerpt from the Biblical history of Abraham with the following paragraph (§ 146) of the Code of Hammurabi :—" If a man takes a wife and she gives a maid to her husband and the maid bears children, then that maid has made herself equal to her mistress; because she has borne children, her mistress shall not sell her for money; she shall put a mark upon her and count her among her maidservants." From this we may conclude at least that at the time when the story of Abraham originated—whenever that may have been—Babylonian laws were known in Israel.

Hence arises the question, What influence had the Code of Hammurabi (CH) upon the legislation of Israel? That the Israelites possessed legal definitions and practices not retained in our present copy of the law is apparent from the example referred to above, but we shall not pursue this subject. Far more important here is the law as expressed in the Pentateuch, more particularly as found in the Book of the Covenant of Exodus xx.–xxxv. and certain chapters of Deuteronomy. If we compare these chapters with the Code of Hammurabi, we cannot be blind to the fact that a remarkable similarity exists between them. It is sufficient for our purpose to point out a few examples.

First of all let us compare the general formula which is common to the individual laws of CH and to many of those found in the Book of the Covenant: "If any one does so and so, then so and so shall he be treated." But further, let us compare the following :—

CH.	Exodus.
§ 196 f. If a man hath caused the loss of another's eye, then someone shall cause his eye to be lost. If he hath broken another man's limb, then one shall break his limb.	xxi. 22 f. If any mischief follow, then thou shalt give life for life, eye for eye, tooth for tooth, hand for hand, foot for foot. . . .
§ 200. If one hath made the tooth of a man who is his equal to fall out, then one shall make his tooth fall out.	
§§ 199, 201. If he hath caused the loss of the eye of a man's servant or hath broken the limb of a man's servant, then shall he pay half his price. If he hath caused the loss of the tooth of a freed slave, then shall he pay one-third of a mina of silver.	xxi. 26 f. If a man smite the eye of his servant or of his maid and destroy it, then he shall let him go for his eye's sake. If he smite out his manservant's tooth or his maidservant's tooth, then shall he let him go for his tooth's sake.
§ 250. If a savage ox in his charge hath gored a man and caused him to die, then that case hath no remedy (as recompense).	xxi. 28. And if an ox gore a man or a woman that they die . . . the owner of the ox shall be quit.
§ 251. If, however, the goring ox hath made known his vice that he gores, and the owner hath not blunted his horns, hath not secured the ox, and this ox gores and slays a freeborn man, then his owner shall pay one-half a mina of silver.	xxi. 29. But if the ox were wont to gore in time past, and it hath been testified to its owner, and he hath not kept him in, but that he hath killed a man or a woman, then shall the ox be stoned and his owner also shall be put to death.
§ 252. If a man's servant,	xxi. 32. If the ox gore a

CH.

the owner shall pay one-third of a mina of silver.

§ 125. If a man hath placed anything on deposit and where he gave it something hath been lost ... then the owner of the house (where the deposit was made) shall make good what has been lost, and then shall seek out and recover it from the thief.

§ 124. If a man hath handed over before witnesses to a man silver or gold or anything on deposit, and he hath disputed with him, then that man shall be called to account, and whatever he hath disputed, he shall make good twice over.

§ 126. If a man, although he hath lost nothing of his, asserts, "I have lost something belonging to me" ... he shall estimate his (reputed) loss before God. Afterwards (when his deception against God hath been proved) he must give double of what he hath claimed.

Exodus.

manservant or a maidservant, then shall he give unto their master thirty shekels of silver, and the ox shall be stoned.

xxii. 7. If a man shall deliver unto his neighbour money or stuff to keep, and it be stolen out of the man's house, if the thief be found, he shall pay double.

xxii. 9. For every matter of trespass, whether it be for ox, for ass, for sheep, for raiment, or for any manner of lost thing, whereof one saith, "This is it," the cause of both parties shall come before God; he whom God shall condemn shall pay double unto his neighbour as recompense.

The question which proposes itself here again is how these striking similarities are to be explained, or, in other words, what conclusions must we come to concerning the origin of the Biblical laws?

As far as the Mosaic Code in general is concerned, I must refer the reader to what will be said later upon this subject. Here I will limit myself to the so-called Book of the Covenant, which, together with the Decalogue, is claimed to be the oldest part of the Law. Of late the opinion has been advanced with increasing confidence that this code (BC), like all the other legislative writings of the Israelites, belongs to a relatively *late* period, but formerly it was regarded as Mosaic, or at least as belonging to the period of the Exodus. It is claimed that in it are to be found traces of the period following the appearance of the first great prophets, according to some critics, of the time towards the end of the pre-exilic period, in the reign of Manasseh. Many have accepted this opinion as so conclusive a result that they have adopted it as an abiding fact, so that it is small wonder that this assumption, together with the general one that all Israelitic legislation originated at a time later than the prophets, became an article of popular belief.

We must definitely—and the sooner the better—break with this opinion. It has its origin in the time and method of regarding the Old Testament from a purely literary point of view, and as though it were derived from purely Israelitic sources; the chief exponent of the method being Wellhausen, of whom we shall have a little to say later on. Since the excavations have considerably widened our field of vision, and have made us familiar with periods which even a few decades ago were still considered as *terra incognita*, our attitude towards this question has undergone a complete change. We know now that, many centuries before Moses, there existed in a civilised country, having many affinities with Canaan, a code of laws which has many parallels with the Book of the Covenant; we know also that Palestine, before and in the days of Moses, was largely under the intellectual influence of the country where the above-mentioned laws were formulated; we know too that in those days the relations between Babylonia and Palestine were very friendly. All these facts are easily authenticated. Further, we can show it to be highly probable that, before and during Moses' time, justice was administered in Canaan upon the

PLATE II.

Massebahs at Gezer. (Reproduced from Kittel's *Studien z. heb. Archäol. usw.*, after the photograph by Dr G. Rothstein.)

[*To face p.* 32.

basis of the Codex Hammurabi, for how otherwise does the narrator of Abraham's history assume that the patriarch's action is in accordance with a good Babylonian principle of justice?

From all these facts we are justified in concluding that Moses, when he was looking for a system of legislation for his people during their march towards Canaan, or the Israelites themselves, after their settlement in Canaan, feeling the need of legislative principles suitable to the conditions of life in that country, found in Canaan itself a living law at their disposal which they could adopt and which was closely related to the ancient Code of Hammurabi. This relation was not such that the one was a simple copy or a mere imitation of the other, but that a special code had been formulated in Canaan, framed on the lines of the gifted work of Hammurabi and having many laws in common with it which were suitable to the country and its peculiar circumstances and requirements.

If we can show it to be probable that the Israelitic Book of the Covenant is better explained as having its origin in the conditions of life during the early, even the earliest, Israelitic period in Canaan than in those of a later date, then we have satisfied all the preliminary conditions to the understanding of this code and its relation to its Babylonian-Canaanitish model, and we have now only to consider more closely the course of the formation of the Book of the Covenant.

We will first of all consider the question of the *age of the Code*. The supposition that it is the product of a late period is true of only a few passages, where—as is easily seen—it has been subjected to a later revision. Excepting these passages, such a claim can be regarded only as the result of a preconceived opinion, which was supported by the idea, which is now proved to be utterly false, that the art of *writing* was unknown to the Israelites in the days of Moses. We shall have more to say concerning this conception later on. With the fall of this premise, fails, of course, the conclusion deduced from it.

When we consider the individual laws of the Book of the Covenant, we find that it presumes simple pastoral conditions of life. It speaks of agriculture, cattle-breeding, garden and vine culture, laws relating to marriage, slavery, persons and things, of the blood vengeance, "eye for eye," and the like, reflecting the conditions of Israelitic life soon after their settlement in Canaan, as we know them from other sources. No mention is made of a king or of a central government. The tribal chief of Exodus xxii. 28 must not be regarded as a national ruler, much less the king of Israel. The conditions are those of the pre-kingly period, when every tribe, district, or clan existed in and for itself. In the Code we find much that harmonises with primitive and particularly pre-Israelitic conditions of life, and the retention of these is easily understood if the Code was framed or was adopted at an early date, but unintelligible if we must date its origin at a later period.

A relic of these primitive times is found in the law pertaining to the altar in Exodus xx. 25, which is closely related to the Book of the Covenant, where it is stated that the stones of the altar might be hewn with a "sword." This peculiar expression is understood only as belonging to a period when the difference between sword, knife, and chisel was unknown, *i.e.* to the relatively early Stone Age. At the time of the invasion of the Israelites the Canaanites had advanced beyond this stage of development, and stood at the end of the Stone Age, using, besides flints, bronze to a large extent, and, in some cases, iron. This would also be the position of the Israelites at the time of their immigration into Canaan, unless they had become acquainted with the use of iron earlier in Egypt or in the ferruginous peninsula of Sinai. The expression referred to must therefore have originated at a much earlier period. Another proof of the primitive conditions reflected in the Book of the Covenant is the precept in Exodus xxii. 29 f., that every male *first-born* belongs to Jahwe. We know that the Israelites, if not always, at least very early in their history, mitigated this command by paying a ransom, *i.e.* the substitution of an animal for the child (*cf.* Exodus xxxiv. 20). Whoever, in Israel, read the words of this command, probably as a rule interpreted and practised it in its milder signification. But the fact that the law was accepted into the Code without any alleviation is sufficient proof that it once existed and was practised in accordance with the letter. And we know that the Canaanites practised the horrible custom of child-sacrifice. We can safely maintain, therefore, that in this case, as in the previous one, we have the remnant of an ancient pre-Israelitic religious precept, which was adopted by the Israelites into their law.

How then do we explain the *origin* of the Book of the Covenant? Everything that we are able to ascertain about this book points to the fact that it was composed in the early period of Israel's settlement in Canaan, and for the conditions of life in that country. In form and contents it has many affinities with the legislation of ancient Babylon as practised among the Canaanites. The book is not formulated to legislate for the Israelites of the nomadic period, and does not meet the requirements of their sojourn in the wilderness. Since we know from other sources that Moses was a lawgiver in Israel (to which fact we shall refer again later), there is no reason why we should not connect this early Israelitic code with him, either in the sense that Moses himself, by reason of his people's immigration into Canaan, altered the laws which already existed in the country, or that—as is more probable—men of the early post-Mosaic period, influenced by the motives and principles of Moses, created this code upon the basis of the laws practised in Canaan. Like all the codes of ancient Israel, this was probably originally intended to be the law of a definite sanctuary (like Bethel or Siloh).

Whilst we are discussing the origin of the

Israelitic code and its connection with Moses, we might add a few words about the *Decalogue* (the so-called Ten Commandments or "words"). These are found in Exodus xx. 1–17, in close connection with the Book of the Covenant. Of late years, principally under the influence of Wellhausen—the idea was first mooted by Goethe, who perhaps did not mean it to be seriously adopted,—the attempt has been made to maintain as a dogma of Old Testament criticism that the real and original Decalogue is not found in Exodus xx. 1–17, but in Exodus xxxiv. 11–26. With this assumption came the other one that we have two distinct and separate Decalogues, neither of which can be traced back to Moses with any degree of certainty.

Notwithstanding this, I regard this claim as everything but an "authentic conclusion" of our research, and must warn you against accepting it. Exodus xxxiv. 11–26 has never been a Decalogue, nor does it claim to be such. It is only a careless recension of *v.* 28 which gives it this semblance, which led Goethe, and many others after him, astray. With certainty it can be maintained, first, that this passage cannot be reduced to ten commandments without omitting parts of the text. As the passage stands it contains twelve or thirteen precepts. Secondly, it is quite certain that the passage is nothing other than a parallel to the Book of the Covenant itself, or is a part of such a work. If one belonged to one sanctuary, perhaps Siloh or Bethel, then the other belonged to another, such as Mispah or Ramah.

If this theory of two Decalogues resolves itself into nothing, we have only to consider the ten commandments of Exodus xx. There is no reason why these should not be ascribed to Moses. The evidence which from time to time has been brought forward to refute this claim, *e.g.* the prohibition to worship Jahwe in the form of an image, is by no means conclusive. In favour of the existence of a collection of such short fundamental laws in early Israel is the fact that the ancient Egyptians also had such a collection in their Book of the Dead. The prohibition of images is explained by the contrast which exists between the Israelitic religion and many other religions, and also by the fact that images were seldom found in the official religion of Canaan. On the other hand, the prohibition against covetousness should not be interpreted as possessing the same force as Jesus gives it when He says, "Every one that looketh at a woman to covet her, etc." That is the deeper signification which Jesus gave to the prohibition, and the meaning *we* must give to it. But to the people of Moses, covetousness meant conspiring to gain possession of another man's property.

Summarising, we may come to this conclusion:—Much relating to the beginnings of Israelitic legislation, which of late years has come to be accepted as authentic conclusions, does not deserve to be so called, or, to say the least, only with great reservations. We may regard it as a fact that the ancient Canaanites were from the earliest times quite familiar with laws and legislation. The traditions that Moses gave his people fundamental laws, and that the so-called Book of the Covenant belongs to the early Israelitic period, find strong support in this fact, and they are further strengthened by the constitution of these laws and by what we know of Moses from other sources (see below).

3. *Tel-el-Amarna.—Gezer, Taanach, Megiddo, and the Civilisation and Religion of Ancient Canaan*

Much of what has been said will be made clearer by what we shall learn under this heading. A true description of the conditions of

PLATE III.

Sacred Tree in Modern Palestine. (Photograph by Prof. Dalman.)

[*To face p.* 40.

ancient Palestine before the invasion of the Israelites under Joshua has only lately been vouchsafed to us through the successful excavations in Palestine itself.

A promising beginning in this respect was made by the discovery at Tel-el-Amarna, in Central Egypt. At this place, in the winter of 1887-8, the really epoch-making discovery was made, that, in the desert sands of Egypt, the political correspondence of the Pharaohs Amenophis III. and IV. with their vassals, the Palestinian princes and the kings of the Near East as far as Babylon, had been preserved until modern times.

The correspondence was written upon clay tablets, one of which is reproduced on Plate VI. (following p. 64). All at once this discovery let in a flood of light upon the political as well as upon other conditions of life in Palestine at the time *c.* 1400 B.C.

From these tablets it was seen that the whole of Syria was at that time subject to Egyptian rule, but in such a way that this supremacy of Egypt was only a nominal one. The numerous petty kings, town and district princes really ruled Syria, and they had made themselves practically independent of Egypt, but always carried on a vain struggle for supremacy with their neighbours.

Their wars consisted of petty feuds and raids, the losers generally appealing to the overlord in Egypt. However, the supremacy of Egypt in Syria was so far decayed that the Pharaoh was not in a position to consider seriously these complaints and prayers for assistance, and certain nomadic robber tribes—comparable to the Hebrews and probably closely related to them—more and more openly and persistently overran the land.

No less significant than the description of the political conditions of Palestine found upon these tablets, is the fact that this correspondence, although carried on between the Egyptian Pharaoh and, for the most part, Canaanitish and neighbouring princes, is in the language and *writing of Babylon*. From this we see not only that writing was familiar to the inhabitants of those lands which soon afterwards were to pass into the hands of the Israelites, but also how powerful and far-reaching Babylonian influence must have been, and was. In spite of many centuries of Egyptian rule, these lands had not been able to cast off the influence of Babylonian civilisation since the time when Babylon was supreme in Syria. Doubtless the land had for a long time been strongly influenced by Egypt—this influence being more powerful towards the south,—yet that was not enough to supplant or to overcome the other to the extent that the Egyptian language and method of writing should be used. We have already referred to the *importance* of this fact in the dissemination of Babylonian thought, legislation, and civilisation in Palestine. Here we shall only remind you of the oft-mentioned and important fact that the discovery of the Babylonian Adapa myth is connected with the finding of the Amarna tablets, so that through the latter we are assured that the Babylonian myths were current and studied in Palestine. At Taanach we find further evidence in support of this.

This brings us to *Palestine* and to a consideration of the modern excavations in that country.

Without mentioning the praiseworthy efforts of earlier explorers, I shall only consider the work of the last few years. Not far from Jerusalem, on the old road to Joppa, where the mountains descend towards the coast plains, lies the hill upon which are the ruins of *Gezer*. That is the town which was once conquered by the Pharaoh, when Solomon sought the hand of his daughter in marriage, that he might give it to his son-in-law as a dowry (1 Kings ix. 16 f.). It must therefore have been a town of some strategical importance, and must have been an ancient town which was able to resist the Israelites for a long time. The results of

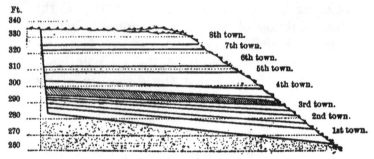

FIG. 1.—A Section through the Hill of the Town of Lachis, in Palestine. (After the report on the English excavations.)

the English excavations there confirm all this. At Gezer it was found—as had been found to be the case on the site of Troy and other places—that a number of towns or settlements had been built in strata one upon the other, each succeeding town being built over the ruins of the previous one, each being in its turn destroyed through some catastrophe or other. The same was also found to be the case at Taanach and Megiddo. By penetrating down to the bottom of these mounds we are able to trace their history back to the time of the first human settlement. We cannot, of course, ascertain the exact age of this settlement, but we can safely say that it lies far back in prehistoric times. (*Cf.* the figure on page 44. It shows clearly the various strata of towns built at different times.)

One of the most important discoveries for our subject was made at Gezer, when the excavators brought to light a complete massebah sanctuary, the like of which had never been found before. By massebahs we mean stone pillars of various sizes which, in olden times, were but roughly hewn columns; but, apart from the crude manner in which they have been fashioned and their stunted size, they may be compared with the Egyptian obelisks. They served as symbols, often perhaps were regarded as seats, of the deity, and, it seems, were considered by the Canaanites to be necessary adjuncts to a complete place of worship. They were adopted afterwards by the Israelites, especially into the popular religion, and are on that account often mentioned in the Old Testament. Luther, in his translation, calls them "monuments," thereby following the customary interpretation of the significance of these sacred stones as symbols, especially as memorial stones, as was done in course of time by the Israelites themselves. (See Plate II., following p. 32.)

Of perhaps still greater importance are the excavations made at *Taanach* by Professor Sellin, formerly of Vienna, now of Rostock. This place is situated a few miles from the better-known town of Megiddo, on the southern edge of the famous plain of Jezreel, which, watered by the Kishon, is the granary of Palestine, and was as such held for a long time in the hands of the Canaanites. The plain was protected by fortified towns, such as Taanach and Megiddo, which had been built upon the hills overlooking it. These two towns are mentioned in the Song of Deborah: "Then fought the kings of Canaan in Taanach by the waters of Megiddo" (Judges v. 19). The most important discovery at Taanach was that of the *archives* of the local king, Ishtarwashur, which were found by Sellin, hidden in a clay receptacle. The archives were written upon clay tablets, in the Babylonian language and script, similar to those found at Tel-el-Amarna, and doubtless belonging to the same period. They contain the correspondence of the king with the neighbouring vassal princes. The contents prove conclusively the correctness of what we said earlier concerning the Amarna discovery. (See Plate VI., following p. 64. It shows the extraordinary resemblance in form and condition which exists between these tablets and those found at Amarna.)

It has been attempted to minimise the importance of the Amarna tablets by saying that they deal with diplomatic affairs only; the fact that they were written in Babylonian proves little more than that Babylonian civilisation had strongly influenced Western Syria; that Babylonian was the diplomatic language of that period just as French is to-day, and that therefore no far-reaching conclusions can be inferred from the tablets. But the discovery at Taanach has removed this objection. The letters of Ishtarwashur are not political, and were not written to foreigners in Babylonia or Egypt, but were sent to his near neighbours, dwelling only a few hours' journey away, and deal with the most commonplace matters, concerning cattle, soldiers, servants, and the like. This means that not only matters pertaining to international commerce and trade, but also everyday affairs, were discussed in the Babylonian language, and were to a very great extent influenced by Babylonian ideals and civilisation.

The excavations at *Megiddo* were carried out by the German Palestine Exploration Society. The geographical position has been already described. It played an important part as a Canaanitish and—from the time of Solomon—as an Israelitic stronghold. Here, as at Taanach and elsewhere, the hill was penetrated down to the natural rock, and the excavators found, as at Gezer, unmistakable relics of the earliest human settlement and worship of God in Palestine. The magnificent town wall with its faultless glacis and ramparts, which the excavators discovered, proves to us—what has been especially confirmed by the discoveries at Jericho—that these inhabitants of ancient Palestine were past masters in the art of building towns and fortresses, and were with reason feared by the Israelites. A number of citadels, palaces, and temple buildings complete the picture which is here, as at Taanach and Megiddo, reproduced by means of the numerous individual discoveries, which include all kinds of sculpture, besides utensils and ornaments in stone, bronze, and iron, and in some cases in gold. The most beautiful find at Megiddo

PLATE IV.

The Great Rock Altar of Zorah (Ṣaʻra). (Photograph by Lohmann.)

[*To face p.* 48.

TEL-EL-AMARNA AND PALESTINE 49

is the splendid seal of Shema, "servant" of Jeroboam. It is probably the state seal, which the minister or wezir of the king—who was probably Jeroboam II.—carried in the name

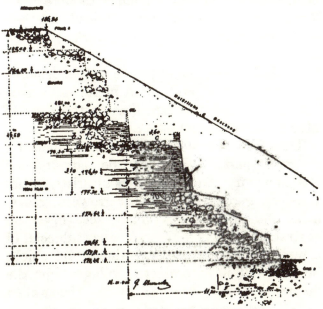

FIG. 2.—Section of the Town Wall of Megiddo. (By Schumacher.)

of his master (see fig. 2 and Plate IX., following p. 104).

The sloping line in the sketch represents the side of the mound before the excavation was made. Having cleared away the earth to the depth of a few yards, the whole splendid fortifications—they can hardly be imagined more perfect—were revealed. We can easily understand, therefore, how difficult it must have been for the invading Israelites to take these fortified towns, which were, indeed, in their way, masterpieces of the art of warfare at that time.

With the foregoing knowledge at our disposal, we are now in a position to picture the *conditions* in which the Israelites of the time of Moses found Canaan.

The Canaanites of that period had, for the most part, ceased to be nomads and had settled down. They were agriculturists, cattle-breeders, gardeners, and vine-growers, tradesmen and merchants. They recognised no central authority, but were the subjects of a number of independent princes and chiefs. Some dwelt in unprotected villages, but the majority betook themselves to the walled towns, which were situated generally upon hills, and which they knew well how to fortify and to defend. They were skilled in many arts and crafts, which they practised for the most part after foreign patterns, but also, in a less perfect manner, in their own way. Assyrian-Babylonian models are found, especially in the south, side by side with Egyptian. Besides these are to be found, especially in pottery, early Cyprian and Cretan influences. They made their utensils (as well as from clay) and their weapons from stone and bronze, and they had begun to use iron for purposes of war. For documents, contracts, legal affairs, and the more important correspondence they used the Babylonian language and script. This language must therefore have been known and used among the upper classes. The mass of the people, of course, spoke their own, the Canaanitish language, which, however, did not possess a script.

In their religion they worshipped the Baal or, better, the local Baalim in the manner found described in the Old Testament (see below), and at altars with which were associated the stone pillars or massebahs described above, and the asherahs. These latter were symbols of Astarte, the female deity associated with Baal. He represented the fertility of the male, and she the fecundity of the female. They were also connected with the sun and the moon. Besides these two they worshipped other deities such as the Aramaic weather-god, Hadad or Ramman, and others. For private worship and sorcery (by means of

52 SCIENCE AND THE OLD TESTAMENT

talismans, etc.), they used a number of small idols, which, for the most part, were of foreign origin, either Babylonian, like the nude figure of the goddess of fecundity, Ishtar, or Egyptian, like Isis and Bes. Some of these images were imported, but others were made in the country after foreign models. They were hardly ever used in public worship. (See figs. 3 and 4 and Plates VI. and X., following pp. 64 and 96 respectively.)

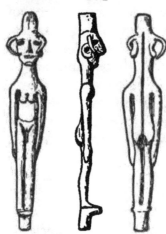

FIG. 3.—Small Images of Astarte from Gezer. Horned, or perhaps fitted with eyelets for the purpose of hanging as amulets.

Characteristic features of their public worship are that it was practised in the open air upon *rising ground* (the so-called high places), and for the most part without any temple buildings, and also that generally no *idols* were used. It must be regarded as being more than chance that, although the excavations have brought to light numerous Babylonian and Egyptian images which were used in private worship,

TEL-EL-AMARNA AND PALESTINE 53

not a single one was found which could be proved to have been intended for public worship, least of all an idol of the principal Canaanitish deities, Baal and Astarte. The only cases which in this respect deserve serious consideration are a few bull images, which, however, like the bull or the so-called golden calf of Bethel or that of the wilderness, did not represent Baal or Hadad, but were mere symbols of deity. Really, they refer neither to Baal nor to Jahwe, but to the Aramaic weather-god Hadad (see Plate X., following p. 96). The significance of this fact in determining the antiquity of the demand for a religion free from idolatry in Israel—which

FIG. 4.—Image of Astarte recovered from the Ruins of Gezer. Cast in clay after an Egyptian pattern, 3 inches high. (From the report of the English excavators.)

is reflected in the chief commandment in the Decalogue—is at once clear.

Of the religious customs of the Canaanites we shall mention only that of *child-sacrifice*, because this practice can be proved directly from the excavations. The discoveries at Gezer and Megiddo conclusively confirm the statements of the Old Testament with reference to the burying of children in walls. Probably the sites of houses were regarded as being the property of the deity, and, to recompense the latter for the injury sustained by erecting a house, a sacrifice was immured in the foundation (see figs. 5 and 6). The manner in which the corpse is buried in the masonry itself (see fig. 5) and not in the foundation soil, that is, is really *immured*, can hardly be explained otherwise than as a sacrifice to the god.

But the Canaanites were probably not the earliest *inhabitants* of the Holy Land, and their worship was not the oldest form in which the deity had been worshipped in this land. On the surface of the earth we find relics of an apparently pre-Semitic civilisation which point to a very ancient pre-Canaanitish population of the land, whilst below the surface, in caves and upon shelves of rock, revealed to us by the work of the excavators, similar indications have been found. Perhaps the numerous dolmens, *i.e.* stone monuments, regarded as the dwelling-places of the dead,

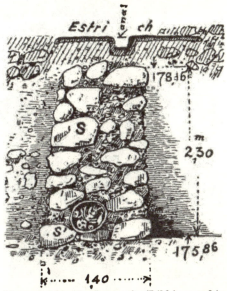

Fig. 5.—Urn containing the Corpse of a Child immured in the Wall of the Northern Citadel of Megiddo. (Drawn by Schumacher.)

which are so commonly found in the country east of the Jordan, as well as the menhirs and cromlechs, *i.e.* stone pillars of a peculiar kind and sacred circles of stone, are also the remains of this primitive population.

It is at least worth noticing that they are

56 SCIENCE AND THE OLD TESTAMENT

not, like the massebahs, confined to Semitic and Mediterranean lands, but are found in many other parts of the globe, from India in the east

Fig. 6.—Child's Grave in the Town Wall of Megiddo.
(Drawn by Schumacher.)

to Brittany, Ireland, and Scandinavia in the west. It is not impossible, therefore, that in prehistoric times Aryan tribes, in the course of their migrations, settled for a time in Palestine

PLATE V.

The Great Rock Altar of Zorah (Ṣa'ra). (Photograph by Lohmann.)

[*To face p.* 56.

TEL-EL-AMARNA AND PALESTINE 57

and left behind them these witnesses of their occupation of the land (Plate X., following p. 96).

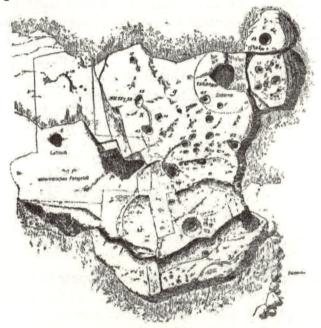

FIG. 7.—Rock Altar at Megiddo with Cup-marks.
(Drawn by Schumacher.)

During the past few years, as the result of the excavations at Gezer and Megiddo, our attention has been drawn to certain *religious sites* which point to a primitive religion belonging to a period long prior to the Baal-worship of the Canaanites—in fact, to the time of the first human settlement in Palestine, far away back in antiquity.

These primitive places of worship seem to have been boulders and flat, open, rocky ledges, with perhaps caves beneath the latter. Peculiar *round holes*—often called cup-marks —seem to have been used to receive the gifts

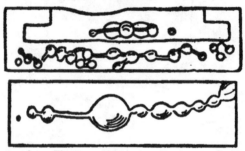

FIGS. 8 and 9.—The Stone of Marmita, showing the Cup-marks. (Drawn by Lohmann.)

of the worshippers. The gods appear to have been conceived as infernal spirits, having their habitations under the earth, in the numerous caves and clefts which abound in that very rugged, mountainous country. (See figs. 7–9 and Plate IX., following p. 88, as well as the peculiar holes seen in the altar represented on Plate V., following p. 56.)

A full description of all the details would take us far away from our subject, so we must be satisfied here with making the statement that the results of the Palestinian excavations confirm, enrich, and often complete the picture given to us by the Bible of Canaan in the days of Moses and Joshua. Further, that they give us important knowledge concerning the later periods; but, above all, that they have given us a new and unexpected vision of early Canaan, and have made known to us the fact that the country had already attained a high state of civilisation when the Israelites invaded it under the leadership of Joshua.

II

RESULTS BASED UPON LITERARY CRITICISM

In the foregoing chapter we endeavoured to give an account of those results of scientific research which are based upon the latest excavations, or at least have been obtained mainly through such means. But Old Testament research is not confined to these. Nor did it wait for the excavators—who have only begun operations during the last few years—to give it a start, but had proceeded on other lines and had developed independently of the excavations. An important field of research, which had long remained untouched, was that of *literary criticism, i.e.* the examination of the Old Testament as the literature of the ancient Hebrews.

There is no necessity that anyone should be astonished, least of all frightened, that this examination of the Biblical works should be called "criticism." There can be no historical research without criticism. Criticism means separating, distinguishing—the separation of the truth of traditional conceptions and theories from the false, and then to establish the former as historical. Without criticism in this sense it is impossible to prove what is historically true or false. That the employment of the critical method occasionally leads us to a premature denial of true traditions, that criticism can be precipitate and lead to untenable conclusions, does not lessen the necessity for using the method. These rather only warn us to be circumspect and cautious in its application.

When we consider this subject more closely we find it necessary to classify the most important Biblical works. We find in the Old Testament legal, historical, prophetical, and poetical literature. This fourfold classification includes all branches of extant Israelitic writings. We will now consider—

1. *The Legal Literature*

This we find in the so-called five books of Moses, which were known collectively to the Greeks as the Pentateuch. The criticism of these books is therefore called Pentateuch

62 SCIENCE AND THE OLD TESTAMENT

criticism (or, since the book of Joshua is closely connected with these five preceding books, one often hears the terms Hexateuch (six books) and Hexateuch criticism mentioned). If I referred to this portion of the Old Testament briefly as "the Law" (Heb. *tōrāh*), as is done in the Jewish synagogues, I would only be describing its main character. As will be seen later, the Pentateuch contains, in addition to legal precepts and commands, also a large number of narratives and stories, which, however, are closely connected with the legal parts.

After the Pentateuch had for many centuries been regarded as the work of Moses, of late years this claim has been more and more disputed, and to-day we can accept as a fact that the whole book at least, whatever may be said of parts of it, *cannot* be ascribed to Moses.

The most important arguments in favour of the latter view are the following:—It is nowhere definitely stated in the Pentateuch that Moses was the author. It is only stated of detached portions that Moses wrote them. These, however, in comparison with the whole work, are insignificant. The statements in Deuteronomy (xxxi. 9, 24 ; xxvii. 8 ; xxviii. 58, 61), granting that they are not later interpolations, did not originally refer either to the whole Pentateuch or to the whole of Deuteronomy, but probably only to a comparatively small book, out of which the book of Deuteronomy was later evolved. It is true that we often meet expressions, as "Jahwe spake to Moses," or "Jahwe commanded Moses," and the like, concerning the various laws, which may mean that the contents of the laws should be ascribed to Moses, but not that Moses wrote them.

The expression "law of Moses," which we so often meet in the later books, or even the expression "law book of Moses," must not be accepted as literally true, although it is not impossible that the writers themselves connected this code with Moses as its author. In the course of time it became an article of faith in the Jewish synagogue, whence it found its way into the later books of the Old Testament, that Moses had written the whole "law," that is, the whole Pentateuch. It was the custom of the later Jews to call the individual groups of their holy scriptures by popular names. Thus the Psalter was referred to as "David" or "the Book of David," because a large number of the psalms were ascribed to David; the books which we still call the "Books of Samuel" were so named because Samuel is the principal figure in the first book, although in the other parts no mention is made of him. In the same way the Pentateuch was ascribed to Moses, because he plays the leading part therein. The evidences which support this claim are found only in writings which are chronologically far removed from the days of Moses, so that they cannot be accepted as historical proofs of the fact itself, but only of the views of later Judaism upon this question.

The latter remark may be made concerning the few remarks found in the New Testament, where Jesus speaks of Moses as the author of a code of laws (John i. 45; v. 46). It did not occur to Jesus to instruct us concerning the circumstances under which the various books of the Old Testament were composed. When he spoke of the writings of Moses, he merely accepted the popular mode of expression, just as he spoke of the rising and setting of the sun, without proceeding to show—as was done by Copernicus—that such an expression is really incorrect. Just as little as the Evangelist, when he stated (Luke iv. 17 f.) that Jesus opened the book of the prophet Isaiah and read lxi. 1, intended to hinder us from recognising that these words did not emanate from the prophet Isaiah but

PLATE VI.

Astarte from Taanach
(⅔ natural size.)

Letter of King Abdichiba of
Jerusalem to Amenophis IV.

[*To face p.* 64.

from a prophet of the Babylonian exile, so little are we bound down with reference to the Pentateuch by such occasional statements. The same remark applies also to John v. 46, where the question concerns the contents of the five books rather than their composition.

Since we are unable to deduce any conclusions concerning the composition of the Pentateuch from its traditional names, we are forced back upon the *internal evidences, i.e.* we must infer the authorship and the date of the work from its contents.

A closer observation of these books proves conclusively that, in their present form, they are not the work of *one and the same person*. This fact is evidenced on all sides both in the historical and the legal parts. In the historical parts we find a large number of duplicate accounts of the same events. We find two narratives of the Creation (Gen. i. and ii. 4 ff.). The story of the Deluge is recounted in such a way that it is often repeated in order to relate anew certain incidents in the story (*cf.* Gen. vi. 5-8 with vi. 9-13, or viii. 20-22 with ix. 11-17, and others). Certain passages of the histories of Abraham and Jacob are related over and over again, some proper names are explained in various ways, etc. (*cf.* Gen. xxi.

31 with xxvi. 33 ; xxxii. 29 with xxxv. 10 ; xxviii. 18 f. with xxxv. 14 f.).

But duplicate accounts of the same events and the like are not conclusive proofs against the unity of the reporter. It is quite possible that the same narrator, either intentionally, to inculcate his teaching, or accidentally, as the result of literary mannerisms or personal weakness for repetition and diffusiveness, may occasionally repeat himself. But such an explanation is only admissible when the repetitions are really *only* repetitions. But if the duplicate narratives recount events from a totally different point of view, then the unity of authorship is obviously open to doubt. If, further, the differences in details are so great that they cannot belong to the same mind, then the unity of the author of both becomes an impossibility.

The second narrative of the *Creation* lets man be created first, and *afterwards* the animal world and the woman were created to serve the man (Gen. ii. 7, 8 f., 19, 21); but in the first narrative (Gen. i.) man is regarded as the crown of the creation, his creation following that of the animals and plants. Contrary to the geocentric—*i.e.* the earth as centre of the universe—point of view of the second chapter, the account in chapter i. is from a cosmo-

THE LAW

centric—*i.e.* regarding the universe as a whole —point of view. The parallel narratives of the *Deluge* differ from one another, in that in the one the flood lasts for a whole solar year, from the 17th day of the second month in one year until the 27th of the same month in the following year, *i.e.* one year (namely, a lunar year = 354) + 11 days, whilst in the other account it lasted only 7 + 40 + 7 + 7 + 7 = 68 days; also that in the one a pair of every species of animals are admitted into the ark, but in the other seven pairs of clean animals, *i.e.* such as were suitable for sacrifice. This latter difference is, of course, explained by the fact that the narrator of the one account does not accept the sacrificial worship of primitive times, whilst the other accepts it (*cf.* Gen. vii. 11; viii. 3–5, 13 f. with vii. 4, 10, 17; viii. 6, 10, 12, and further vii. 2 f. with vi. 19 f.; vii. 8 f., 14 f.).

We find the same differences in the histories of Joseph, Moses, and many others. In the story of Joseph we are told in one place that Joseph was given to Midianite, in another place to Ishmaelite, merchants; whilst in one account Reuben is said to be the leader of his brethren, in the other, Judah. There are many differences between the various accounts which we have of Moses in Exodus and elsewhere; but here I must content myself with drawing your attention to the following. Should anyone read through the account of the events at Sinai, and then try to answer the question as to how the narrator was able to describe the course of events, he will readily admit that it cannot be easily answered. It can only be explained by assuming a plurality of narratives which were compiled and revised by a later hand. One narrator would naturally have sought to relate the events in chronological order and continuity, and write his account from the same point of view, so that his readers would be able to follow the story from beginning to end. But in the history of Moses this is impossible. When we try to follow the course of events we at once see that the continuity of the narrative is again and again broken, and a new line of thought taken up. Moses ascends the mountain, then descends; he reascends and descends again, only to ascend again, etc. That is clearly not the original form of the narrative, and proves a plurality of chroniclers.[1]

[1] In Exodus xix. 3, Moses ascends the mountain; in xix. 14, he descends to the people; in xix. 20, he ascends; xix. 21, 25, he descends; xx. 21, ascends into the clouds; xxiv. 1, he stands upon the mountain; xxiv. 3, he descends to the people; xxiv. 9, he ascends; xxiv. 12 f., ascends

We may say that if we persist in regarding the narrative as the work of one man, much of it remains dark, and in some cases objectionable. But as soon as we decide to look upon it as the result of the compilation of a plurality of sources, much of what was obscure becomes clear.

What applies to the historical passages is true also of the *legal* parts. They also show a plurality of sources. We find injunctions concerning sacrifice, the festivals, the priests and Levites, and many other institutions, not once but several times; but they are such that they cannot have belonged to one and the same period of time, to the same stage of religious and social development. Examine the following examples. Exodus xx. 24

once more; xxiv. 18, he ascends a third time (to receive the law); xxxi. 7, 15, he descends; xxxii. 31, he goes to meet Jahwe (upon the mountain?); xxxiv. 2, 4, he ascends; xxxiv. 29, he descends. He then publishes the laws given to him upon the mountain, xxxiv.-xl. Later he receives laws in the tabernacle, Leviticus i.-iii., and later again (iv.-viii.), without mention being made where the laws were received, but, as it seems, not in the tabernacle, for in iv. 3 we are told that Moses is to proceed thither with the people. Then follow further laws of the same kind (Lev. xi.-xvi., xvii.-xxiv.), and in Lev. xxv. 1 we find Moses once more upon Sinai, and xxvi. 46, xxvii. 34 seem to imply that *all* the laws in the book of Leviticus were given upon Mount Sinai. The narrative is full of such contradictions.

permits an altar to be built in every place where Jahwe causes His name to be remembered, *i.e.* every place which He deems worthy for purposes of sacrifice. Deut. xii. 1 ff., on the contrary, declares emphatically that sacrifices can be made only at that place which Jahwe has chosen. Further, Exodus xxiii. 14 f., xxxiv. 28 assume three chief festivals which Israel is to celebrate annually by a pilgrimage to the sanctuary, the Passover, the feast of Weeks, and the feast of the Tabernacles. Lev. xxiii. and Num. xxviii. f. speak of five great annual festivals which obviously, at least as far as the sacrificial side is concerned, are celebrated at the sanctuary. The book of Deuteronomy, when it speaks of the priests, refers to them as the "Levitical priests," without making any hard and fast distinction between priests and Levites. Other parts of the Pentateuch, however, such as Num. iii. 5 ff., xviii. 1 ff., and others, distinguish between the priests, as the sons of Aaron and the rest of the Levites, whose position was a subordinate one, and their duties those of attendants to the priests at the altar. It is impossible to conceive that these fundamental differences should have been introduced at various periods during the lifetime of Moses, and the explanation that he gave one command at the commencement of the sojourn in the desert and substituted it by the other at a later period, is therefore unsatisfactory. For the differences are so fundamental that it is quite inconceivable that any abrogation of one law in favour of another by the man who issued the first could have taken place. Such discrepancies could only have originated in the course of time, through changes in the mode of life of the people and the presence of entirely different conditions and ideas.

The first to conceive the really epoch-making idea that the Pentateuch is a compilation of different records, which had at one time an independent existence, was, strange to say, a layman in the world of Biblical research, namely, Jean Astruc, physician-in-ordinary to his Majesty Louis XIV. of France (1753). His clever conclusion is now almost universally accepted, in spite of all that has justly or unjustly been brought against it. He observed that in the narratives of the book of Genesis—to which book he confined himself—the name of the Deity changed, in what seemed an arbitrary and inexplicable manner, from "God" (Heb. Elohîm) to "the Lord" (Heb. Jahwe), and *vice versa*, and he concluded that two independent *records* must have been compiled to form the present book. He therefore distinguished between an Elohist and a Jahwist document. These, of course, must have been compiled by a third as redactor (R). The fact that they (J and E) favoured two different religious ideals, and that on that account they must have lived at different periods and moved in different circles, strengthened Astruc's theory. A comparison between Exod. vi. 3 and Gen. iv. 26 illustrates the force of this argument. In the former passage we are told that prior to the days of Moses the patriarchs knew God only as the omnipotent One, but that His name, Jahwe, had not been revealed to them; but according to Gen. iv. 26, God was invoked in the name of Jahwe even in antediluvian times. Both these statements cannot be ascribed to the same person.

This theory of two records or "sources" was later developed by Ilgen (1798). He believed that he could perceive two separate sources within the Elohist document, an older and a younger. Later scholars recognised one of these Elohist sources as a priestly document or Priestly Code, and so we have a triad of narrative and legal writings, which the editor

PLATE VII.

Clay Tablet from Taanach.

Small Bēs Idol from Taanach. (Light green porcelain. After Sellin.)

[*To face p.* 72.

(R) compiled—a Jahwist (J), an Elohist (E), and a second Elohist which was also a Priestly Code (P or PC).

P begins with the Creation in Gen. i., narrates later on the story of the Deluge, and then very briefly the events which lead up to the great Levitical laws which we find in Exodus xxv.–xxxi. and xxxv.–xl., the whole of Leviticus, and a great part of Numbers. J, on the other hand, tells us the stories of the Creation and Paradise in Gen. ii. f., then of the Deluge and the tower of Babel; to him belong the beautiful and interesting narratives of Abraham, Jacob, and Joseph in Gen. xviii., xxiv., etc., whilst he shows but little interest in legislation. E is first introduced in Gen. xx., and then can be traced throughout the whole Pentateuch as a parallel to J. The legislative standpoint of E is found reflected in the Book of the Covenant (BC). In addition to this book and the great Priestly Code (P) we find other legal writings in Deuteronomy (D) and the so-called Law of Holiness (at one time an independent code, but later absorbed into P), Lev. xvii.–xxv. (H).

For a long time P, because its narratives introduced the Bible, was regarded as the oldest document, and it was claimed that

J, E, and D, or E, J, and D, respectively followed it. The theory which is often (not rightly, perhaps) called the Grafian hypothesis, after Karl Heinr. Graf, at one time professor at Meissen, soon disproved this. The Grafian theory did not become popular, however, until it was adopted by *Wellhausen* (1878), by whose name it was afterwards — wrongly — called, whilst the real authors were Edward Reuss of Strassburg, Vatke and George. The hypothesis is briefly this: that P, which had for so long a time been accepted as the fundamental and therefore the oldest document in the Pentateuch, is really the latest, and belongs probably to the exilic and post-exilic period; that is, is later than the destruction of Jerusalem and the Temple by Nebuchadnezzar.

After Wellhausen adopted and had forcefully restated it, the hypothesis was readily accepted; but it has never lacked opponents, who have asserted their opinions against some of its most important points, and have emphasised the weakness of Wellhausen's position. To-day, after thirty years have passed by, we can try to sum up the results of the controversy, and more impartially than in the days when the cry was, "For or against Wellhausen," to consider the right and wrong of this theory. We may, I think, without depreciating or exaggerating the benefits gained, make the following remark. Old Testament criticism owes more to Wellhausen than to any living man. But this theory of the Pentateuch as formulated by him has not proved itself to be tenable. The objections to it proffered by many scholars, among them being the writer of these lines, have been clearly justified.

We may ignore as unworthy of our notice the blustering of the over-sanguine, who speak of Wellhausen's theory as being *in extremis*, or already dead. They who most confidently say this are generally those who have contributed least towards the realisation of their hope. It is true that the tendency to regard all the Biblical texts as the product of exilic and post-exilic times, which prevailed some twenty years ago, and which, although distrusted by the more prudent scholars, was quite natural considering the position of Biblical research in those days, has, among a wide circle of investigators, given place to a sounder theory. At that time our sources were confined entirely to the Biblical records themselves. Although these documents could not make the theories propounded other than probabilities, they were accepted because we had only a few authorities outside the Old Testament to refute them. To-day, however, the limits of our science have been considerably enlarged. We now have at our disposal a number of facts formerly unknown, and they have justified the general point of view of the conservative thinkers of two decades ago.

These preliminary remarks bring us to the main question of the *authentic conclusions* and the future *problems* of Pentateuch criticism.

Speaking generally, we may say of all literary criticism, that we do not possess documents which contain "records" in the strict sense of the term. We have no direct proofs for the existence of the different sources, such as the Jahwist, the Elohist, and the Priestly. It is only when someone discovers a fragment of the Jahwist or Elohist writings in the original, or a reliable copy thereof on leather or papyrus,[1] that we shall possess such direct proofs. As long as this very remote

[1] The kind of writing which we would expect to find upon such a document may be seen on the seal of Shema which we have reproduced upon Plate XI. (p. 104). The script in which the present Bible was written is shown in fig. 10, which is reproduced from the oldest extant manuscript, viz. the great manuscript of the prophetic writings (date 916 A.D.), now at St Petersburg.

THE LAW

possibility is not realised, we must content ourselves with a *hypothesis*, that is, an assumption based upon observations and facts.

But the hypothesis or assumption which we shall make use of is one which is based upon

Fig. 10.—A Specimen from the St Petersburg Manuscript of the Prophets, A.D. 916 (Hosea iii. 4).

such well-founded observations, and which serves to elucidate so many problems which without it are difficult to interpret, that we may ascribe to it a high degree of probability, and claim it as an authentic result of Biblical research, in so far as any hypothesis which has survived the test of many decades may be regarded as an authentic result. If, contrary to our expectation, we meet facts which refute our hypothesis, we must, of course, consider them.

Among the authentic results of Pentateuch criticism the most important is the existence of several records, historical and legislative, from which the present Pentateuch has been compiled; further, that the chief sources of antediluvian as well as patriarchal and Mosaic histories are J, E, and P, and that J and E represent an older tradition than P—a conclusion which I had formed after studying Graf's exposition, long before it was proposed by Wellhausen. Of the legal writings, as we have already heard, the Book of the Covenant forms the oldest part and belongs to a very early period; then comes the book of Deuteronomy (D) and the Law of Holiness (H); whilst P, at least, taken as a whole, represents the latest addition to this class of literature. As another authentic conclusion, I maintain that J and E, in respect of their authorship, at least as regards their real authors, belong to the ninth and eighth centuries B.C. respectively.

Although most critics are ready to accept these conclusions, there still remains much diversity of opinion with respect to others.

In spite of all that has already been done, Pentateuch criticism has still many problems to solve. The question of the formation and authorship of D, and with it the question of the age of P, still awaits a satisfactory answer. Both questions are closely connected. Since Graf and Wellhausen, and others before them, it has been regarded as a fixed axiom that Deuteronomy is the fixed point from which the age of P could be determined, and that this Archimedean point should be fixed in the reign of King Josiah—more accurately, in the year 621 B.C. If P is in the main later than D, it follows naturally that the former was composed during the exilic or post-exilic period.

But it can be shown that Deuteronomy was neither composed in the days of Josiah, nor was it a fixed, complete unity. It is therefore not well adapted as a fixed point of departure for the determination of P. As this statement is an important one, I must ask your permission to explain it more fully.

In the second book of Kings, ch. xxii. f., we find a narrative which tells us that on the occasion of a complete restoration of the Temple, the high priest Hilkiah claimed to have found a law code in the Temple which he recognised at once as the law book of Moses, and which, after he had read it to the king, was soon afterwards made the basis of a far-reaching reform of religious worship. The most important reform was the abolition of the high places or local (country) sanctuaries in favour of the Temple at Jerusalem.

Does this narrative contain historical truth? This question must be answered in the affirmative. The account has probably undergone revision, but in the main it is intact and historical. But what code does it refer to? and how did it originate? It was for a long time held that the whole Pentateuch is meant. But the very fact that the book was read so often in a short time precludes the possibility of its being such a voluminous work as the Pentateuch, or even the parts thereof which deal with legislation. It must have been a comparatively small book. But still more decidedly in favour of its being the book of Deuteronomy, or some code closely resembling it, is the fact that the reforms appointed by King Josiah, in accordance with the contents of the newly discovered code, are based upon an innovation in which the lawgiver of Deuteronomy was closely interested, viz. the centralisation of worship in the capital and the aboli-

Plate VIII.

The Great Altar of Baalbek. (After Kittel's *Studien z. hebr. Archäol.*
From a photograph by the author.)

[*To face p.* 80.

tion of the local sanctuaries with their altars, massebahs, and asherahs.

But how did the book get into the Temple? How was it formed? It does not require much ingenuity to come to the conclusion that the whole affair was a hoax, a barefaced forgery. It is no wonder, therefore, that this has been conceived as the true explanation. The book is supposed to have been composed by Hilkiah, its "discoverer," or an intimate of his. At least, he is supposed to have known beforehand all about its history; he smuggled it into the Temple, and later "found" it without any difficulty, in order to influence the susceptible king and thus secure his assistance to carry out the decisive reforms commanded in the code.

This opinion, which I am sorry to find expressed again and again in modern publications, even in the latest issue (3rd) of Kautzsch's edition of the Bible, is certainly wrong. If Hilkiah, or anyone moving in his circle, were the author, the code would have been quite different from what it is. In it, it is stipulated (Deut. xviii. 6 f.) that the deposed local priests, because they were destitute, if they should come to the central sanctuary—which is the Temple at Jerusalem—should be permitted to sacrifice there and have a share of the sacrifice for themselves. Say that a code of laws were discovered in the Roman Catholic or, more precisely, in the Italian Church, according to which the country priests of the whole of Italy were to leave their churches and to come to Rome, and their sustenance, after the loss of their benefices, to be guaranteed from the income of the Vatican, more especially from the Peter's pence, which they would share in common with the priests of Rome. Is it probable that such a precept could have been commanded by the Vatican and the Pope?

The attitude of Hilkiah and his fellow-priests towards this code, which also gives us an idea as to what it would have been had it been formulated by them, is seen from 2 Kings xxiii. 8 f., where it is stated that when King Josiah sought to establish the reforms stipulated in the code, and to bring the local priests to Jerusalem, the Temple priests protested against it and hindered him. When we read again that the priests of the high places, although they came to Jerusalem, were not permitted to take part in the altar services, we are justified in reading between the lines and in assuming that the hierarchical views and the avarice of the aristocratic priesthood of the capital opposed the king's reforms. Thus we have conclusive proofs that Hilkiah cannot have been the author.

Nor is it possible that it was the work of any member of the Temple priesthood. It is far more probable that the author belonged to the humbler class of priests. Despite his moral and religious greatness and his very great spiritual significance, he was a man of lowly position, a genius of the type of Jeremiah, who was the son of a simple country priest, but was nevertheless a genius of the very highest order.

When was the book composed? To answer this question, it is first of all necessary to remember that the present D cannot possibly have been the book found in Josiah's reign. The latter is contained in Deuteronomy, but they are not one and the same. The book found in the Temple has been enlarged, the present D being the result of subsequent revisions. The book found by Hilkiah may have been composed in the days of Hezekiah, in whose reign the idea of centralising worship seems to have taken root. But it may be taken for granted that the book did not then receive its first form. The sanctuary at

Jerusalem, as probably every other important sanctuary, had its special ordinances from the earliest times, at least from the time of Solomon. They regulated the sacrificial and other religious customs and the behaviour of the worshippers. It is obvious that these sacred laws were, in course of time, restated, added to, and revised. Thus, in Hezekiah's day, the demand for a united worship was incorporated. Some of the commands, however, are very old, and seem to be based upon a code parallel to the Book of the Covenant, and the whole book was on that account ascribed to Moses.

In course of time this code, not without reason called *the* code by Hilkiah, disappeared, until it was discovered on the occasion of the restoration of the Temple.

Such discoveries are by no means uncommon. We occasionally find accounts, in ancient Egyptian records, of how the ancient rules of a sanctuary have been rediscovered after a lapse of centuries, whilst Origen tells of a similar find at Jericho. But to determine the true form of the older Deuteronomy, the one found by Hilkiah, as well as of the book based upon it, is the task of future research, for the questions are, so far, unanswered.

If it is shown, and I think it is, that our present D is not the product of one person, but is a compilation of various sources, it obviously follows that it does not merit the position allotted to it, viz. the norm whereby we may determine the age of the other documents, especially the *Priestly Code*. The idea of the centralisation of worship may still be referred to as a norm, but otherwise other independent signs must be sought for the determination of dates.

You must remember that neither P nor D represents a perfect fixed unity. P, like D, is the product of various editions in successive periods. Its legislation represents a many-sided ritual which must have taken many centuries to develop. The legislative and historical books which we refer to as P received their present form and many of their constituent parts during the exilic and the early post-exilic periods. In this respect the Graf-Wellhausen hypothesis is justified. But it is an exaggeration, and must on no account be accepted as an authentic conclusion, to ascribe the whole of P to exilic or post-exilic times. We cannot over-emphasise the fact that a great many parts of P, such as the so-called Law of Holiness (H) and the laws relating to sacrifices in Lev. i. ff., very probably belong to an *early* period.

There is nothing to support the opinion, which is so often confidently asserted, that these laws were first formulated after the fall of the state and the restoration was at hand. On the other hand, everything is in favour of the view that, as was the case among other nations, Israel had from the earliest times regulated its worship and matters pertaining thereto. And since we know that the art of writing was familiar to the priests, it is but natural to assume that these laws had been reduced to writing at an early date. The same remark applies to the historical passages of P. We need only recall what was said of the Creation story, to feel convinced that all the narrative parts of P are not to be regarded as late productions, even though some of them may be. Although I consider that Gen. i. in its present form may probably be ascribed to the time of the Exile, that does not exclude the existence of a much earlier form (or forms). Here again we have a wide field of research, which so far has not been satisfactorily investigated.

Our position with reference to the two older narratives, the *Jahwist* (J) and the *Elohist* (E), is somewhat similar, since the work of determining their authorship and date is far from being completed. Most of our scholars content themselves with classifying the verses and parts of verses which belong to J or E, and then stating that J speaks here, and E speaks there. But this process of separation becomes more and more subjective and uncertain the more it is applied to details and the less it supposes great independent streams of tradition. But the distinguishing between J and E is only the commencement of our work. What we want to know is, where did J and E find their material? whether they were copyists or not? but above all, how far can we regard them as individuals, as literary and religious personalities?

To prevent myself from being prolix, I shall here confine myself to a few suggestions as to where we should seek the solution of these problems.

We completely err if we—as is the general custom these days—regard J not as an individual but as a "school." As true as that he had followers, pupils, and sympathisers, and therefore that he had his school, is it that he was an individual of flesh and blood, indeed a very pronounced personality. In like manner those who regard him as a mere "collector of legends" fail to do justice by him, for he is not that. Rather is the Jahwist a collector of traditions, narrator and poet, philosopher and religious teacher of his nation.

As a collector he compiled the various traditions which were current in his day—indigenous as well as those of foreign origin. The Israelites found in the land of Canaan narratives which from antiquity were connected with some particular spots in the country. Such was the story of the formation of the Dead Sea and the destruction of Sodom and Gomorrah. This narrative has probably some connection with certain reminiscences of some terrible natural upheavals in ancient times which occurred long after the formation of the Dead Sea, but which caused its extension towards the south. Another narrative of this kind is that of Jacob's struggle with the Deity at Mahanaim (in the country east of the Jordan), which describes how the founder of the Israelitic race wrestled with God and at last compelled Him to bestow a blessing. Quite early, perhaps as early as the time of the collector, this story was interpreted symbolically as describing a mental struggle, Jacob wrestling with God in prayer. It is quite possible that without this symbolical interpretation it would never have

PLATE IX.

The Northern Block of the Rock Altar of Megiddo. (After Schumacher.)

[*To face p.* 88.

been handed down to us. But there is no doubt but that originally it was believed literally.

Many traditions, as we have already seen, were adopted by the Israelites under the influence of the early Babylonians. These were known to J in their original form, and were collected and recast by him. There are other traditions which seem to have their origin on the steppes of South Palestine and the Sinai peninsula. They are probably to be connected with natural phenomena peculiar to those parts, whence they were brought into Canaan by the Israelites, and there collected and elaborated by J. Such are some of the Mosaic stories, that of the burning bush, and the pillar of cloud and fire.

In all these instances J appears as a collector. But his work of compiling was not mechanical and slavish; he revised the traditions without, however, doing violence to them. Everywhere we find traces of his creative, poetical, and controlling hand, and note the piety and tolerance with which he treats religious ideas which reflect conceptions of God which had been superseded in his day. Boldly—fully conscious of his superiority to such notions—he represents God as descending to the earth, as walking through the garden of Eden and speaking with men as though He were a man. Everything is described so naturally and impartially that it was at one time believed—and perhaps is still believed by some—that he expressed his own opinions in the narratives, and that he was nothing else than a narrator of folk-lore.

How unjust such a conclusion is, is best seen where he appears as a narrator and not as a compiler. Here he reveals himself not only as a true *artist* and poet, possessing superior charm and freshness and an unrivalled descriptive faculty, but also as a *religious personality* of a very pronounced type. J the narrator does not conceive God as walking on the earth; His abode is in heaven, and He appears to men only in visions or through the medium of angelic messengers; He is not confined to any one place, but accompanies Jacob and Eliezer to Mesopotamia, Moses and the Israelites into the wilderness, smites Pharaoh in Egypt; in short, wherever the pious seeks and needs Him, there is He present with His mighty arm to aid and protect him. These differences help us to distinguish between the passages in which J himself speaks and those which he has merely adopted.

When he shows himself thus in his true colours, we clearly see that he is far more than a mere narrator or a sublime artist. Although his narratives are full of æsthetic charm, yet art is not the end he has in view. The charm which characterises his narratives is not an end in itself, but only the means to attain a higher goal. What he relates are not always mere stories; they are *philosophical* problems in the guise of narratives. He is nothing else than the philosopher and the religious and moral teacher of his nation. The vital questions which affect the human soul, such as: Why must man die? Why have sorrow and pain and sin ever come into the world? Why is man doomed to eat his bread in the sweat of his face? Why is woman compelled to purchase the happiest hour of her existence at the price of the severest pain? Why is it that men, who are descended from the same parents, are separated into nations with different languages, so that they do not understand each other? —these and many others are the questions which interest J and absorb his nature; and what he as a sage, the wisest among the wise men of his nation, deems to be the answer to them, he has recorded in his narratives.

What we find in J is not altogether his

own creation, still less the product of his imagination. He adopted the poems and legends which had been transmitted to his days and gave them a suitable setting. And what he found in the way of myths and narratives concerning the fatal serpent, the garden of Paradise, the tree and water of life, the tower of Babel, etc., he adopted as a foundation upon which to build up his ideas, or made use of them to support his conceptions. From this material, or rather what this suggested, this *incomparable* religious genius created a masterpiece among the profane as well as among the religious literature of all ages, which will be regarded as a gem among the products of the human intellect as long as true beauty and piety are cherished among men.

Whilst reflecting upon these vital questions, he rises above the dross of traditional mythology and he gives his people a higher conception of religion in a manner worthy of a *prophet*. This he is able to do because he has meditated deeply on the nature and existence of God—the God of Israel who is also our God —and because he referred the questions which inspired him to God Himself, and answered them in accordance with his idea of God and the moral commands which had their origin in Him. He thus creates a work—rather it was presented to him by God—in which, it is true, we find both myths and legends, but which, however, infinitely transcends these, and cannot be called either the one or the other. The only way to realise its true significance is to regard it as a kind of prophetic intuition, the work of a prophet, even a *prophetic revelation*.[1]

In what has been said we have taken for granted that J, even though his work may be ascribed to the time of the prophet Elijah, is based upon much older *sources*. The same may be said of E. Of course it would be extremely valuable to be able to determine these sources still more closely, especially in respect of their age. But as yet everything connected with these problems is in its infancy, scholars not yet having realised that we have here a field for research which demands special attention. We shall consider the subject further in our next chapter (pp. 97 f., 158).

2. *Nature and Method of Hebrew History Writing*

History, in the modern sense of the term, cannot be looked for in the Old Testament,

[1] See further pp. 256 ff.

at least only to a limited degree. The narrators of past events did not, as a rule, consider it their duty to criticise the historicity of the traditions which had been handed down to them, and to distinguish between what was true and what was false, to separate the legendary from the historical. If they did criticise at all, they only did so in the sense that they quietly ignored what seemed to be untrue. The finer differences between popular legends and strict history were unknown to most of them. Where they, or rather the compilers, do exercise criticism, it is, as we shall point out later, in a different sense. Therefore, what we find in the historical writings of the Old Testament, generally, is a compilation of narratives, describing the nation's past, its great men, and its religious traditions, which were current among the Israelites and had been gradually collected. What we have to do is to examine how far these narratives reflect the true course of events.

The Hebrew historical writings, as is the case in other literatures, have been developed from *ballads* and *epic poems*. The ancient Israelites must have been a music-loving people. Ordinary everyday experiences moved them to give expression to their feelings in poetry and song. Marriage and death, victory and pillage, harvest and vintage, festival and feast, were all celebrated in song. When the victorious general returned from the wars he was accompanied to his home by crowds who danced to the music of stringed instruments and songs. The great deeds of the nation's heroes were commemorated in songs, and thus the great ones of the past lived again in the memory of posterity, and their deeds endured for centuries.

It is said that, when Israel had crossed through the Red Sea, Aaron and Miriam celebrated their triumph in a song, the opening lines of which are found in Exodus xv. 21 :—

Sing ye to Jahwe, for He is highly exalted,
The horse and his rider hath He thrown into the sea.

When Deborah had won the battle which freed Israel from the power of the Canaanites, she is supposed to have commemorated her victory in that stirring song which bears her name, and which has made her and her act of deliverance immortal (see Judges v.). After the fall of Saul and Jonathan upon the battlefield on Mount Gilboa, David seized his harp and lamented over them in song (see 2 Sam. i. 17 ff.). This dirge affords a striking testimony to David's genius and magnanimity, and also to his unfortunate rival's fame. And when David himself returned from victory, the women of Israel sang this song in his honour :—

> Saul hath slain his thousands,
> But David his ten thousands (1 Sam. xxi. 11).

These examples show how popular the ballad must have been in ancient Israel. We certainly shall not be far wrong if we assume that the private and the wandering *minstrel* or *storyteller* was regarded as an indispensable member of society, and his position one of honour in Israel, as in the Orient of our days, where these men are everywhere found and their calling highly respected. At sacred festivals, in fairs and markets, at every meeting-place of men, on the open squares of the town, at caravansaries, at the table of the king, in the banquets of the great—in fact, everywhere and always where an opportunity was offered, the minstrel and storyteller was sure to be found, singing the praises of former heroes, narrating the history of the sacred sanctuary, giving an account of its fortunes, how it was attacked by formidable enemies and how these enemies were repulsed ; or the subject may be the ancestors of Israel, whose

PLATE X.

Dolmen from the country east of the Jordan. (After Eckhardt, Fenner, Zickermann, *Paläst. Kulturbilder*, 1907.)

Image of the God Ramman (Hadad) from er-Rummāne. (After Eckhardt, Fenner, Zickermann, *Paläst. Kulturbilder*, 1907.)

[*To face p.* 96.

great deeds were recited, how they were led by Jahwe into the promised land, etc. As is the case in the East to-day, in places where newspapers and books are unknown, the minstrel and the storyteller compensate the want of these, so also in olden times were these people made welcome wherever they went.

The stories and songs were transmitted from mouth to mouth and from generation to generation: the more fixed their form was, the more trustworthy was the tradition. That is the virtue of verse. A simple narrative, when dependent upon mere oral tradition, generally undergoes change unless its contents are regarded as sacred, in which case it is carefully preserved. It is true that even in the case of poems additions have been made to the original tradition, and in some cases (although this is seldom) the poems have been completely recast. But when a narrative has once been cast into verse, it is more easily remembered, and thus guarantees a more trustworthy tradition, and at the same time checks any arbitrary and haphazard changes.

Of this kind may have been the oldest narratives—of which but a few have been handed down to us—of the adventures and fortunes of David and Saul, the great deeds and victories of the Judges and the great heroes of ancient Israel, and the stories of Moses and the patriarchs. Wandering minstrels brought them from place to place, each generation of minstrels passing them on to the next. We may, I think, safely assume that the sources of the Pentateuch referred to above, J and E, as well as the contents of the books of Judges and Samuel, are based upon *sources* for the most part in verse, which were orally transmitted from age to age, *i.e.* upon a kind of *epic poetry*. The age of the sources varies, of course, but some of them, like those found in J and E, carry us back to the very earliest times. We find examples of this phenomenon among other nations than the Israelites, where family trees and sacred texts have been transmitted from generation to generation for centuries merely by means of oral tradition.

But it is difficult to retain faithfully a tradition which is merely orally transmitted, even when it takes the form of verse. As soon, therefore, as the art of writing began to become familiar among a people, it would naturally be made use of, first as an aid to the memory for purposes of dictation, but in course of time as a means of transmitting traditions.

Verbal tradition became *written* tradition. It began with recording individual songs and poems, traditions concerning the sanctuary, stories relating the origin of sacred sites, which were perhaps committed to writing at the sanctuary, lists of warriors, heroes and their great deeds, state officials and princes, family histories or episodes in the lives of the great national leaders, etc.

Of this kind are the oldest parts of the earliest *historical* books of the Old Testament. These books, as we now see them, are not in their original form, nor were their authors contemporary with the events narrated therein. The *present* form was acquired at a comparatively late date. But probably they contain examples of all the older and oldest primitive forms of historical portraiture.

In them we find songs and poems of the kind mentioned above, we find lists of David's heroes, the officers of Solomon, and narratives of all manner of heroic deeds; in them are traditions concerning the ancient Ark of the Covenant, the numerous severe trials it underwent, and the manner in which it finally triumphed over the enemies of Israel. We read therein of the deeds of the Judges, particularly of Barak and Deborah, Gideon and his son

Abimelech, Jephthah and Samson; we find in them David's family history, how his sin recoiled upon himself and his house, accounts of the wars and victories of the great kings, of Samuel and Saul, and the madness of this unfortunate king. These and like narratives represent the basis of the older historical literature outside the Pentateuch, with the narrators of which, especially J and E, many of the writers of both seem to stand in close relation. Joined on to these earlier narratives we find accounts of Solomon's treasures, his wisdom and his justice, of the prophets and the kings and their deeds in Israel and Judah, of the inroads of foreign nations, first the Syrians, then the Assyrians, and of the fortunes of the two kingdoms until their fall.

This enumeration is by no means complete, but is only a brief outline of the most important material which constitutes the older parts of the books of Judges, Samuel, and Kings. But if it were complete it would not include all that existed at one time in Israel in the form of songs and poems, lists, records, and histories of all kinds. We know that at one time there existed in Israel many other collections than those found in the Old Testament, for we find references in the Bible

THE HISTORICAL WRITINGS 101

to books and collections which we only know by name, *e.g.* the "Book of the Upright," *i.e.* of the bold heroes, and the "Book of the Wars of Jahwe," which probably gave an account of the great wars of the heroic age of Israel. And we can assume with certainty that, besides those collections which are expressly mentioned, there were others, at least a large number of songs and stories which have not come down to us.

We shall now make a few remarks on the *redaction* which gave these books the form in which we now find them. The materials referred to above, which form the constituent parts of these books, vary considerably in respect to the place and time of their composition, as well as in contents and style. But they are all alike in that the later compilers thought they were all worthy to be handed down to posterity. To this alone do we owe it that they are now extant. How did this happen, and what determined the compiler's choice?

If we read the present books of Judges, Samuel, and Kings attentively, we at once perceive that they are the products of a thorough compilation and revision. Our remark concerning the Pentateuch, that the books are not—as it might at first appear—the work of one and the same person, but that different records, each one being independent of the other, have been compiled by a *third*, may be made concerning these books also.

Although we are not able to trace the various sources in these books with the same reliance as in the Pentateuch, after what has been said of the diverse character of the contents of these books, the plausibility of this conclusion is at once clear.

The manner in which the compilers, who were also the redactors, have collected their materials together, is peculiar to these books. This is best observed in the books of *Judges* and *Kings*. In both books, more particularly in the latter, we see that the present author presents to the reader certain sketches—which in the main the author found in a completed form—portraying the life of the individual judges or the age in which they lived, but in a peculiar way, in that he puts them all, as it were, in a certain definite *setting*. One is reminded of the truth which has again come into special prominence, namely, that it is important in what frame a picture is placed if it is to have the proper effect, and to convey to those who look at it the true meaning of it as intended by the artist: only that in this case the frame is perhaps not the work of the artist himself, but of someone else who, by means of a harmonising frame, connects the whole together and enables all who look at the picture to obtain the proper effect.

Thus the author of the present book of Judges has framed his stories of the individual judges throughout the whole book with similar, almost stereotyped, *prescribed forms* of preface and conclusion. He wishes thereby to convey to his readers the important points to the correct understanding and appreciation of what he writes. Almost every account is introduced by: " The children of Israel did that which was evil in the sight of Jahwe, and they forsook Him and served the Ashteroth. Therefore He delivered them into the hands of their enemies, and they served them for a long time. But when the children of Israel cried unto Jahwe and turned to Him again, He raised up a Saviour for them." The setting is the moral-religious scheme within which is set the historical pragmatism of one who criticises the history of the past from the point of view of national piety. A similar kind of stereotyped setting is found in the books of Kings: " King N—— reigned so and so many years.

He did that which was right in the eyes of Jahwe, only he did not take away the high places, or, "he did that which was evil in the eyes of Jahwe, because he made the people to sin at the high places." In this way the character of each king is summed up and his history judged from a particular point of view, which, however, reflects quite a distinct ideal, in this case that of the Deuteronomic school, which regarded all worship of God, except at the place which He had chosen, as sinful and leading to destruction.

In this scheme we recognise the spirit which inspired the compiler, and the principle according to which the material at his disposal was either accepted or rejected. This redaction is rightly called Deuteronomic or Deuteronomistic (Dt or D^2). The influence of the D school is seen most clearly in the preface and conclusion of the individual narratives, that is, in their peculiar setting and the connecting together of the various details so as to form a complete picture. But it did not confine itself to these additions, but occasionally abridged some of the older narratives or added to them—always from the point of view described above. The whole subject-matter was in this way imbued with a spirit

PLATE XI.

The Royal Seal of King Jeroboam of Israel.

[*To face p.* 104.

THE HISTORICAL WRITINGS 105

of moral earnestness and an awe-inspiring, almost terrible, precision, narratives which were at one time popular being thereby refined and made the instruments of moral edification. The spirit of serious introspection, inspired by the thought of the many calamities which had befallen the nation, pervades the whole recension. During the years immediately preceding the fall of the state, men sought to moralise upon the past and thus save the future generations from God's judgment, which was exemplified in the history of the nation.

This was the manner in which the leading men of the time interpreted the past, and they desired that posterity should see with their eyes, in order that it should learn and be warned. One sees, therefore, that these Deuteronomic editors did not regard their subject-matter from the purely historical standpoint, but rather from that of their own characteristic principles, which, in their view, history as a whole is to exemplify. The end they had in view was not the compilation of historical facts, but history is consciously and deliberately made a teacher of life. Past events are not related merely in order to make known what the condition of things was in days gone by, but to show how the future could be made better, and how the errors of the past may be avoided. On this account the *selection* of the material is naturally biassed. A redaction influenced by such ideals as those of the Deuteronomic school, could not make use of everything at hand, but was compelled to select only what seemed to be suitable, and to reject what did not conform to their ideas.

The ancient religion of Israel, particularly the popular religion, contained, as will be seen later, much that was repellent in nature to a refined religious and moral thinker. Hence it followed, naturally, that the redactors approached these things — concerning which Judges ii. is especially instructive,—when it seemed possible or necessary, in the light of their advanced religious and moral conceptions. On this account the offence which could be taken with them is mitigated. It follows, further, that the compilers, whenever they were unable to, or would not, select certain narratives, rejected them. They did not mind if the narrative was not a continuous one; they were not concerned with the narrative itself, but with the lesson it conveyed; it was the edifying character of the story that was important to them. Their ambition was not to be historians in the usual sense, but helpers and restorers of their degenerate fellow-countrymen.

We can therefore understand why so much has been *lost* to us, why what we know has been presented to us in such a peculiar light.

We often hear complaints and adverse comments about the narrow-mindedness of these Deuteronomic editors, to whose limitations we owe it not only that what we have has been presented to us in a prejudiced light, but also that so much invaluable historical matter has been lost. We regret that books like the Book of the Upright and the Book of the Wars of Jahwe are irretrievably lost because the compilers of the sacred scriptures did not think they were worth preserving. But here again to understand is to forgive. Rather than deplore and lament because so much has been lost, we ought to thank these editors for what we have. And for this we must thank their onesidedness and limitations, which are so often condemned. It is just these qualities, and these alone, which induced these men to compile and preserve what has come down to us. Only their zeal — blind, perhaps — prompted them to collect what they deemed to be valuable in a religious sense. Had they not had this zeal, we would know nothing of a period in which history in the modern sense was unknown; as there would be no *motive* to make the past known to future generations. If we did not possess what we have, and if it had not been cast in the form in which we now find it, it is quite probable that we would know *nothing* about ancient Israel—and then, indeed, we would have no reason to be incensed against these editors, for then all traces of them would have disappeared for all time in the universal darkness of a past without a history.

As these sentences may sound strange, I must explain what I mean more clearly.

What made the prophets of Israel great, and what enabled them to inspire new life into the dying nation and to preserve it through the dark days of adverse fortunes even to the present day, was the passionate and intense *one-sidedness* with which they judged everything, even everyday life, from the purely religious point of view. Life in its relation to God was the only thing that mattered; everything else was unimportant. Breathing this spirit into their fellow-countrymen, they made the nation proof against the introduction of heathen customs whilst dwelling among pagan people, and thus preserved the Israelitic religion intact through the Babylonian exile. (In the same way did Elijah, by his passionate opposition to the Baal-worship, save his people from being absorbed into the Canaanites, and so from being lost in history.) It was its religion alone which saved the nation of Israel from extinction, just as the Church is the only factor which keeps together some of the small politically dead nations of the East to-day.[1] Thus the strength of these men lay in their weakness, and their sight in their blindness. For they were not ordinary men, but personalities of an extraordinary type, consciously harsh in their condemnation of malpractices. They were compelled to be harsh and uncompromising, otherwise they would have been of no account among so uncouth a people as the Israelites of their days were. They were consciously blunt, consciously "blind"; they *wanted* to be one-sided.

What is true of the prophets is also true of their followers, the compilers of the texts which we are now considering. Had they been men who took an "objective" interest

[1] *E.g.*, the Armenians and the Greeks within the Turkish Empire.

in history, had they collected their materials impartially in the sense of disinterested profane history, it is quite possible, on account of the perishable character of the materials used for writing purposes in Israel, that nothing would have come down to us, as is the case with the archives of the Phœnician Canaanites, the Aramæans, and the Philistines, which must have existed at one time. The storms of the times and the fall of the two kingdoms would have swept them away just as surely and completely as these heathen records. It was the *religious* idea, and that in its characteristic onesidedness, which caused the Israelitic writings to be preserved. The same power which dominated the compilers dominated the nation in exile also, namely, enthusiasm for *sacred* conceptions and the *holy* scriptures. These were taken with the nation into exile although money and property had to be sacrificed for them; the writings were recovered from the plundered towns at the risk of life, and were carried and treasured through the centuries—but always because they were *onesidedly holy*. Life and property would not have been endangered for the sake of mere " profane " history.

In this characteristic of the Deuteronomic

writings is to be seen their peculiar value for purposes of *instruction* in church and school. The compilers were men to whom history as such was of less importance than the moral and religious teaching reflected therein. Facts as such did not interest them except in so far as they were the expression of the Divine will and His plan for the salvation of mankind. In church and school also the teaching of Israelitic and Biblical history as such should never be made an end in itself, but only a means to the attainment of a true knowledge of God's plan of salvation among the Israelites, and the preparation of the world for the coming of the complete revelation in Jesus Christ. To attain this end, the religious pragmatism of the historical books of the Old Testament can be used as a profitable guide. Of course, it does not necessarily follow that we must accept the authority of these redactors even when they reject historical facts. We differ from them in that we live in the age of historical criticism, and we are in duty bound to accept its conclusions. But, without neglecting these conclusions, we can always learn from these men that historical details are not of paramount importance to religion, except in so far as they have moral and religious significance, and point towards the religious end of human history.

After what we have said, it will not be difficult to estimate the *historical* value of these books. That the value of the Deuteronomic parts does not exist in its historical, at least in its political, significance has already been shown. This probably accounts for the fact that kings whose political activity — from all we can gather—was considerable, have either been dismissed with just a few words, as in the case of Jeroboam II., or, like Ahab, have been mentioned only with blame.

Of greater historical significance is the *material* which the D school have transmitted to us. Songs like the Song of Deborah or David's lament over Saul and Jonathan are of inestimable worth. No less valuable are narratives such as those about Gideon in Judges viii., about Abimelech in Judges ix., and the history of the migration of the tribe of Dan in Judges xvii. and xviii., which is important alike to the history of civilisation and of religion. In the history of David's campaigns, together with the account of his private life (2 Sam. ix.–xx. and 1 Kings i. f.) we possess a record of the very highest importance. It must have been written by one who was intimately acquainted with the events which he describes, by a man who was very well informed concerning David's character. Even to-day we cannot but marvel and admire the impartiality with which the narrator depicts David's personality. He openly declares himself to be an admirer and a partisan of the great king, whose magnanimity he has put in the best possible light; but at the same time he has not made any attempt to hide his hero's weaknesses and criminal acts, but describes them relentlessly and candidly, in a manner which, under other circumstances, could be ascribed to hatred or party spirit. Among the other passages which possess very high historical significance are many extracts from the books of Kings, some of which have been remarkably confirmed by the inscriptions, especially the Assyrian (whilst, on the other hand, it is true that other passages in these books have been refuted).

Although we are thus in a position to regard all these as historical records of the first rank, we also find a large number of narratives which can be regarded as possessing only the second degree of historical certainty, and some of the third degree, which nevertheless contain valuable and, in a sense, very important information. To this class belong some of the narratives concerning David at Hebron and in Jerusalem, found in the first chapters of 2 Samuel; also the narratives concerning Saul's first acts; those concerning Ahab and other kings; others again which were written at a time long after the occurrence of the events narrated, such as the later history of Saul and his relation towards David, the histories of Samuel, Elijah, and others. On the whole, we may say that, despite important gaps in the tradition, we are nevertheless far better informed concerning these important periods and events from the Israelites than from most of the other nations of that time.

Only a few words need be added concerning *the later historical writings.* In the books of Chronicles we have a parallel to a large part of the earlier historical books. But the value of Chronicles is much less than that of the latter. Where the Chronicles go their own way, they often follow a very late tradition, which is not always unbiassed.

The chroniclers either omitted the displeasing or disturbing features in the traditions at their disposal, or altered them and thus presented quite a different picture from that conveyed in the original. Above all, the

Chronicles have been strongly influenced by very pronounced priestly ideals, so that on this account the older traditions have undergone changes to harmonise with the priestly teaching. Although this book can, therefore, only be accepted with great reservation as a record of history, the books of Ezra and Nehemiah, which are probably from the the same hand as the book of Chronicles, are, however, of a quite different type. It is true that we must regard certain parts of these books with distrust, but in this case the books relate the history of a much later period than the Chronicles, and the narrator therefore is in a much better position, in that he speaks of events which were nearer to him in time than the events described in the Chronicles.

3 *The Peculiarity of the Prophetical Books*

Besides the legal and historical literature, the prophetical literature, as we see, represents a special branch of the Hebrew scriptures. This separation of the prophetical writings into a distinct class is but natural. For since prophecy was a quite peculiar phenomenon in the national life of Israel, which took up an independent position among the people, and exerted an influence which is only explicable from the nature of prophecy itself, then we may naturally expect the writings, which are in a special sense the product of this phenomenon, to be peculiar as well. But if we wish to understand these writings, we must first of all distinguish between prophetic writings as extant in the Old Testament and the prophetic writings in their earliest form.

In order to be in a position to estimate the earliest activity of the prophets as authors, we must try to observe them in their several rôles of *speakers, poets,* and *writers.* What they were in respect of their calling will be considered later in a separate paragraph. We will, however, anticipate one conclusion, viz. that they claimed to be men of God, who felt that they had been commissioned to communicate the will of Jahwe to the Israelites. Just now, whilst we are considering literature, we are interested in them as writers only, and in the circumstances which caused them to apply their energies to literary work. On that account we shall consider only those prophets whose books or fragments of books are found in the Old Testament.

If we inquire how these prophets, the earlier as well as the later, who felt that they were the heralds of God's will to the Israelitic

THE PROPHETICAL WRITINGS   117

nation, discharged this commission, we will find that they were not writers from the beginning, but became such from necessity in the course of time. As the age in which they lived became more literary, when the art of writing began to become familiar among the people, and the knowledge of reading more prevalent, these heralds of God's will were naturally eager to reduce their messages into writing. For, if they wished to justify their high calling, they were of necessity compelled to make use of such means as seemed to be most suitable to get into touch with the people and to propagate their teaching among them. Once the art of reading became general, there was no better means of attaining this end than through the medium of writing.

The earliest means which the prophets adopted to express the will of God, besides the short sentence or oracular response, was probably the *sign*, the symbolic act. In order to attract attention, the prophet would do something peculiar which made the people regard him with surprise and ask one another why he did it. The symbol chosen was such that its meaning became clear as soon as it was recognised to be symbolic of something, so that there was no necessity for the prophet to utter many words. The prophets knew how to deliver their message by this means, and to express themselves in a manner easily comprehended by the average man. We can well imagine, therefore, that even the later prophets were inclined to revert at times to this primitive form of communication. As examples of symbolic acts on the part of the prophets we may cite the following:—A prophet of the time of Ahab made a pair of horns for himself, in order to say to the king, " With these shalt thou push the Syrians until they be consumed " (1 Kings xxii. 11); Isaiah walked naked and barefoot for a long time in order to tell Judah what would happen to Egypt, and probably to Judah as well (Is. xx. 1 ff.); Jeremiah carried a yoke upon his neck, Ezekiel laid siege against a picture of Jerusalem portrayed upon a tile, the former in order to foreshadow the Babylonian exile, the latter to signify the siege of the capital (Jer. xxvii. 1 ff.; Ezek. iv. 1 ff.).

Although the later prophets made use of these symbolic acts on account of their powerful and direct appeal to the senses, there is a great difference between these men and earlier seers. These later prophets adapted themselves to the conditions which prevailed in their days, and, in accordance with the progressive evolution of public life, became *orators*. They were no longer content to utter short sentences or oracular responses; consequently the sign was no longer made to serve for a sermon, but only as a text or for purposes of illustration.

They did not become popular speakers all at once. At first the less developed forms of oratory were probably more favoured; we still find some indications in the Bible that the visionary experience—which is described below—often expressed itself outwardly in short, broken words or sentences. But it was soon the rule for the prophet (*cf.* Isaiah) to meditate upon what he saw and heard in his vision, before communicating it to others, either in short oracular sentences or in a lengthy oration. If the prophet was desirous that the people generally should hear what he had to say, he had to go where he could find them in large numbers, such as the court of the temple, the square at the town gate, and such like places where people gather together. His speech, be it long or short, would then become an address, and he himself an orator.

How the orator who does not wish his words to be forgotten, or the knowledge of them to be confined to the few who happened to hear him, but wishes them to be disseminated among a wide circle, becomes of necessity an *author* as soon as reading has become familiar to a people, has already been explained. But that the prophets did not begin by writing "books," and that their first literary productions were of a more modest kind, is in accordance with the natural course of things. A proverb, a short address, detached fragments of some kind or other, would be committed to writing so as to give an opportunity to the hearers to read what they had heard and to impart it to others. Then other writings of the same nature follow—distributed among the people in the form of pamphlets—and after a time these fragments are collected, first of all into small separate collections, which are in turn gradually collected together to form one book.

We see, therefore, that the formation of the prophetical books—perhaps the course adopted was not always the same, but in the case of most books the process of compilation was that described above — is partly the result of a thoroughly developed process. From what we have said, it seems quite probable that the collecting of the separate parts, and the completing of the book, and perhaps even the writing down of the sayings and speeches themselves, were not done by the prophet himself, but by his *disciples*. If we assume—and there is much to be said in favour of our doing so—that the prophet was surrounded during his lifetime by a circle of disciples, and that these continued their master's work after his death, we can easily understand that a special field of work was opened for the "school" in recording the sayings of their teacher.

The *present form* of the prophetical books is in accordance with this assumption. If we examine them carefully, we will find that in some of them—*e.g.* in Isaiah and Jeremiah—consecutive reading is difficult, that the individual chapters are often very loosely connected, and that it is often enough quite impossible to perceive a clear, connected sequence of thought. This is quite true, and a still closer examination reveals to us that fragments of a very different character and belonging to very different periods in the life of a prophet are to-day placed side by side, whilst the real continuation of one paragraph must often be looked for in a quite different part of the book in its present form.

Of course the explanation of this is that the individual parts which form the books have not been transmitted to us in their proper sequence, and that the prophets themselves never set them in the order in which we find them. If we recall what was said about the manner in which these books were compiled and the presumed activity of the prophetic "schools," this characteristic of the writings under consideration will be still further explained by assuming that within the individual books we find many *separate collections*, of which formerly one collection contained one fragment and another another, and so forth; until at a later period, out of respect for the collections which were already compiled, they were added on to the latter just as they came to hand.

A careful analysis of these prophetical books enables us to state confidently that in some of them are to be found many passages which cannot be ascribed to the person whose name they bear to-day. The best known, although by no means the only example of this, is the whole of the latter part of the book of Isaiah (chs. xl.–lx.). One cannot on that account accuse the compilers of these books of forgery and deceit, for the reason probably is that these writings were collected at a time when it was impossible to state exactly what ought to be ascribed to this or to that prophet. In other cases the presence of extraneous matter may be due to later recensions, as is the case in the Pentateuch and the historical books.

What has been said above is true of the majority of the prophetical books. It can be maintained that the contents of these are derived from the personal sayings of the prophets. But we cannot fail to recognise the fact that, the more general the use of writing became, and, on the other hand, the more difficult it became for the prophet to address the people — *e.g.* during the Exile, when it was almost impossible to do so,—the prophets became more and more authors as distinct from orators. Some chapters in the books of Ezekiel and Zechariah can never have been delivered orally. In the case of the exilic Isaiah it is more than questionable whether the whole of his book, or even the greater part of it, was ever addressed to the people by word of mouth. During the centuries after prophecy had ceased to be active and its place had been gradually usurped by the scribes, the transition to the new period is characterised by the fact that prophecy passed from active speech into a literary phenomenon, *i.e.* into book prophecy.

A much-discussed question of the past as

well as of the present day, is whether the prophetical writings are poetry or prose. That we do occasionally find a few scattered songs and poems (*e.g.* Is. v. 1 ff.) is not disputed. Granting this, it cannot be denied but that we again and again find whole chapters which can only be described as prose, although its style often differs from that of simple narrative prose. The subject influenced the writer in such a way that he unconsciously affected the elevated style of rhetorical prose.

But if we maintain that all the prophetical writings are of this kind, we hardly do justice to them. In them we find many chapters whose style is superior to that of elevated prose, and which can be described as poetry in the strictest sense of the term. The question as to what extent this is the case in, *e.g.*, Jeremiah or Haggai, cannot be decided, but the presence of poetical passages in these and other prophetical writings cannot be disputed. And it is quite natural that it should be so. If, as we saw, the longer speeches of the prophets are evolved from the short oracular saying, and the course in which the speeches developed was outwardly like the development of the ancient oracular and seer aphorisms, then the form also will be analogous to and comparable with that of the ancient oracular and seer aphorisms. These latter are generally found expressed in verse, as distichs, epigrams, and the like. Again, on the other hand, if the prophetic utterances were the expressions of an ecstatic state of mind, we may assume that this exalted mood often reflected itself in rhythmical speech.

4. *The Hebrew Lyric, especially the Poetry of the Psalms*

We have already heard that the ancient Israelites were a music-loving people, so much so that there was scarcely any occasion, whether sad or joyful, which was not reflected in song. So far we have only considered the epic poetry of Israel, the songs celebrating the noble deeds of former heroes. Judging from the evidence found in the Old Testament, the lyric as well as the epic must have attained a high degree of perfection. We find songs in which the author sings his own or another's praises, like that of Lamech, in which he boasts of his own courage and his passion for revenge to the terror of all those who might be able to injure him (Gen. iv. 23 f.). We find execratory and defamatory songs — like those the Arabs affect, in which one disparages his opponent—*e.g.* those parts of the so-called Blessing of Jacob which refer to Reuben, Simeon, and Levi, or that portion of the Song of Deborah where the indolent and self-seeking tribes who refused to join their fellows against the enemy are vituperated (see Gen. xlix. 1 ff.; Judges v. 16 f.; *cf.* Numbers xxi. 27-30). We find also harvest songs in which the rejoicing over the produce of the earth is reflected (Judges ix. 27; Isaiah ix. 2); well songs, which were sung by those who went to draw the water, composed perhaps when the well was being sunk (Numbers xxi. 17 f.); and drinking songs, which were sung at banquets and feasts (Is. v. 12; Amos vi. 5; 2 Sam. xix. 36).

But above all else, weddings and love affairs on the one hand, and death and burial on the other, offered excellent opportunities to develop poetical endowments. The "Song of Songs," wrongly ascribed to Solomon, is nothing else than a collection of love or wedding songs, which, though in a sense voluptuous, yet reflect the most refined and tenderest feelings. At a time when their simplicity was no longer understood, these songs have been allegorically interpreted, and this misunderstanding probably accounts for the presence of this precious collection of true poetry and beauty—which, however, should not be abused by being put into the hands of children and the immature —in the Old Testament. The attempt has been made of late — in pursuance of the popular tendency already referred to — to ascribe these songs to a very late date, without there being any good reasons for so doing. Many signs point to the fact that the basis of the collection belongs to the earlier period of Israelitic history.

No less important is the place given to lamentation for the dead and to *threnody* in general, by the ancient Israelites. Even today, loud, noisy lamentation for the departed is an important part of the ceremonies which belong to the correct form of burial. It was the same in ancient times, and oftentimes not only was the pain and sorrow of separation expressed in these loud laments, but also all kinds of superstitious beliefs and ideas. In course of time, from complaints and groans, a rhythmical, melodious form of lament, the elegy, was developed. The most beautiful example of this form of poetry is the grand poem which David composed when he heard of the deaths of Saul and Jonathan. Almost as beautiful is the collection of elegiac songs which we find in the book of Lamentations, which bewail the fall of Jerusalem, the suffering during the siege and the pillage of the city by the hordes of Nebuchadnezzar.

More important than all these, however, is that collection which we call collectively *the Psalms* or the Psalter. The songs and collections already referred to are profane, secular lyrics, but the Psalter is a collection of religious songs which were current among the Israelites, and in course of time became the religious song-book, the "hymn-book" of the Jewish community. How was this book compiled?

To answer this question we must first consider the age and origin of Israelitic *religious lyrics* in general.

Under the influence of the tendency already referred to, and which we criticised when considering the origin and development of the Pentateuch, namely, the tendency to ascribe great portions of the Old Testament to the latest Israelitic-Jewish period, modern scholars, led by Wellhausen, have sought to date the psalms, almost without exception, in the post-exilic period. As the most important reason for this argument, they maintain that only the profane lyric was known to the earlier Israelites; that the religious lyric, the most important examples of which are found in the Psalter, is altogether the product of post-exilic times.

For all its popularity, I cannot regard this hypothesis as an authentic conclusion of Old Testament research, but rather as the consequence of a great and unfortunate error.

As a matter of fact, the religious lyric among the Israelites, as among all other ancient nations, is quite as old as the profane. If there were a difference in the age of the two, it would not be in the order maintained by the above-mentioned theory, but rather the contrary, the religious lyric, judging from all we can gather on the subject, being the older of the two. The belief that it took nearly a thousand years for the religious lyric to develop from the profane, is, in my estimation, to be regarded as erroneous and most improbable.

Religion had always the highest significance to the Israelites. There is absolutely no truth in the theory that it is a product of the Exile in Babylon. The only influence the Exile had upon the religious life of Israel was to lead it into new paths. Religious life was quite as powerful in ancient as in later times. It would therefore seem very strange if poetry, which was, at an early date, in the service of joy and sorrow, the glorification of heroes and of war, had not offered itself at the same time to the service of the God of these heroes and wars.

It can be seen, therefore, that there is no necessity to refer to any *foreign* examples of religious poetry in order to support the antiquity of the religious lyric in Israel. However, we shall very briefly refer to them.

We find very early traces of religious poetry in Egypt, which has many affinities with the poetry of the psalms, and in the Babylonian penitential psalms we are taken back to a period prior to 3000 B.C. Arguing by analogy from these facts, and remembering the close relation which existed between Israel and the countries of Babylon and Egypt, the theory propounded by Wellhausen and his school becomes still more improbable. Moreover, it is positively refuted by certain facts which are very clearly presented to us in the history of Israel itself.

In one of the most pathetic songs which describe the suffering of the Exile, the author relates that, when the exiles had set themselves in mute sorrow beside the waters of Babylon and had suspended their harps idly upon the willows on the banks of the stream, the Babylonians begged them to sing one of "the songs of Zion." Indignantly they replied, "How shall we sing the songs of Jahwe in a strange land?" (Ps. cxxxvii. 1-4). What are these songs of Zion? They are the songs of Jahwe, *i.e.* songs of praise to the God of Israel, religious songs. To sing these on foreign, heathen soil would have been a sacrilege. It follows of necessity, therefore, that these songs had been sung in Palestine—in other words, that Israel possessed religious songs before the Exile, which they doubtless used in the Temple for purposes of worship.

Amos tells us the same thing. Whilst he complains of the outward show of religious worship, he exclaims (v. 23 f.):

Take thou away from me the noise of thy songs,
For I will not hear the melody of thy viols.

The whole context speaks of public worship, how festivals and sacred gatherings, sacrifices of all kinds, as practised by the people, are repulsive to Jahwe, and no less are their songs. By the latter the prophet can only mean the religious songs, the hymns sung in divine worship, *i.e.* what we call psalms. The religious lyric, then, was known in the days of Amos, and at Bethel, the scene of the prophet's ministry. And it may be taken for granted that, if it was known at Bethel, it was known in Jerusalem and Judah generally.

There is no lack of examples which point to a *pre-exilic* origin of the religious lyric. When David conveyed the Ark of the Covenant to Jerusalem, a ceremonial procession was organised. According to 2 Sam. vi. 5 the procession went up to Zion to the accompaniment of "harps and psalteries and timbrels and castanets. . . ." There can be no doubt but that these psalteries were religious songs, which proclaimed the praise of Jahwe and His holy Ark. These examples by no means exhaust the number which are at our disposal, but they will suffice to prove that we are justified in assuming that religious lyric poetry was known long before the fall of the kingdoms, not only in isolated cases, but developed to the same extent as the profane.

Although we therefore claim that psalmody was known to the early Israelites, that is no proof that the songs which we find collected in our Psalter contain these ancient poems even in part. So far we have only proved the possibility of this assumption. To find out whether it is true, we must consider the problem more closely. For that purpose we must refer ourselves to the Psalter itself. The first question to be considered is to what extent the tradition that David is the author of the greater part of our Psalter can be confirmed.

According to the *titles*, no less than seventy-three psalms, *i.e.* almost one-half of the whole collection, are to be ascribed to David. But it is not quite certain that these titles were originally intended to designate the author, although in later times it became the custom to interpret them in that sense. On account of the latter fact, the tradition was enlarged into a statement that David had composed all the psalms, and the Psalter was briefly referred to as the book of David. We must admit that these titles are very obscure and uncertain sources. It can be proved that they form no part of the earliest texts of the psalms, but were added at a very much later date. It can be shown further that some of the psalms which, according to their titles, are to be ascribed to David, *cannot*, in the light of their contents, be referred to him at all. It is better, therefore, to ignore the titles, and to consider the question of the authorship of the psalms in the light of internal evidences, *i.e.* according to their contents. The titles are not on that account worthless; they represent an old tradition, which is always valuable; but they cannot be accepted as satisfactory sources of information.

How much truth is there, then, in this tradition concerning David? It may be maintained as a historical fact that he was a poet. Not only does the narrative of the books of Samuel recognise him as a singer of renown—and the singer is generally a poet,—but we have certain (although they are only a few) songs outside the Psalter which can be traced back to David. Even though there was but the one—undeniably genuine—song which he composed on the occasion of the deaths of Saul and Jonathan (2 Sam. i. 17 ff.), that alone would be sufficient to prove that he was a master of the art of poetry. Should anyone set out to collect the gems of literature belonging to all nations and times, he could not possibly overlook this song.

It may be claimed, further, as a historical fact that David was deeply religious. David's human character is not without its blots, and there is no reason why the Biblical investigator should palliate them. David seduced Bathsheba; he became a common murderer in the affair of Uriah. And in other instances he was not free from despotic caprice and human weakness. But all these shortcomings only prove that he was a man of flesh and blood, such a man as those days and a princely throne might be expected to produce. It shows further that our narrators give us a true description of him in the main, a picture true to life and not as a model man, nor yet as an ordinary personality. On that account we have every right to believe them when they depict him in his greatness.

And when they do this, they describe him as a man of extraordinary genius, head and shoulders above his contemporaries, both as a man and as a religious personality. As a man full of genuine magnanimity, he laments the death of his bitterest enemy in accents of unalloyed sorrow, is chivalrously faithful to a friend even unto death, and he frankly admits his guilt to the prophet. And as a religious personality he is in keeping with the spirit of his day, which he truly reflects, and is not free from superstitious and eccentric religious tendencies. He reveals this side of his character in his lifelong childlike simplicity, which was more pronounced perhaps in David than in any other of his contemporaries—in this respect again proclaiming himself to be a man in the truest sense of the term. But this characteristic of his nature is due to the influence of true religion. It is the expression of strong, genuine, deep piety. Of this we have ample proofs. Although a king, he acknowledges the will of Jahwe as supreme. Jahwe's honour is above everything, even above his own interests (2 Sam. vi. 22). To restore this is David's chief aim in life, and it was with this end in view that he brought the sacred Ark which Saul had dishonoured by leaving it in a remote corner of the land, to Jerusalem, thus making the capital of his kingdom the chief habitation of his God. The tradition that he intended to build a temple, and that he reorganised public worship, not forgetting the musical side thereof (*cf.* 2 Sam. vi. 5 with Amos vi. 5), is not altogether without foundation.

Considering all these facts, then, we are perfectly justified in regarding David as a *religious poet*. It would indeed be astonishing if he had not placed his harp in the service of Jahwe, whose honour lay so near his heart. If therefore we find a tradition to this effect either within or without the Psalter, we are quite justified in crediting it.

But that fact does not enable us to conclude that, if in the present Psalter a number of psalms are ascribed to David, they all, or even any of them, are really from his hand. The genuine psalms of David may have been lost, or, through having been recast, have become unrecognisable. If, on the other hand, some psalms are found in the Psalter which in form and contents seem to suit the age in which David lived, there is no necessity for serious scruples against ascribing them to him. Of course they must be songs in which, besides the poetical power and peculiarity which belong to the style of David's dirge in 2 Sam. i. 17 ff., we find a certain unbroken naturalness and originality of religious conception, such as is displayed in other places by David. And such songs are still found in our Psalter. Formerly there may have been still more.

As examples of what I mean, take the latter part of Ps. xxiv. (*vv.* 7–10). In this beautiful chant the ancient gates of Jerusalem, as though they were living beings, are commanded to lift themselves up as high as they can, and proudly to hold aloft their heads, so as to enable the majestic king to pass through them. His majesty is so exalted that the gates, however high they may be, seem too small to admit him. The powerful king threatens to burst them. Such is the one chorus. The other asks, "Who is this king of glory?" The first answers, "He is Jahwe strong and mighty, Jahwe who is mighty in battle." Doubtless this song celebrates the entrance of the Ark, the home-coming of the God of war from a victorious campaign. After the time of Solomon, the Ark was hardly ever carried to the field of battle, but probably was in the days of David. With this song its home-coming may have been celebrated. It is not a late imitation, for here one breathes the air of ancient Israel and of the Book of the wars of Jahwe.

Or we may take the 29th Psalm. In it the "sons of God" are called upon to honour and praise Jahwe. Then Jahwe is extolled as the majestic storm-god, and His might is described with wonderful poetical beauty—how His voice of thunder breaks the cedars, makes Lebanon and Hermon "skip like calves," and "makes the hinds to calve." In accordance with a primitive conception of nature, the loud-roaring, fear-awakening thunder was regarded as the essential part of a storm. Or the 19th Psalm, in which the sun, like Helios and his chariot, is conceived as a hero, almost as a sun-god, who runs his course from end to end of the heavens. These are poems of consummate poetic skill and the highest religious power, but reflecting a form of religion which still abounds in elementary conceptions of a mythological character. These are the type of songs which we might expect from such a man as David.

Naturally psalmody developed itself in the course of time. After David's day, others composed songs in which they reflected the spirit of their own times and in accordance with their own poetic and religious abilities. During the periods of the Exile and the restoration to Jerusalem the collection was increased, and the great agitation of the Maccabean period added yet new songs to the older ones. It is conceivable—but we must beware lest this admission leads us to false conclusions—that most of the songs of the later, especially of the post-exilic, times have been preserved to us. Their own religion and the spirit which prevailed in their own day concerned the collectors of these psalms more than the religious ideas expressed in the older songs. We are probably indebted for the few examples of the earlier psalmody—as in the case of the early narratives and the secular songs—to a large extent to favourable circumstances, and it is by no means impossible that many a late psalm at one time read otherwise than at present, and that its original form was changed to conform to the higher ideals of the time.

It has of late become the custom to regard the community, and not the poet himself—who is supposed to be only the mouthpiece of the people,—as the *subject* in the majority of psalms. This opinion, in my estimation, makes it all the more difficult to understand many of the songs. It is based upon the false assumption that all the psalms were originally intended to be used in religious worship. Surely all the psalms cannot be included in this category, for some, like the penitential psalms and others, present purely personal matters before God. To overcome this objection, it is claimed that this personal individual character only represents the form in which the poet expresses the thoughts of the praying community. But the supposition is a false one. Our Psalter contains very many songs which cannot be imagined as having been composed for purposes of religious worship. Just imagine Psalm cxix. as having been sung at a sacred service, or at least as having been composed for that purpose! This applies to many other psalms, which strictly speaking cannot be called "hymns," but instructive productions of a literary muse.

Since the hypothesis is false, it follows that the conclusion is also false. As a matter of fact, there are a large number of psalms which can only be understood, if we would do justice to their contents, when we assume that they express the mood and feelings of a definite person, and of a definite moment in the life of that person. Songs like the 32nd or the 51st Psalm are treasured because in them we hear the sighs and groans of a soul in anguish, we see the innermost depths of the heart, we experience its remorse, but also the feeling of freedom and joy which follows. If we say that they do not reflect personal individual experiences, then their peculiar vitality is destroyed, for then they are merely productions of religious art, lacking the vigour of sincerity and truth even in the most important matters.

The fact that the Psalter does contain a few songs of this kind does not prove that its best and most profound psalms were thus composed. And that a hymn which is the expression of the innermost nature of an inspired soul, when others hear it and respond to its influence, should become the hymn of others, even of *everybody*, does not prove that it was composed as the hymn of a community. For the best and profoundest qualities which thrill and exalt the human heart, because they are also the truest and purest human characteristics, of necessity affect other hearts as well. The oppression of sorrow, the joy of deliverance, the distress of sin, and the rapture of salvation are universal. If a poet describes them so vividly that he really and truly reflects his own soul, he will always find others who will select him as the interpreter of their own feelings. His song becomes the song of all.

If the psalms are properly understood in this respect, their *religious significance* is seen in its true light. And that cannot be overestimated. Not that all the psalms are equally valuable. They vary both in poetic and religious value. In the Psalter we find the works of authors, as in our modern hymn-books, who are masters of the art of poetry; others who are novices therein, but in whose hearts the Creator has written the laws of beauty; others again who work after strange models and laboriously wrestle with the forms. And we find among the various authors some who are no less masters of religious thought and men of intense piety, whose thoughts are true, and spring directly from their souls—men like the great prophets of Israel. But there are not wanting those who, after the manner of the scribes, are superficial, or, like the mean-spirited persons who are to be found among the pious of all times, think only of rewards, or thirst after conquest and revenge. From such the notorious imprecatory psalms originated. They are a historical, instructive witness to what was at one time accredited to God. It is not necessary to excuse them; they belong to the past; to palliate them would be quite as foolish as to blame them; to repeat them would be blasphemy, and not to be thought of in these days.

But what the Psalter is, and what it again can be to us, is not seen in its inferior psalms, which belong to a primitive stage in the evolution of religious knowledge, but in its best songs, which transcend all time. In them, as in the writings of the prophets, speak the true *classics of religion*, the great men of Israel, the masters and leaders of the religious life of all ages, men who have realised in their own lives what a complete resignation to the will of God can make of the human heart.

Luther's verdict on the Psalter is eternally true: "There thou lookest into the innermost souls of all the saints." The whole range of genuine religious feelings, from sublime exultation consequent upon the possession of God's grace and a clear conscience, down through the state of anxious longing of the soul for God and His guidance and assistance in temptation and suffering, to the deepest depths of human misery and wretchedness due to being rejected of God and being thrust back upon oneself, and the unceasing, terrible torments of an accusing conscience, is reflected in these songs, and stirs up similar feelings in our own souls when we read them.

One should read a good translation of psalms like the 32nd or the 51st. A more affecting and truer description of the consuming power of an evil conscience which stirs the body and the soul in their uttermost depths, which is like a fire burning in the inward parts, with its scorching flame causing both body and soul to waste away, can hardly be found in any other religious writings; nor a truer picture of human impotence to escape from the torments of unexpiated guilt: "When I would silence it, my bones waxed old." Or, one should realise for himself the painful insight given to the author of Ps. li. into the deep entanglement of human nature in "original sin," the inability to prevail over the ingrained disposition to evil in the human soul, and the plaintive but hopeful prayer for a pure heart and the unquestioning faith in God's readiness to assist: "Create in me a clean heart, O God; and renew a right spirit within me."

Or we should read the latter part of the 73rd Psalm, where the psalmist, after anxious doubts, struggles through to an acknowledgment of God which is based upon the deepest conviction: "Whom have I in heaven but thee? And there is none upon earth that I desire beside thee. My flesh and my heart faileth: but God is the strength of my heart and my portion for ever." Religious idealism and complete self-denial attain their highest perfection in these words. We can appreciate the spirit of these words only when we consider how often worldly affairs, even in these days, crowd out from our lives all thoughts of God and communion with Him. To see God, to gain heaven, is even now to many people synonymous with freedom from temporal sorrow and pain, or with the bliss of paradise or the reunion with the departed. That is how they imagine heaven to be, and *on that account* desire it. But here, in this psalm, we have an Israelite who, to the shame of thousands of Christians, ventures to say that heaven would be nothing without God—it would not be a heaven, with all its pleasures it would be nothing—more, it would be a hell—if God was not in it. Only He, only His presence in the heart, and communion with Him in spirit, *i.e.* only spiritual possessions, make heaven a place of happiness and joy. If we have these possessions no earthly sorrows can assail us, even though body and soul perish.

Here we have a pure and lofty ideal which has not been surpassed either in the Old Testament or the New, nor could it be surpassed. Even Paul, when he rejoices to depart and be with Christ, can but echo it, and can add nothing to it other than that salvation is through Christ. This shows us that such psalms as these contain the highest and best thoughts which, from a religious point of view, have ever been vouchsafed to the human heart. Naturally, they know nothing of that which effects and guarantees the possession of God to the Christian. But apart from this limitation they stand as prominent monuments of purest piety and true religious ideals, whose influence reaches far beyond the limits of the Israelitic nation and the religion of the Old Testament, and leads us into regions where all distinctions of nationality and time are unknown, into the regions of *eternal truth*.

It has often been attempted, without complete success, to establish the *date* of the individual psalms, and the circumstances under which they were composed. Some psalms seem to imply a definite period, and we try to the best of our ability to interpret their contents in relation to their historical background. Others defy every attempt to limit them to any time or place. Nor do they require to be interpreted as though they reflect any definite and fixed conditions, even though we must assume that such did exist. This fact is the strength of these psalms, not their weakness. They are like certain ballads of which none know or ask whence they are, by whom they were composed, when and where they were first sung, but which, nevertheless, everybody loves and sings. Just as these popular songs came directly from the hearts of the people and are their common heritage for all time, so also did these psalms emanate from the soul of the Israelitic nation at various periods of its history. They have by this time long ceased to be the peculiar property of that people, and are now treasured by other nations as songs of *eternal* beauty and, what is more, of eternal truth and greatness. In this they bear the stamp of true religion, which is not confined to any one nation or generation, but belongs to the whole world and eternity.

III

RESULTS BASED UPON HISTORICAL (GENERAL AND RELIGIOUS) RESEARCH

1. *The So-called Patriarchs*

THE history of the so-called patriarchs, Abraham, Isaac, and Jacob, as found in Genesis xii.–l., has in recent times become the subject of a spirited critical discussion. The first question considered is how these personalities are in general to be explained. Three opinions have been expressed, each one directly opposed to the others. According to one, these patriarchs were ancient *gods*, degraded to the ranks of men; the second opinion regards the patriarchal narratives as representing the histories of tribes, the patriarchs themselves as personified tribes and not real persons; whilst according to the third opinion the patriarchs are real individuals, *i.e.* this opinion supports the traditional interpretation which in the past was accepted as a self-evident fact. Which of these three views is the true one ?

Let us examine the first. According to it, there were deities of the names Abraham, Isaac, Jacob, etc., who were worshipped by the Israelites before they had any knowledge of Jahwe as God. In course of time, when the worship of Jahwe became known, they receded into the background and were regarded more and more as heroes or demigods. At a still later stage they were degraded to the rank of men, and as such they afterwards received the dignity of being the progenitors of the Israelitic tribes. Such in outline is the substance of this theory. But there are many things to be said against such a hypothesis; and to maintain that there are positive proofs in favour of it, is *far* from being true.

Generally speaking, it must be admitted that such an occurrence as that maintained by those who uphold this theory—regarded from a purely abstract point of view—is quite imaginable (it is maintained by some scholars that similar transitions took place in Greece and elsewhere). But, on the other hand, in all cases, in our special field of research and those which are closely related to it, where we are able to observe—and not merely to imagine—the course of events, we find that as a rule the order is reversed. Just as, in Rome, divine attributes were ascribed to the emperor, *i.e.* he was raised to the dignity of a god, so also was the king of Egypt regarded as the incarnate sun-god, whilst the kings of Assyria were exalted to the rank of gods, at least after their death. The Arabs believe in innumerable saints and demigods, whose graves are regarded as sanctuaries. They are throughout regarded as men who have been raised to the dignity of gods, or at least supernal beings. In many cases it can be proved that they did at one time really exist as men. The same evolution of ideas can be proved in the case of notable men in ancient Egypt. All these instances support the contention that the rule, at least, was to elevate man to the position of a god, and not to degrade gods to the ranks of men, for which we have not a single really certain proof in Israel.

Consequently, all arguments which are maintained in favour of regarding Abraham, Isaac, and Jacob as ancient gods are highly uncertain, because they all admit of other interpretations. The whole theory is a very improbable one. Nowhere in Israelitic history do we find even the slightest intimation that Abraham, Isaac, and Jacob were ever worshipped, or that a temple was dedicated to one of them, or a sanctuary erected to their honour, or again that they performed supernatural acts, miracles and the like. There is no mention made that they accomplished such mighty deeds as those ascribed to Samson, Hercules, and others. The only fact that might be brought forward in favour of this theory is that the *tombs* of these patriarchs were held sacred in antiquity, and, to some extent, in these days as well. But this is anything but a proof, for Moses, Jonah, and others, whom no one thinks of regarding as gods, share this honour in common with the patriarchs.

Indeed, it is argued of *Abraham* that he reminds one forcibly of the Arab-Edomitic god Dusares. The name signifies "he of Sarah," and the latter name is supposed to be that of a goddess, who afterwards became Abraham's wife. But the existence of a goddess of the name Sarah cannot be proved. We only know of a range of mountains of this name, and "he of Sarah" would in that case be the god whom the Edomites worshipped upon these mountains, not the husband of

Sarah, *i.e.* Abraham. No tangible connection between Abraham and the god Dusares has been proved, nor is it probable that it will. The position of some other scholars (following Winckler and Jensen) is no better. This school maintain that Abraham was a Babylonian or an Egyptian god. In proof of this they point out the fact that Ur of the Chaldees and Haran, the most important stations of the nomadic life of Abraham, prior to his coming to Canaan, were places which in olden times were famous as centres of the worship of the moon, and they refer us to other facts connected with the life of this patriarch in which they believe they find traces of moon-worship. These arguments, however, are often —especially those of Jensen, but also those which introduce Egyptian mythology into the discussion—based upon quite secondary matters which can prove nothing; in other cases their conclusions are uncertain and far from being sufficiently confirmed. As far as the reference to these moon sanctuaries is concerned, not only were they scarcely more highly esteemed in Babylon than in other sanctuaries — and even though they were, that does not prove that Abraham was a moon-god,—but we do not know where this

Ur of Abraham was really situated, or whether it was mentioned in the earliest tradition of the patriarch.

The position is very much the same in respect to *Isaac* and *Jacob*. In the case of the former we are particularly requested to note that in Gen. xxxi. 42, 53, the " fear of Isaac " is mentioned ; and, in the case of Jacob, that in the same book, ch. xxxii. 24 f., his fight with God is described. This fear of Isaac is interpreted as the fear which people had of him, and consequently he is supposed to have been a terrible demon. But recently it has been pointed out that in the verses cited Jacob swears by the fear of " his father " Isaac. This statement cannot possibly mean the fear which he had of his father Isaac. For when Jacob calls Isaac his father he can scarcely regard him as a god as well. This shows that Isaac was conceived throughout as a man, and that the expression " fear of Isaac " must be understood in some sense other than the above. The fear of Isaac simply means the one whom Isaac, Jacob's father, feared, *i.e.* his (Isaac's) God, as is confirmed by the fact that this expression interchanges with " God of my father " (see Gen. xxxi. 42). As for the fight which, according to the legend, took place between Jacob and God, however else we may explain the narrative, this much is clear, that the thought of Jacob as being anything other than a man—endowed with exceptional powers, it is true—is far removed from the narrative.

But what of the theory which interprets the patriarchs as personified *tribes*? Speaking generally, we can say that it has many analogies in its favour, *e.g.* the Greeks often refer to men, as the progenitors of their tribes, who apparently are nothing else than subsequent personifications of the tribes themselves. Thus they spoke of Hellene, the founder of the Hellenes; Ion, the founder of the Ionians; Æolus, the founder of the Æolian tribes. The substitution of an individual for a tribe or nation is not unknown to the Old Testament writers, *e.g.* Eber is referred to as the founder of the Hebrew peoples, whilst in the ethnological table in Gen. x. 15 f. expressions like, " Canaan begat Sidon, and the Jebusite, and the Amorite, and the Girgashite, and the Hivite," are used, and in Gen. xxv. 13 f. desert oases like Dumah and Tima are spoken of as the " sons " of Ishmael. Consequently some Old Testament names can be explained in this way. But it does not follow that this method of interpretation can be universally applied, and that all names should be explained by means of it.[1] In a few cases it may be justified. Thus Israel is certainly the name of a nation or a tribe. It is quite possible that this name was only transferred to Jacob at a comparatively late date from the nation or from one of its leading tribes, because he was regarded as the ancestor of the nation or the particular tribe which was known by this name. The tradition that Jacob was not always known by the name Israel supports this view. There may be other names which should be interpreted in this way, but it is not always easy to bring forward clear proof; but we should not overlook the fact that there are a number of names, such as Hamor, Abiezer, Jerachmeël, Caleb, Machir, Manasseh, Zebulon, Simeon, and others, which can be proved conclusively to have always been the names of individuals.

Even though such an interpretation of the patriarchs is not in principle excluded, it is

[1] If we try to explain every marriage of the patriarchs as a union of tribes, every death as the extinction of a tribe, every family quarrel as a tribal feud, every journey as a migration, as has, as a matter of fact, been done, with the intention to write "history," we will land ourselves in unnatural, unnecessary difficulties.

nevertheless *in reality* improbable, and in a sense impossible. We can maintain with certainty, in the case of Abraham, that his name never occurs as the name of a tribe. We never find any mention made of either a nation or a tribe called Abraham. But we can prove that Abraham in its older and shorter form, Abram or Abiram, was in general use as a personal name both among the Israelites and the Assyrians. Even in an Egyptian inscription belonging to the tenth century B.C. we find the expression "field of Abram," which again points to the use of this name as designating a person. The same may be said of the names Isaac and Jacob. It is true that these names are occasionally used to designate the nation, as parallel names to Israel. But it is well to notice that the name Isaac, with this signification, is only found in Amos vii. 9, 16, and the name Jacob almost exclusively in prophetical and poetical writings, *i.e.* in places where the writer consciously substitutes it for the more usual name Israel. In support of this is the fact that the name Jacob is often used from the very earliest times, in nations other than Israel, as a person's name.

If we now try to outline the true *historical facts* of the case, we may conclude from what has been said that the patriarchs were neither deities nor tribes, and that the mere examination of the names has conclusively proved that we have to do with real individuals. We find abundant evidence in favour of this conclusion. We have already heard that the narrative books, in which we find the histories of the patriarchs recorded, the Jahwist and the Elohist documents, which, in their present form, belong to the ninth century B.C. or thereabouts, depend upon older sources, either oral or written, either prose or poetry, which, in turn, belong to a much older period. If this be the case, it follows that we, although the narratives contain much that is legendary in character, can expect to find in them a *historical nucleus* with much greater confidence than if they were such late creations as some modern scholars would have us believe.

In favour of this is the fact that we can prove in many cases that the tradition of the patriarchal history has preserved here and there very *good reminiscences,* or has abstained from idealising the past, and therefore, in the main, rests upon a good historical basis. As proofs I shall cite facts like the following: that Abraham and the other patriarchs are never described in these histories other than as strangers who had immigrated into the Holy Land, who did not claim any rights to the possession of the land; further, that their moral shortcomings are frankly admitted in the account of Abraham's untruthfulness in the affair of Sarah, and of Jacob's deception upon his father. A fiction composed subsequent to the time of Saul and David would probably have made Israel indigenous to the land, and would have avoided all references to defects in the characters of the patriarchs. Since this is not the case in these narratives, we may confidently assume that they were *current* at least in the early kingly period. We may further assume that Israel's reminiscences of pre-Mosaic times are closely connected with the land of Canaan, for how otherwise are we to understand the histories of the various places and tribes as recorded in these documents? That Simeon and Levi are regarded as accursed in the so-called Blessing of Jacob (Gen. xlix. 5-7), and that they only played an insignificant part in the conquest of Canaan (see the Song of Deborah and the story of Gideon), can only be explained if we assume that these tribes had suffered great hardships in pre-Mosaic times, of the kind described in Gen. xxxiv. In the same way we can only understand the story of

Shechem if we assume that it belonged to Israel in ancient times, for it became an Israelitic possession by conquest only after Saul's death. Gen. xxxiv. is unintelligible as a reflection of the time of the Judges. Again, the high position of some of the sanctuaries in the south and further north (Hebron, Beersheba, Bethel, and Mahanaim) is explicable only when we assume that they were religious centres in olden times. It may be said that the *inscriptions* seem to support this opinion. In the lists of Dhutmes III. (*c.* B.C. 1430) we find mention made of a Canaanitish place or district of the name of Jacob (Jacobel), and also of a place called Joseph. About B.C. 1250, in the reign of Meremptah, we find a tribe of Israel in Canaan. In the days of Pharaoh Seti or Rameses II. a mountainous district in Galilee is referred to by the name of Asher. In Biblical times we only know of a tribe of this name, but we are told that they dwelt in the north, so that probably their habitations are meant in the reference cited.

If this is the case, and we are able to maintain that the Biblical legends dealing with the history of the patriarchs, despite the freedom with which they record details, represent on the whole a reliable historical tradition, then surely this applies to the chief characters in this tradition, the patriarchs. Since we have seen that these patriarchs cannot be explained as having been either deities or tribes, and have heard that the names Abraham and Jacob were commonly used in antiquity as personal names, then we are quite justified in reverting to the only possible conclusion, viz. that these patriarchs were *real persons*, and that such persons did at one time *exist*.

We may therefore assume that Abraham, Isaac, and Jacob were chiefs and leaders of small tribes or clans, sheikhs of nomad tribes which had migrated from the East and had settled in Canaan. These tribes in course of time would have increased in strength through alliance, by marriage and otherwise, with other tribes, but they also suffered temporary losses through separation and emigration of some of their own families. The most important instance of the latter was the emigration into Egypt under Joseph, which attracted a considerable part of the tribes, but hardly the whole. Tribes like Asher and the group belonging to it, who had settled in northern Canaan, and perhaps also that tribe which later gave Israel its name, seem to have remained in the land.

However, a possible misunderstanding must not be overlooked. Even if we are able to maintain that the principal figures in the patriarchal history are historical, it does not necessarily follow that we are in a position to establish the historicity of *every detail* of this history. We do not possess the standards whereby we might test the truth of the narratives. We are able to establish the individual existence of the principal figures, and to give an account of the chief events in their lives in the light of the general historical conditions of the times and a few well-authenticated records. It is on these that we base their historical reality. In the case of details, however, we lack such authorities, and are therefore unable to assert positive conclusions. They *can*, but may not, be historical. Only in cases where the narratives testify for themselves—such as the account in Gen. xiv.—or when they are in such close connection with the principal facts that they are dependent upon them, can we hope to establish their historical truth. In all other cases we must assume nothing.

It follows from what we have heard that our *sources of information* concerning primitive times are not such that we can claim them to be historical in every detail. I have no doubts

THE PATRIARCHS 163

in my own mind but that the sources at our disposal are in the main much older than the documents J and E, and that we, in these sources, are less removed from the events themselves than if we did not possess them. But they are not " records " in the truest sense, and therefore they ought not to be accepted as historical, if we want to keep within the limits of truth and certainty.

They are not records, because, for the most part, if not altogether, they are founded upon traditions which were verbally current among the Israelites, *i.e.* upon popular legends, which should never be used as historical sources without being thoroughly confirmed by other sources. Another argument against their being accepted as sources is that we often find, even in J and E, duplicate traditions, differing from each other in details, of the same events. When this occurs, naturally, in accordance with every logical and historical principle, only one of the two accounts can be assumed to be giving the true course of events. Which gives us the true account, we are generally not in a position to decide. We cannot repudiate this conclusion, nor have we any right to hide it from intelligent adults and mature school-children who are capable of grasping it.

2. *Moses and the Israelites in Egypt*

If we wish to examine closely the history of the Mosaic period, which is found mostly in Exodus i.–xx., we must first of all direct our attention to the *desert tribes* and the *migration* into and out of Egypt. We must adopt the same attitude towards the sources of this history as we did in the case of the patriarchal history, for the nature of the records at our disposal is the same in both.

It is true that these sources are not so far removed in time from the events recorded of the Mosaic age as in the case of the patriarchal narratives, but the space is still great enough. And even although we possess some ancient and reliable accounts which place us in a position to describe the principal phases of this period, we must not suppose that we can regard these narratives, without further proofs, as records in the strict sense. In the Mosaic history, as in the patriarchal history, we only possess a tradition, which is by no means uniform. Independent streams of tradition flow together, and in them are many elements which cannot be regarded as historical, but belong to a later development of the tradition, or are such as cannot be ascribed to any known historical period. A few examples will demonstrate my meaning.

The desert of Sinai consists for the most part of sand and stones, and has but few oases. It is improbable that such a large number of people as one tradition in the book of Exodus maintains, namely, 600,000 men, besides the old men, women, and children, could have existed in it for so long a time, apart from the question of sustenance. At the time of Deborah the Israelites numbered, as we know from Judges v. 8, at most 40,000 spears. And this number is probably an exaggerated one. The number must have been very much less in the wilderness, so that we must regard the number quoted in Exodus as the extravagant representation of a later period. As soon as we try to read the course of the history at Sinai and in the wilderness from Exodus xviii. or xix. to Exodus xxxv., and note the way in which the events follow one another—how Moses ascends the mountain, what he does there, and how he descends again—we perceive that it is quite impossible to discover a continuous sequence of events in the narrative.[1] A certain line of thought is taken up, which is

[1] See above, p. 68 f.

suddenly discontinued and replaced by another, to be afterwards renewed in another place. This proves that different traditions concerning the course of events existed, and that to-day it is probably impossible to say which is the oldest tradition or which represents the true tradition, least of all to say what the real course of events may have been.

Again, in connection with the story of the Egyptian plagues, we have to admit that we have no means of establishing their historicity. However, by that I do not mean that they are unhistorical. It is quite possible that, at the time of the Exodus, Egypt was devastated by some great plagues, which caused Pharaoh to grant permission to the Israelites to depart. Moreover, many of the events narrated can perhaps be interpreted as the results of natural phenomena peculiar to the land of Egypt. But to prove the historical character of the details is impossible with our present knowledge of this period. It is seen, therefore, that the same confusion which we found in the earlier history exists also in the history of the Mosaic period. We must often be content with seeking out the *historical nucleus* of the tradition.

In these days two opposing opinions claim

followers among Old Testament scholars—the strictly conservative view that the whole tradition of the Mosaic period is historical, and the critical view which declares that no part of this account is historical. That the former is untenable we have already seen; the latter is far from being established.

We will first of all consider the tradition of the *sojourn in Egypt*. Did any Israelitic tribes dwell in Egypt in the Mosaic period? It is often doubted whether Israel did migrate into Egypt. Is the tradition true, then? We can answer: Yes, but the fact must be properly understood. It may at least be declared that the tribes which eventually formed the Hebrew nation can, in all probability, be divided into three groups: the Canaanitish tribes, who never emigrated from Canaan, the tribes who did migrate into Egypt, and, thirdly, the Arabian-Sinaitic tribes, who never were in Egypt, but had settled upon the steppes of Sinai.

The theory that the Israelites never were in Egypt is so far justified, in that presumably all the tribes did not emigrate there. It is quite probable that a few clans journeyed only as far as the steppes, and there remained until they were joined by the tribes which came out of Egypt. To these belong parts of the tribe which was later known by the name of Judah, at least important units, which at a later period were incorporated with it. We have also good reasons for supposing that clans like Asher, and perhaps parts of the tribe of Manasseh and some others, were settled in Canaan even in pre-Mosaic times, and had never emigrated. Consequently, when the Israelites entered the country, they found there many related tribes upon whose support they could rely. Lastly, we cannot dispute the historical contents of the tradition that certain tribes, known as Joseph (Ephraim and Manasseh), Benjamin, Simeon, and Levi, in consequence of dissensions and persecutions, emigrated into Egypt. It is quite possible that they were under the leadership of a man called Joseph. The story of Joseph, on the other hand—how, according to Genesis, he was carried into Egypt—must be regarded as belonging to those narratives which cannot be historically confirmed in every detail. We know, it is true, of great famines and of measures adopted to counteract the evils of the great dearth, which are comparable with those recounted in the book of Genesis, in the history of ancient Egypt; but whether we can refer them to the time and influence of Joseph, we are unable to decide.

What, then, are we to conclude with respect to the sojourn in Egypt? What are our grounds for believing that any Israelitic tribes were at one time settled in Egypt? I shall mention two principal reasons:—*Firstly*, the tradition is not confined to any one part or time, but represents a continuous, abiding Israelitic belief. It is mentioned by all the chief chroniclers of the book of Exodus and by all the prophets from Amos down. Such a confident and uniform tradition deserves every attention, and should not be ignored unless we have excellent reasons for doing so. *Secondly*, it would be difficult to find a nation which is so self-reliant as the Jewish. If, then, the Jewish tradition introduces their history by referring to so great a humiliation as the subjugation of the nation by the Egyptians, the sojourn in the "house of bondage," as it is often called, it would be very strange if the Jews merely invented this story. If they only desired to make a beginning to their history, they would certainly have adopted different means. How easy it would have been for the fictitious legend to spare Israel this black blot in their past! This is a strong proof that the sojourn of Israelitic tribes in Egypt is a historical fact.

But the history of this period would be incomplete without some remarks upon the principal figure of those times—*Moses.* How are we to regard him?

In general, modern Old Testament scholars are agreed to regard Moses as a historical personality; but there are some who oppose this view, so that a few words may be necessary on this subject. I may say beforehand that, to me, Moses is a real historical character, nor do I think that this fact can possibly be disproved.

That Moses is a historical person is proved by the description—assumed to be historical —of the state of affairs at the time of the Exodus. The tribes which were dwelling in Egypt were a disorganised crowd, a conglomeration of isolated families, each taking its own course, without any idea of patriotism or of unity. These were first inspired into the people by Moses, who in this way accomplished a deed of incalculable importance to the race. He instilled into them strength, courage, and enthusiasm, and inspired them to oppose the Egyptians. Whenever a whole nation begins to be formed from a group of tribes and clans, it is not the work of the tribes themselves, but that of an individual, who imparts his own enthusiasm to the crowd.

Italy did not combine of its own accord, but Cavour created the united Italy; it was not the German tribes who effected the German Empire, but Bismarck inspired them to bring it about. If tradition said nothing of such a person as Moses, we would have to assume his existence; since the tradition is definite and positive on this point, we are compelled to accept it as historical.

It may be added that Moses is undoubtedly an Egyptian name. Moses does not mean, as the tradition wants us to believe, "the one who was drawn out from the water." This is merely a case of popular etymology, examples of which we often find everywhere. We are all of us familiar with the popular local derivations of the names of persons, villages, hills, and rivers. Generally they are artless attempts to interpret the names and then connect them with definite events. The events themselves may have occurred, but their connection with the names is a figment of the imagination. The name Moses, interpreted as a Hebrew word, would mean really "the one who draws out," *i.e.* the deliverer, redeemer. But this is a case of the assimilation of a foreign word to the Hebrew language, influenced by the thought of Moses' life-work. The word, however, is really Egyptian, and means "child." It is the same word which we find in Egyptian compound names, *e.g.* Dhutmoses. The fact that the leading figure in the Israelitic history of this period does not bear a native but a foreign name, is strong proof that he is historical, and also that the Israelites did sojourn in Egypt.

We have a few further remarks to make concerning the personality of Moses as we estimate it to be. *Politically* regarded, he is the uniter of the tribes, their leader out from Egypt over the steppes, and their organiser. Some of the chief events in his life can be historically confirmed, or at least shown to be highly probable, such as the exodus from Egypt and the crossing of the Red Sea. In Exodus xv. we have a song of triumph, which, although its present form is the result of a later revision, contains a portion of the original poem, and reads as follows:—

Sing ye to Jahwe, for He is highly exalted;
The horse and his rider hath He thrown into the sea.

After what we know of song-composing in ancient Israel, especially the war and victory songs, there is no reason why we should regard this song differently from that of Deborah and some others which have come down to us. This song furnishes us with a proof that a great catastrophe, like that described in Exodus, befell the Egyptians in the Red Sea. What we know of the character of the northern point of the Gulf of Suez, and the perils experienced by the army of Napoleon I. in this part, supports the historicity of the fate of the Egyptian soldiers. With the destruction of the Egyptians, its cause, namely, the exodus of the Israelites, is historically established. Then comes the march over the steppes to the mountain of Sinai, the position of which we are unable to determine definitely. At Sinai the new revelation of God was made to Moses. Afterwards follows the further march to the oasis of Kadesh and the rebellion of the people, a prolonged stay at the oasis, where further laws were promulgated. The springs there are occasionally called the well of judgment and the waters of judgment (see Gen. xiv. 7, and *cf.* Exod. xv. 25), Moses having judged there. This points to the fact that an organisation of the people took place here, like that which is described in Exodus xviii. After this long halt at Kadesh, the history goes on to speak of the march in the neighbourhood of the Red Sea, the fight against the Amorites, and the raid into the country east of the Jordan. All these are events which are to be accepted as historical, and which can be established without any difficulty.

A description of Moses as a *religious* personality may be gathered from the account of the events at Sinai and Kadesh. It agrees with the traditional estimate of this side of Moses' character, and it is quite probable that Moses obtained a special revelation upon one or another of the mountains in that region, which we are unable to locate definitely. So that he is indeed the founder of the religion and the legislation of the Israelitic nation.

Of what kind is this religious revelation? It is closely connected with the name of Jahwe, and expresses itself in certain religious and moral commands. The latter are set down in laws which we have in the preceding pages ascribed to Moses, the most important among them being the Ten Commandments. It is immaterial whether Moses revealed the name of Jahwe to the people or not; therefore we need not discuss this question. What is material is that we understand what the name conveyed to Moses, and the idea of God represented in it. We can say that the essential article of the faith of the later Israelites was that the God of Israel was a unique and moral God. The germs of this highest development of the Israelitic religion must have existed beforehand in the idea of God expressed by Moses. That was the determining principle of the Mosaic revelation and its real nature.

It is sometimes maintained that Moses obtained his idea of God from the Kenites, but a proof of this cannot be produced. But it probably can be said that, if Jahwe had been a Kenite god, then in our opinion the Kenites would have become the leading nation and Israel would have been absorbed into it. For it was religion, the characteristic belief in God, which to a large extent determined the national peculiarity of the ancient nations and tribes. That Israel became the leading nation is due to its religion. So the Kenites were absorbed into the Israelites.

Whence Moses obtained this idea of God and the ideals dependent thereon is the secret of his religious genius and his religious experience. For religion is experienced in the innermost depths of one's personality, in those hidden parts of the spiritual life of man which exclusively share the communion with God. It is sufficient for us to know that Moses, because such experiences fell to his lot at certain periods of his life, appears as the pioneer of those men whom we recognise as the religious leaders and masters of the Israelitic nation, viz. its *prophets*.[1]

3. *Idea of God, Religion, and Morality among the Early Israelites*

If we wish to consider this important theme thoroughly, it is advisable, first of all, to direct our attention to Israel's *connection with the Canaanites* and its influence upon the former people.

Speaking generally, we may say that the Mosaic God was the one worshipped by the Israelites after their settlement in the land of Canaan. At least that was their intention. Nevertheless the religion of the masses did not escape profanation, so that many innovations of Canaanitish origin were introduced into it. In order to understand this we must remember that during the first generations after the conquest the Israelites were closely associated with the Canaanites. In this way new ideas were adopted into the Israelitic religion.

[1] See further pp. 224 f., 233.

The history of the conquest of Canaan was not so complete as some parts of the book of Joshua might lead us to believe, as though Israel under Joshua had conquered the whole of the land, so that Joshua was able to allot the whole country among the tribes. If there was a division at all, it was only a partition of an abstract kind. In Judges i. we have the true account of the conquest. Joshua and the tribes of his days had made some progress towards conquest. A number of strategical points had been won, but many remained in the possession of the Canaanites. Generally the possessions of the Israelites were mountain districts, but the fruitful plains and a number of fortified towns were held by the Canaanites. In many places where both peoples lived side by side, without one being able to gain supremacy over the other, there developed a peaceful social life, as, for example, was the case at Shechem (Judges ix.). They made a virtue of necessity, and sought to establish themselves side by side. In this way they formed mutual commercial and religious intercourse. Naturally this close association enabled the Israelites to obtain a knowledge of the Canaanitish religion. The civilisation of the Israelites at this time was in many respects inferior to that of the Canaanites, so that the latter became their teachers in many things. The Israelites were mostly cattle-breeders; the Canaanites, on the other hand, were agriculturists, town-dwellers, craftsmen, and, as we have previously heard, possessed a comparatively high civilisation, and many peaceful and warlike arts, which the Israelites eagerly adopted from them. Thus it happens that, although politically the Israelites subjugated the Canaanites, intellectually the conquered remained conquerors. This is most evident in the domain of religion.

The Canaanitish *religion* was, more particularly, a religion of husbandmen, vine-dressers, and gardeners. It was in a special sense a religion of a rural people, connected with rustic occupations, and was to a large extent developed from them. The principal deity, Baal, signifies the owner, particularly the owner of fruit-giving natural objects and localities, of wells, trees, and fertile tracts of land. Local deities were to be found everywhere, the Baalim of a particular district, mountain, well, or field. The worship of this Baal took the form of sacrifices of fruit and the produce of the land (Hosea ii. 8). Here was something new to the Israelites. Their

Deity was a majestic God of heaven and earth, but He was not a God who had instructed Israel in the art of husbandry, which had never—at least not for a long time—been practised by them. Therefore this Baal impressed them. The consequence was that the Canaanitish cult did not long remain unknown to the Israelites. They saw the Baal cult practised everywhere by their neighbours and acquaintances; what wonder, then, that they imitated the Canaanites in this as in other respects? But generally they did *not* adopt these pagan rites in the sense that they *denied* their Mosaic God. While they participated in the forms of the Baal-worship, the God they worshipped was their own hereditary God, Jahwe. Thus the popular religion of the Israelites of this period was established—the popular religion in contradistinction to the more spiritual religion.

Before I pass on to describe this *popular religion*, I wish to refute a serious misapprehension which is unfortunately current—that is, the idea that this mixture of the Israelitic religion with the Canaanitish cult is nothing else than the religion of Israel in the erroneously called pre-prophetic period—more correctly, the time prior to the great canonical or literary prophets. It is true that the lower, illiterate members of the Israelitic community never did grasp clearly the difference between the pagan Canaanitish worship and the worship of Jahwe, but conceived their God Jahwe in accordance with the Canaanitish model. Later, the influences of this fatal interchange of both cults affected more or less even the upper and the ruling classes, but never to the extent that the feeling that it was improper died away completely.

Sacrificial feasts like those held by the Canaanites were celebrated in honour of Jahwe. Canaanitish sanctuaries, which have already been referred to, were often dedicated to Jahwe—a course not unknown in other religions; *e.g.*, Christian shrines and places of pilgrimage are found in places where formerly Roman, Celtic, German, or Slavonic deities were worshipped. Whenever the Israelites obtained possession of a district, they took possession also of its "high places," as these sanctuaries are often called in the Old Testament, but only that they might be dedicated to Jahwe. It may have been that in certain places, where the population was made up of both Israelites and Canaanites, the former would join his pagan neighbour and worship at the Baal altar, but apparently this was not the rule. In principle the sacrifice was made to Jahwe, but the form of worship and the sacrificial places were oftentimes not essentially different from those of the Baal cult.

Besides the altars, the Israelites retained the oft-mentioned *massebahs* or stone pillars, the nature of which we are now able to determine as the result of recent discoveries at Gezer and elsewhere. These were symbols of the Baal. Likewise they took possession of the sacred trees, the symbols of fertility, and the artificial tree-stumps or sacred stakes, called in Hebrew *asherahs*, and translated by Luther " groves," which represented the sacred tree where no trees would grow. They were originally dedicated to the worship of Astarte. The ancient cup-holes, the relics of a much older period than the conquest of Canaan, were also appropriated to the worship of Jahwe, and some other institutions of the Baal cult. Occasionally the Israelites sacrificed first-born children. The narrative of the sacrifice of Isaac (Gen. xxii.) has been misinterpreted by those who are indignant because the God represented there and the spirit of the narrative seem to extenuate and even to uphold child-sacrifice. The aim of this story is in quite the contrary direction, and would *abolish* this horrible custom. The narrator wishes to teach that the offering of one's own child is indeed the greatest sacrifice man can make to God, and the faith which prompts such a sacrifice is worthy of an Abraham; but the God of Israel does not require such a sacrifice, He having appointed animals for this purpose. Some explain the narrative by saying that God demanded the sacrifice of Isaac only in order to test Abraham. However that may have been, the strong protest against the custom expressed in the narrative proves that it was practised at times among the Israelites.

Photographs and sketches illustrating the objects referred to above are reproduced in figs. 7–9 on p. 57 f., Plates III., IV., and V., opposite pp. 40, 48, and 56. It is the custom even in these days to hang offerings, especially pieces of cloth, upon the sacred trees, in order to propitiate the supernatural being who is supposed to dwell in them.

In general, then, the religion of Jahwe did indeed adopt many Canaanitish rites and customs, so that sometimes Jahwe is distinguished from the Canaanitish gods only by His name. The lofty and pure conception of Jahwe in the days of Moses degenerated later into an idea of God which *limited* His sphere of influence to a certain people and country, and which was not unlike the idea they had of the Baal. Jahwe became a national God who was supreme only in the land of Israel, who recognised that other lands belonged to other gods. Just as, in days gone by, the principle, "Cujus regio ejus religio," was admitted in our own states and among our own people, it was applied by the ancient world to the various deities. An example of this custom is offered in Judges xi. 24, where Jephthah compares Chemosh, the god of the Ammonites (more correctly, of the Moabites), with Jahwe, the God of Israel, as though they were of similar rank. He regards them both as *national deities*: Chemosh is the lord of the land which he has given to his chosen people, but the land of Israel belongs to Jahwe—as though Chemosh were really a God like Jahwe.

Again, in 1 Sam. xxvi. 19 f., David, when persecuted by Saul, and meditating flight into the land of the Philistines, utters these words: "Now therefore, I pray thee, let my lord the king hear the words of his servant. Let those who have stirred thee up against me be accursed. They have driven me out this day from the inheritance of Jahwe, and they say:

Go, serve other gods." It is immaterial whether David uttered these words or whether they were merely put into his mouth by the narrator, or whether David, if he is the speaker, expressed his own belief or only that of a certain class of the Israelitic people: the latter may well have been the case. The fact remains that the narrator assumes that there were people in Israel who did believe what is recorded in this story. People counselled Saul to persecute David, and thus compel him to flee to the land of the Philistines, in whose territory he would have to sacrifice to other gods, for there Dagon and the other Philistine gods were supreme. Since these examples show that Jahwe was conceived as being limited to a special territory, it is not improbable that His power was limited *in other respects* as well. In some of the narratives which the Jahwist adopted from the older legends, God is represented as walking in Paradise, "walking in the evening breezes" (as the literal translation would express it), as descending from heaven to convince Himself whether the tower of Babel or the wickedness of Sodom were really what He had heard they were. He visits Abraham, eats food and takes a walk with him. He was also conceived as being spiritually imperfect; He is angered when people approach too closely to His sacred ark (1 Sam. vi. 19; 2 Sam. vi. 6–10). He stirs up men against each other (1 Sam. xxvi. 19), or He tempts people to do evil; the disastrous census which was David's great sin was prompted by God Himself (2 Sam. xxiv. 1).[1] However, God is not regarded here as the author of evil, but only as the absolute cause of all things. It is a crude way of expressing the conception that God is all in all, and that even in the wicked acts of men God is not to be thought of as permitting or preventing them. But the very fact that this expression took this form, in the mouth of a popular narrator, proves that there was something wanting in his idea of God's nature.

We know, further, that the Canaanitish *sacrificial feasts* were accompanied by wild orgies, that not only did they hold great banquets on these occasions, but also that the customs thereat were of a Dionysiac-Bacchanal character, among others that of religious prostitution. We have already heard that Baal was a god of fertility, and that

[1] The Chronicler perceives the danger of such a mode of expression, and substitutes Satan for Jahwe as the tempter of David (1 Chr. xxi. 1).

Astarte, his spouse, represented fecundity in all its forms, including that of animals and man. It was believed on that account, as in other Asiatic religions, that the god of fertility should be worshipped by means of religious prostitution.

However harsh it may sound, and however deplorable this worst illusion of the erring conscience may be, those who know the power of the lower instincts over the human soul can understand how these customs were admitted into the popular religion of the Israelites. There were at times Temple girls, women who sacrificed their chastity at the altar, and even prostitutors. Amos and other writers candidly admit the existence of this evil. It is from this point of view that we are to understand the story of the Midianites at the end of the book of Numbers (Num. xxv.). On account of this thing the lewdness of Ham, the father of Canaan, is, in Gen. ix., accursed; and more particularly for this same reason is it said, in Gen. xv. f., that the iniquity of the Amorites was "not yet full," but soon would be, and in ch. xix. of the same book the wickedness of the Canaanites is described as sodomy. The narrator of these stories knows well, while he accuses the Canaanites of committing these sins, that every man and woman in Israel is by no means innocent—in public worship and elsewhere; but he also knows that such acts as these are not in compliance with the religion of Jahwe, and that the Canaanitish religion and morals are the source of a terrible and *abiding danger* to Israel. So that we understand the harsh and inexorable opposition towards the Canaanites, and the seemingly cruel measures which we find recorded in the books of the Old Testament which reflect these periods of Israelitic history.

The picture presented to us is by no means pleasant, but it will be shown that it does not represent the whole of Israel, to which fact the nation owes its development and preservation.

However general, particularly in the period prior to 800 B.C., this so-called popular religion had become, it was never adopted by the whole nation as such. The official religion as practised at the principal sanctuaries had, at an early period, rejected many of the excrescences of the popular religion, which had been condemned on principle by the more spiritually-minded Israelites.

The *official religion* of Israel during this period was the religion of the priests and kings as the official leaders and sponsors of divine worship. Even these now and then adopted some parts of the ritual of the popular religion, but this religion was far from being the one they acknowledged. This can be proved from incidents in the lives of Saul and David. Saul was not altogether free from some of the superstitious ideas of his time, and was clearly favourable to the popular religion. But—at least as long as he retained his mental faculties—he was willing to be guided by Samuel, and had, under the influence of Samuel, declared war against the unclean excrescences of the inferior popular beliefs and superstitions. And David also shows now and then traces of an eccentric, imperfect piety (see 2 Sam. vi.), which are probably due to the influence of the popular religion, but his religion is by no means confined to these shortcomings. The fact that he restored the ancient ark, the shrine of the Mosaic period, at which Samuel also had become great, and which had been unduly neglected by Saul, to its early position of honour, shows that he was zealous to uphold the traditions of Moses and Samuel, and to preserve the true religion of Jahwe from complete contamination. A better proof of his sincerity in this respect is the manner in which he placed himself in the hands of the prophet Nathan, thus showing that he was willing to acknowledge the higher characteristics of Jahwe's nature.[1]

We should also bear in mind that the Levites belonged to the tribe of Moses, and that they, on that account, even though a few of them may perhaps have gone their own way, would regard it as their special task to foster the traditions of Moses. From the beginning of the period of the Judges they were continually in the van of religious progress. In the days of Eli, Shiloh was a Levitic sanctuary. It contained the Ark of the Covenant, but no images. Nor did the Temple at Jerusalem possess an image of Jahwe beside the Ark. Eli, Samuel, David, and Solomon were therefore champions of the higher cult. Also Jehu, although he did not destroy the high places, removed the worst excrescences of the popular religion. The priest Jehoiada (2 Kings xi. 17) cleansed the Temple from the Baal forms of worship which had been introduced. It should be said also that the tribe of Judah, in the south, probably protested against the introduction of Canaanitish rites into the religion of Jahwe. The members of this tribe had in

[1] See above, p. 134 f.

190 SCIENCE AND THE OLD TESTAMENT

general not yet become husbandmen, and were at the time only newly settled, so that they never —at least only to a small extent—participated in the endeavour to introduce the Baal ritual into the Israelitic religion.

The sacrifices at the important shrines may have been made upon altars like that of Zorah, shown on Plates IV. and V., opposite pp. 48 and 56, and the great altar of Baalbek, shown on Plate VIII., opposite p. 80. Zorah is the place mentioned in Judges xiii., and connected with the early history of Samson.

We can go still further and say that the religion of the leading intellectual classes was even purer than the official religion. This is the religion of the earlier *prophets*, *i.e.* the non-literary prophets and their associates. They were the leaders of the people from the time of the Judges, and at the same time upholders of the Mosaic traditions.

As time advanced the number of these champions of the pure Mosaic religion increased—men like the prophet Nathan, who had doubtless advanced far beyond the stage at which it was believed that Jahwe tempts a man to do evil (as the popular narrator of the history of David puts it in 2 Sam. xxiv. 1). From all that we read of him, he accepted the fundamental principle of the old Mosaic conception of a moral and spiritual God. This proves to us that even in the early period of the monarchy the popular religion was in principle overcome.

In the period following David's time this fact becomes more and more evident, for then the prophets undertook the leadership of the people. Elijah fought with all the strength of a strong man against the Baal, when Ahab and Jezebel sought to make the religion of the lower classes the national religion. He protested vehemently against such a course. He and his followers prepared once more the path for the advance of the monotheistic ideal, which had been degraded and soiled from continued contact with the Canaanitish ideas; not in the sense that they or that Moses had declared all that the later great prophets said, but in the sense that they pointed out once more the great fundamental principles of religion, and the direction in which the idea and the worship of God would have to move, if Israel was to retain the great heritage of its past. And while such men set themselves at the head of the people, they would, as a matter of course, influence a wide circle to abstain more and more thoroughly from the excrescences of the popular religion. Among the followers of Elijah were men like the *Jahwist* and the *Elohist*, who were also the guides of the people at this time. They all opposed the popular religion.

The Jahwist singles out the customs and beliefs of the popular religion and records them in his book, and shows how these things, when once they have been adopted by wide circles, should be spiritually overcome.[1] In J's estimation the massebahs, even worship itself, are not essential to religion. The massebahs become to him only memorial stones. Worship does not consist of ritual, but is a state of the mind. He demands a spiritual worship: obedience is better than sacrifice—this statement, although not expressed by him, illustrates his attitude well. Although he records narratives according to which God walks in the Garden of Eden, visits various men and dwells in particular places, yet to himself God is the *One* who dwells in heaven. He is everywhere where the pious seek Him, and He is a purely moral God. These ideas are found expressed throughout the whole of his book. The method which he follows in his history of the antediluvian period, from the Fall to the Flood,

[1] See above, pp. 89 f., 91 f.

RELIGION OF ISRAEL AND CANAAN 193

shows what his aim is. His conceptions culminate in Gen. xxxix. 9, where he makes Joseph say: "How then can I do this great wickedness, and sin against God?" In the Book of the Covenant he recommends leniency towards enemies and benevolence towards the poor and the feeble. The popular religion did not teach such virtues as these; only the pious are capable of such exalted ideas, only men who were more closely related to the great prophets than to the popular religion.

But our description of this period would be incomplete did we not consider the *moral standpoint* of the time down to the appearance of the canonical prophets.

The morality reflected in the popular religion of Jahwe or the morality of the pious ones of that period cannot, of course, be compared to our Christian morality. After what we have heard, we could scarcely expect it to be otherwise. Nay, we may perhaps consider it strange that even among the champions of the higher and the highest ideals of the time we occasionally find moral conceptions which we would hesitate to adopt as our own. I do not, of course, refer to the cases where the narrator, and with him the Bible itself, directly disapproves of some questionable deed of a leading person, or at least indirectly takes exception to it, in that he causes the consequences of the act to recoil upon the sinner and indicates these consequences to the reader, as in the case of Abraham's lie (Gen. xx. 10 ff., xxvi. 10) and Jacob's deception (Gen. xxvii. 42 ff.).

In all these cases the narrator does not adopt the point of view of the evildoer, but lets us know that such deeds are the immoral or questionable acts of men who were otherwise pious, that is, that they are isolated sins.

The position is quite different, however, in cases where pious men, or the whole Israelitic nation, are recorded, with the approval of the narrator, to have performed acts in accordance with God's will, or at His *bidding*, which, in the opinion of the narrator or of the period generally, may have been permissible, but which we would condemn as immoral. In these cases the difficulty can only be overcome by breaking away once and for all time from the idea that Christian and Old Testament morality are *one and the same*. This is not the case—for how otherwise would the Old Covenant represent the stage of preparatory revelation, unless it was under the law, unless it was under the rule of an only partially complete knowledge of God? Nor is the standard of morality of the Old Testament itself uniform. Not only does the popular religion obviously stand upon a lower plane than that of the great prophets or men of kindred thought, but even within the circle of the latter we find men who are in other respects highly spiritual and religious, still encumbered, on some one point, by the limitations of an inferior conception of religion and morality, and yet believe their teachings to be consonant with God's eternal will.

In the Book of the Covenant the law, "Eye for eye, tooth for tooth" (Exod. xxi. 24), is still in force, and of course appears in the name of Jahwe. The blood-vengeance is, indeed, often opposed, but is occasionally sanctioned. The well-known imprecatory psalms, the approval of the bloodthirsty expressions of which I regard as an offence against the Bible, need no further consideration.[1] These expressions are a relapse on the part of otherwise pious poets into material, carnal ways of thinking. Nor is it necessary to refer at length to the cruel treatment—consistent with the spirit of the age—which was meted out to conquered foes by the Israelites as by other nations.

[1] See pp. 143, 289.

196 SCIENCE AND THE OLD TESTAMENT

We shall only mention a few special cases. What shall we say to the fact that even an Elijah permitted the vanquished priests of Baal to be murdered in cold blood—and that in the name of Jahwe? or that Jahwe permitted Israel to steal what they had borrowed from the Egyptians? or, lastly, that Samuel blamed Saul—again in the name of God—because he had not exterminated the Amalekites root and branch? The fact that Samuel made this demand in the name of God, or that the narrator ascribes the permission to make this demand to God, is significant, and compels us to reflect, even though we may be able to justify the historical necessity of Samuel's action on the ground of the great danger to religion which threatened Israel on all sides from its heathen neighbours. (See 1 Kings xviii. 40; Exod. xii. 35 f.; 1 Sam. xv. 19 f., 32 f.).

Perhaps some of you feel inclined to ask: Did Samuel and the Israelites worship the Christian God, *our* God? My answer must be expressed as follows: The knowledge of God in the days of Samuel and of the leading spirits of that period was not in *every* respect equivalent to our knowledge; still less is the knowledge of the narrator of the history of

Moses comparable to ours. Fundamentally, He is certainly the same God whom we worship and who revealed Himself in Samuel, but in a dimmed, imperfect way.

I do not wish to remind you of certain dark ages in the history of the Christian Church in order to illustrate what has been said. But is not the God of Luther and Calvin our God, because we know that they also did things in the name of God which we nowadays cannot but condemn—or, better, must condemn, if we do not interpret them in the light of the times of these reformers? Or are the peculiar ideas of God which are entertained by pious men who, in other respects, deserve our esteem —think, for example, how Oliver Cromwell and the pious Boer President, Krüger, were wont to chant their psalms—proofs that they were not Christians and that their God was not our God? What applies to Calvin and Luther and many other great men in the kingdom of God must apply also to the pious ones of the Old Testament.

We must therefore judge God's revelation and the knowledge of His nature in relation to the ability of a certain period and people to apprehend divine truth. It must have some relation to the general knowledge of the time, and cannot, under any condition, be separated from it, if the revelation is to be intelligible to men. In Israel it was the prevailing—even sanctified—custom to humiliate captured foes. Historically, and in view of the religious danger which we have already referred to, we can very well understand the existence of this custom, which was practised in the name of the Deity. We are not surprised that at the time this custom prevailed the leading men of the nation should have lent their support to it until the time was ripe for them and their followers to attain a higher plane, and, in the light of their new revelation, to teach their fellow-countrymen the heinousness of such a custom. The same remark applies to the custom which prevailed in antiquity to injure enemies and opponents, should an opportunity be offered, by underhand means. We ought not to forget, however, before we blame the Old Testament, our own customs in war and politics.

We shall not find these things strange if we apprehend clearly that there are ideas in the Holy Scriptures which are not, nor can be, understood at once, because they are closely connected with the general knowledge of the period in which they prevailed. On that account we, as commentators, must be able, under the circumstances, to tell the public that certain moral conceptions in the Old Testament, however exalted they may be in comparison with the conceptions of other nations, still require to be explained, because they were not given in their highest perfection to the Israelites. We will go further and say that a complete, pure idea of God would have been a stone instead of bread at certain periods when the general knowledge of the community was of an inferior kind. They would perforce have missed it, because they would not have been able to comprehend it. Certain fundamental ideas, once they became prevalent, could not be obliterated from the minds of the people without destroying the coherence and the orderly course of their national life, except by means of the slow process of evolution. Thus it is a proof of special divine *educative* Wisdom that the divine dispensation, even in the highest champions of religion, occasionally starts from inferior ideas, yet in them develops its greatness and grandeur. Samuel and Elijah still remain the prophets and instruments of *our* God as well as Luther and Calvin, despite some dross and imperfections connected with their idea of the divine nature.

4. *The Great Prophets of Israel*

That there were people among the Israelites who strenuously opposed the popular religious practices was clearly demonstrated in the preceding section. We saw there that a serious-minded circle, under the leadership of high-spirited men, had fought against the popular religion, and sought to raise the religious life of the nation to a higher plane.

The great prophets of Israel were men who, imbued with the same spirit which enabled Elijah and Elisha to wage war against the Tyrian Baal cult, dedicated their lives to the task of attacking the popular religion on all sides, and effecting a reformation of the national life of Israel. They flourished during the eighth and ninth centuries, Amos being the first of a long line (*c.* 760 B.C.), and after him come Hosea, Isaiah, and Micah, the culminating point of pre-exilic prophecy being attained in Jeremiah. During the Exile the reformation movement was taken up anew by the second Isaiah and Ezekiel, and after the return was continued by men like Haggai and Zechariah, who, however, unconsciously led prophecy in the direction of that spiritual condition which was destined eventually to replace it, namely, the domination of the priests and scribes.

These great prophets took their stand against the overwhelming majority of their fellow-countrymen, they accomplished most of their work in the face of strong opposition, and they, almost without exception, died without seeing much fruit of their labours; nevertheless, they did not live in vain. They did not arrest the downfall of the State; some were even accused—and not always without reason—that they hastened it. But the fact that Israel still continued to exist even when the outward form of a united government was destroyed, that the nation survived the exile in Babylon and the generations of oppression which followed it down to the time of Jesus Christ, and even to our days, is due to these great leaders more than to any other men, although they never ceased to preach the destruction of the nation. But although they seemed to wish the fall of the State, their only thought was its preservation in a newer and better form. Their enthusiasm inspired the declining nation to believe in God and in itself, and to hope for a redeemer in the future—a hope which has always been the mainstay of the Jews, even in the days of their deepest humiliation. It is a *scene without a parallel* in history that a nation, apparently wasting away under the eyes of its religious leaders, should yet become more active and powerful, and that its death as a nation should be only a means whereby it might be revived to a newer and more exalted life.[1]

There are two things which we must not forget when we consider the *active ministry* of these prophets: the fact that the moral and religious condition of the nation was utterly corrupt, and that the political conditions seemed to foreshadow the fall of the State.

Our prophets were in a position to arrive at a true estimate of the *religious* conditions from Elijah and Elisha and some other prophets of Israel's past history. We shall find that they attacked the root of the evil. To them the religion of Israel no longer deserved the name of Jahwe-worship; it was not a worship of God but idolatry; it had degenerated into paganism and natural religion. It was but natural, therefore, that Jahwe refused to recognise the nation as His people, that He would no longer acknowledge those who profess His name, and that the doom of the nation was sealed. In the past such perverse

[1] See above, p. 108 f.

behaviour in divine worship was punished by some temporary visitation upon the king and his people, but now the only adequate punishment was the downfall of the nation.

With respect to the *moral* conditions, again, their conclusions were the same. Moral evils prevailed in Israel at all times. As time advanced these evils undoubtedly gained more and more supremacy and became more and more public. Since the time when Israel became acquainted, through international commerce and intercourse, with foreign civilisations and strange customs and practices, when the country became wealthy through successful business transactions, the strict morality of the Fathers was naturally loosened. Voluptuous and luxurious modes of life, refined pleasures, immorality, and vice obtained, in the course of time, an entry into Israel, especially into its two capital towns.

As trade increased and riches were accumulated in the land, since many of the Israelites were infected by the fever of speculation and gambling, naturally the *social* contrasts became more and more pronounced. The early Israelites, as a simple agricultural people, knew but little of the distinction between rich and poor. But now all this was changed. The new era probably commenced in the reign of Solomon, but the consequences only gradually became perceptible, although in the days of the prophets they were so far developed that we can speak of a crisis, at least of a social danger, with reference to the great gap which separated the rich and poor. Certain expressions of the prophets concerning this state of affairs sound so harsh that we are reminded of the rough and forcible sayings of a social agitator of these days, and we might feel inclined to mistake the prophets—as some have done—for popular tribunes, and thus misjudge their true mission.

There can hardly be any doubt but that the moral and social conditions of Israel did not become pronounced only just at the time when we hear of them, as the writings of the prophets seem to imply. We must assume that they were prevalent long before the prophets began to preach against them. There need be no doubt, either, but that there were champions of the people before Amos, Hosea, and Isaiah, who raised their voices against evil, but their method was different. They may have preached the necessity of repentance and reformation, and may have referred to the probability of punishment and judgment. But when they mentioned the manner of divine visitation, they thought only of a temporary affliction, affecting a town or district, the king, or some of the people, in the way of pestilence and drought, bad harvests, and famine and the like. But Amos and the other prophets announced quite a new manner of judgment; the nation shall not merely suffer temporary punishment, but it must be *destroyed*.

How are we to explain the conception of this final and extreme idea in the minds of the prophets? The answer is: through their far-sightedness in respect to *political* conditions of their time, more particularly with reference to Assyria.

It is necessary here to give a brief outline of the development of the *Assyrian empire* up to the point when it comes in contact with the Israelites, and then, further, to the time when the relation of friendship became one of enmity, and the weaker nation fell under the supremacy of the stronger. We must confine ourselves to the most important facts.

Palestine was, as we have already heard, formerly under Babylonian and Egyptian supremacy. In the course of the twentieth century B.C. both of these world-powers gradually became weaker and weaker, and at last ceased to be. About the middle of the twelfth century a new power, viz. Assyria, coming from the East, began to assert itself. Even at that time Tiglath-Pileser had borne his standard as far as Lebanon. From this point onwards Assyria asserted its claims to Syria and the coast-lands of the Mediterranean Sea as far as Carmel. But Assyria was soon to pass through a period of weakness and incapacity which prevented it from extending its conquests in Syria. This alone is the reason why David and Solomon were able to develop their power in Syria unimpeded. But some time after the schism of the kingdom, in the days of Omri of Israel, the Assyrian kings again took up their ancient policy, never to abandon it.

In the meantime, Israel had other troubles to meet which claimed her first attention. During the period subsequent to the reign of Solomon, at the time when she was weak, a state which became a more and more dangerous opponent, more especially to the northern of the two Israelitic states, established itself on the northern frontier. This was *Syria* or Aram, which had Damascus as its capital. Its successive kings waged incessant war against the kings of Israel from the time of Baasha, and especially from the time of Ahab onwards. The Syrian kings often gained the upper hand, and at times treated the Israelites —especially those who dwelt on the frontier— with ruthless cruelty. The history of the Israelitic kings from Ahab onwards, especially the kings of the house of Jehu, is, with some exceptions, a telling proof of this fact, as are also the history of the prophet Elisha and the statements found in the book of Amos. When Elisha once came to Damascus—so recounts the tradition in 2 Kings—in order to announce to King Benhadad that he would soon die, and to Hazael that he would succeed his master, he burst into tears before Hazael. When he was asked why it was that he wept, he answered the pretender, "Because I know the evil thou wilt do unto the Israelites. Their strongholds thou wilt set on fire, and their young men thou wilt slay with the sword, and wilt dash in pieces their little ones, and rip up their women with child" (2 Kings viii. 12). These words show what manner of treatment the Israelites expected from the Syrians—and doubtless they had every reason for fearing.

These facts enable us to understand an event which we would otherwise be scarcely in a position to explain. Since the time of

Omri, when the Assyrians raided Syria again and again, they were occasionally opposed by the allied forces of the Israelites and the neighbouring Syrian states, naturally without much success. Generally, however, they were *welcomed* by the Israelites, because together they were better able to keep the hostile Syrians in check than the Israelites could alone. We find no evidence whatever, at least in the records prior to the days of Amos, that the Israelites anticipated any danger which might threaten them from Assyria. The favour of the lord of Nineveh was sought as a protection against internal enemies, and he was regarded as the only one who was capable of coping with the troublesome Syrians. Israel had no foreboding that the advantage it expected from Assyria was the same as Homer's "beneficium Polyphemi," the privilege to be the last to be consumed. And yet it was a very clear deduction. If the Assyrians desired to possess the western country and thus gain an outlet into the Mediterranean, the conquest of Israel was but a question of time once Syria had fallen. As long as Syria prevailed, it was a protection to Israel; but when it fell, Israel and Assyria became neighbours, and the fate of Israel would not long remain doubtful.

The fact that such a possibility did not occur to the Israelites for a long time simply proves how little they were accustomed as a nation to look beyond the near future, and also how short-sighted the majority of the people must have been. But there were a few men in Israel who were clear-sighted enough to see things as they really were, and who possessed the moral strength to declare openly before king and people how great the danger was. These men were the *prophets* of that period.

Doubtless they had learnt to regard things in their true light as the result of a careful consideration of the political events of their time. But they did not speak as politicians, in the sense generally ascribed to this word, but spoke in the service of their God, as the religious and moral watchmen and admonishers of the nation, and as the voice of God in the midst of the people. Thus they were naturally the spiritual, in some respects also the political, guides and advisers of the nation. Although they predicted the fall of the nation, and regarded this destruction as good and necessary, because God willed it; although they were thus apparently, and in the thoughts of many, the enemies of their country, yet they were really the noblest and purest *patriots* any nation could ever possess; they were not patriots, indeed, in the narrow national sense, but in that higher sense which transcends all national limitations, which, indeed, does not consider temporal interests, but honours the eternal will of God and the moral laws expressed therein over and above the existence even of their own beloved country.

The English people are said to have a proverb which says: "Right or wrong—my country." I do not know whether this proverb is really current in England—hardly, I should say, among the high-minded and far-seeing members of the English nation. Such a statement as this cannot be imagined as uttered by any of these Israelitic prophets. Their maxim was: When Israel is just, and as long as it continues to be just it may exist; but once the nation ceases to do right and to act in accordance with the will of God, it may cease to be—it does *not deserve* to exist any longer.

But how was it possible that Israelites could conceive such a horrible thought, that Jahwe Himself would accomplish the downfall of the nation? All that the Israelites had conceived of Jahwe and had expected from Him, previous to the preaching of these prophets, was quite the contrary to such an idea. To the *popular religion* it was self-evident that Jahwe would always be gracious to Israel, and would always help it whenever it was in need, if only sufficient sacrifices and worship were offered to Him. If, then, He would not vindicate Israel, it was because He lacked the power. If ever the Assyrians or any other enemies overpowered the Israelites, it was accepted as conclusive proof by the great majority of the people that the strange gods, those of Assyria or other heathens, were more powerful than Jahwe. The natural and practical consequence of such a mode of argument was that these deities were worshipped.

Such was the argument of the popular religion, but it was not the argument of all the Israelites. Men like Elijah and the prophetical schools connected with him, or men like the great Jahwist and his pupils and their contemporaries, had advanced far beyond this inferior form of religion. But even they were loath to think that Jahwe would destroy His own peculiar people. It is, however, an exaggeration—although a common one—to say that Amos was the first to teach that Jahwe is a moral Deity. It is no less an exaggeration to say that Amos was the first "discoverer" of monotheism in Israel, or of the conception that Jahwe is the God of the whole universe. Amos "discovered" neither the one nor the other conception. It is more correct to maintain that the earlier prophets had not advanced beyond the thought that Jahwe would punish His people for their sins, but would not cast the *nation as such* away from Him. They conceived the idea of a moral God by itself, and the idea of His unity and uniqueness by itself. Therefore they advanced no further than to a conception of a moral national organisation under the protection of God, or of a divine cosmic system which was occasionally active. The conception of a universal moral government of the world was unknown to them.

This conception was discovered, if we can refer to it as a discovery, by Amos and men like him. They saw the political necessity and the inevitableness thereof, that Israel's fate would be accomplished by the eastern world-power. They saw also that Israel's moral, social, and religious condition was not such that it could be looked upon with favour by Jahwe. Jahwe was known, moreover, to be a moral God who punished sinners. Since they were unwilling to believe as the followers of the popular religion did, and to forsake the religion of Jahwe whenever Israel sustained a reverse of some kind—and that they could not do because the spirit of God was in them,—there remained to them only the other alternative that the punishing, moral, judging God and the one who does not prevent the destruction of the nation are one and the same. But not in the sense that Jahwe *could* not prevent the downfall of Israel, nor in the sense that He *would* not prevent it; on the contrary, He Himself has ordained it, on account of His people's guilt.

In this way the great riddle of Israel's fate was solved. Assyria is not the primary cause of Israel's misfortunes; least of all is it because Jahwe is weaker than the Assyrian gods. Jahwe Himself and Israel's sins are the primary cause, and Assyria is only an instrument in Jahwe's hand, the rod of correction and the scourge of God for the Israelites.

In this way also was the great riddle of the idea of God solved, or brought nearer to a solution, and an act accomplished which placed the prophets in the very first ranks of the religious leaders of all ages. Even though they are not the discoverers of the unity and the moral character of God, still it was they who brought them out from their obscurity and gave them a content which previous to this had only been dim and uncertainly felt, more surmised than clearly conceived. They established completely and clearly the moral side of God's nature, and, taking this as a standpoint, they explained everything which happened in the world in accordance with this conception, and thereby exalted the uncertain, imperfect idea of God current in their days to the idea of a universal *moral monotheism* which governs the whole world.

Thus they were the heirs of the Mosaic creation, and it was they who made it more perfect. They are the men from whom the human race received the highest possible idea of God — God as absolute goodness, moral holiness, and—since Hosea and Jeremiah—holy love. This idea of God had never been conceived before. There may be isolated instances in Assyrian, Babylonian, or Egyptian literature which seem to approximate to this idea of God, theoretical assumptions and premises; but an ethical monotheism of the kind conceived by the great prophets of Israel is not known, except in the Old Testament, to any people or religion. Even Jesus has not excelled it, nor did He wish to do so. His conception of God was in no way different from that of the prophets. Even to Him God is moral holiness, holy love. What He did was to show that He Himself was the way to this God and the living revelation thereof. In this respect He is greater than even the greatest of the prophets.

The *consequences* of such a conception of God as they had now attained were perfectly clear to the prophets. Religion as practised by the masses, with its pagan Canaanitish practices, and the consequent desecration of the pure Mosaic idea of God, was no longer Jahwe-worship but Baal-worship. Jahwe was, in the estimation of these prophets, degraded to the level of an idol, and His worship had become heathenish.

The main feature in *natural religion* is that it confounds the spiritual Deity with objects or forces of inanimate or material nature. If men are able to influence nature's forces or subdue them by cunning or by force, they will do so. If their power and ability be insufficient to accomplish this, they resign themselves to the inevitable. The compulsion which religion is believed to bring to bear upon these divine natural forces is effected by means of worship, particularly by means of sacrifices.

216 SCIENCE AND THE OLD TESTAMENT

If the god receives an abundance of sacrifices, then he will, or even must, render assistance and grant favours to his worshippers (unless he has special reasons against doing so, or he lacks the necessary power). Whether he who sacrifices is *worthy* of assistance, whether the heart and the soul are inspired to the act of worshipping, is not at all important.

That is the nature of natural religion, and in the same way public worship was emphasised above all else in the Israelitic popular religion, more especially the external *acts* of worship. Sacrifices, prayers, pilgrimages to the sanctuary constituted piety. Morality and spiritual piety were of course desirable, and were in principle esteemed; but they were not necessary in order to obtain a hearing by the god and to receive the divine blessing.

In the estimation of the prophets, such a religion was unworthy of the name. They desired to sweep away with an iron broom every vestige of such idolatry. They could not protest too loudly against such practices. When we read their words, we feel as though we saw Luther in the chapel of Wittenberg Castle exposing and condemning ecclesiastical indulgence and the so-called "opus operatum" —the external action in the place of the inner consciousness; we feel as though we saw Jesus of Nazareth standing upon the hill and saying to His faithful followers: " Leave there thy gift before the altar, and go thy way, first be reconciled to thy brother, and then come and offer thy gift " (Matt. v. 24); or condemning His opponents: " Ye say, If a man shall say to his father or his mother, that wherewith thou mightest have been profited by me is Corban, that is to say, Given to God; ye no longer suffer him to do aught for his father or his mother; making void the word of God by your tradition" (Mark vii. 11).

With this compare Isaiah (i. 11 f.):

> To what purpose is the multitude of your sacrifices unto Me? saith Jahwe:
> I am full of the burnt offerings of rams, and the fat of fed beasts;
> And I delight not in the blood of bullocks, lambs, or of he-goats.
> Your new moon and sabbath and the calling of assembly My soul doth abominate:
> They are a cumbrance to Me; I am weary to bear them.

Or Amos (v. 21 ff.):

> I hate, I despise your feasts,
> And I will take no delight in your solemn assemblies.
> Take thou away from Me the noise of thy songs;
> For I will not hear the melody of thy viols.
> But let judgment roll down as waters,
> And righteousness as a mighty stream.

It is indeed no exaggeration to say that the words of Luther concerning dead works, the words which Paul and even Jesus Himself uttered concerning faith and the relation of the heart to outward acts, are really based upon the statements of these great prophets. The principle they express was known to the prophets, but of course the Old Testament writers had not apprehended the specific contents of faith as revealed in the New Testament.

In one respect the prophets might be misunderstood, as indeed has been done by some recent writers upon the time and work of the prophets. I refer to the tendency to explain the attitude of the prophets towards worship and outward religious practices as though they regarded these things as being of no account *in themselves.* Even though some of their expressions seem to imply that such was really their attitude, and their denunciation of the malpractices in public worship sounds so earnest that the confirmation of even a correct observation of it seems to be denied, in reality this confirmation is as little wanting as the confirmation of good works by Luther, which has so often been denied. If the prophets insisted upon the abolition of all devotional rites and customs, they would be offering a stone instead of bread to the nation. If a proof is wanted that their attitude was quite the contrary to this, we need only to turn to the passage from Isaiah which we have just quoted and see what he says about prayer. There the prophet condemns—just as Jesus did later—the manner in which his contemporaries pray with the same decisiveness and severity as he condemns their sacrifices. But would anyone seriously believe that Jesus or one of the prophets ever intended to do away with the prayer of the faithful?

One result of their exalted idea of God was that they strenuously opposed the popular religion, and sought to teach the people that the Deity was a spirit. Another result of this idea, which we must now consider, is their loud protest against the *moral* and *social* conditions of the time, and the way in which they are to be reformed.

The severity with which Isaiah, Amos, and others criticise these evils is well known to all, so we shall only quote one example. Isaiah, when he sees the thoughtless accumulation of property and the ruthless exploitation of the poor, cries out (v. 8 ff.):

> Woe to them that join house to house,
> That lay field to field,
> Till there be no more room, and ye be made to dwell
> Alone in the midst of the land!
> Thus hath Jahwe of the hosts sworn in my hearing,—
> Of a truth many houses shall be desolate,
> Even the great and the fair shall be without inhabitant.

In these verses it is clearly stated that the punishment for such conduct is the destruction of the State. The society of the time was so very corrupt, its constitution so diseased, that gentle measures were of no avail. There was no other cure but that the State, and with it the whole social system of that time, should be destroyed (Is. iii. 1 ff., 8 ff.). But the fall of the State is not an end in itself; destruction is not the goal of divine dispensation. The prophets were not in vain men of *faith* who had heard the voice of the living God in their hearts. The God whose voice they heard was, and would continue to be, the God of Israel. Even though the State be destroyed, He would still remain, and would find ways and means to continue in that relation. Hence they concluded that this belief in the God of Israel, who is not only holiness but also love, guaranteed to them a *future* purified and cleansed from all the existing defects and evils.

Before proceeding to consider further the idea of a future hope just referred to, we must try to answer a question which has probably proposed itself to many of you. We have spoken at length of the mission of the prophets of the classical period, but we have not yet considered the question: *What* constitutes *prophecy*? What is the *peculiarity* and the distinguishing mark of so remarkable a phenomenon?

History tells us that there were prophets in Israel at all times from the very beginning, in the days of Moses, down to the early period of Judaism. But they were not all alike. Moses, the leading figure at the commencement of the national history of the Israelites, is referred to, in the various Old Testament records, as a prophet, or as the man of God in a peculiar sense. As a revealer of the Deity, as the religious leader of his nation, and as a religious mediator he displays the characteristics of a true prophet. After him comes Samuel, the reformer and purifier of divine worship, which during the period of the Judges had degenerated under the influence of Canaanitish sites and customs. He was probably the founder of the prophetic "schools" also. In his days, it appears that the prophets had united together to make a common cause against the Canaanitish influences. Bands of ecstatic men — looking like madmen—went through the land preaching a holy war, and sweeping away everything which hindered their progress. Political disturbances, which were at the same time religious disturbances, were probably the cause of their appearance. Samuel gathered them together and took them into his service, and so began to refine their innate passionate and unruly natures and to guide their energies to new paths.

From that time prophecy was able to hold its own for many centuries, its champions approximating now to the older prophets, as represented by Moses and Samuel, and thoroughly Israelitic in character, now approximating to the later prophets and influenced by Canaanitish thought. Of the former kind were men like Nathan, the prophet of David's day; of the latter, men like Elijah and Elisha. With the advance of time the method of prophecy was also changed. The independent roving bands of prophets having been united under the leadership of a master, fostered the religious ideals, and perhaps sought to discover new means of ascertaining the will of God. But prophecy attained its climax and its classical period in the days of men like Amos, Hosea, Isaiah, and the other great literary prophets. In the writings of these men we have sufficient witnesses to enable us to comprehend the historical character of the whole movement. To answer the question stated above, we must, therefore, turn to the prophetical writings and let them supply their own witnesses.

The prophets have often been described as patriots, in the strict sense, and their peculiar characteristic as patriotism. They have been compared with men, like Ernst Moritz Arndt and Fichte in Germany, or Demosthenes in Athens, who, through their eloquence, called upon their people to free their native country from the yoke of the foreigner. Others picture the prophets as popular tribunes, men of the people, the friends of the poor and the oppressed, and their champions; and in support of this view, its upholders refer to the harsh and occasionally agitative utterances of the prophets against the exploitation of the poor. They were both patriots and the friends of the people (see pp. 209 and 219 f.). But neither the one nor the other of these characteristics expresses the real nature of their activity or indicates what they, *above all else,* desired to be recognised as. They themselves tell us what they really were when they describe themselves as the mouths of God, or the speakers of God, and call themselves *men of God.*

It is clear that to them the first thing and the last was religion—God Himself. Him they, as "men of God," wanted, and to announce His will to others as His "speakers." The representatives and the champions of the Deity among the people, religious and moral leaders and teachers of the nation, was what they desired *most* to be. Their patriotism and their love towards the people were secondary. If the people were guided and treated contrary to the will of God, the prophets censured it; and when the country and its policy forsook the paths of God, as they conceived them, these prophets seemingly *opposed* it.

But how did they *become* men of God and His speakers? Possibly because they in some way understood God's language. It is only in this way that we are able to understand the manner in which they introduced their various prophecies with, "Thus spake Jahwe (to me)," or concluded them with, "That is what Jahwe spake." We must therefore believe, unless we regard these words as mere forms of speech, that they were really conscious that their words — either literally or metaphorically — were not their own, but those of their Master, that is, the "inspiration" of Jahwe.

They are more explicit still, and confidently say that *what* they preach to the people, and the reason *why* they do preach, is not determined by their own wills. They are determined by a higher will than their own, and are compelled to preach. The prophet may or may not desire to give utterance to the divine command, but when he hears Jahwe's voice within him he *must* testify. He must do so just as one must obey a natural law or an unconditional categorical imperative.

> The lion hath roared, who *will* not fear?
> The Lord Jahwe hath spoken, who can but prophesy?

cried Amos (iii. 8). In the book of Jeremiah we read, more than once, how the prophet refused and shrank from his prophetic task, and how he on each occasion succumbed to the higher will of God.

The question as to the objective truth of this consciousness we need not discuss. It is undoubtedly true subjectively. The prophets themselves thought so, and were indeed conscious of the inner voice compelling them to undertake their divine calling. The question of the *objective* reality of their consciousness is not a historical problem, nor a question to be dealt with in an exact science. We can only say that during periods of *exalted emotion* these men were conscious of the divine activity as a power which completely subjugated their wills. This experience, which is the mystery of the religious soul and its God, made them prophets, and ordained them to the service of the Deity. He who is able to see traces of living God in the world, and believes that He interferes in human affairs, will, of necessity, regard the consciousness of these prophets differently from him who has no knowledge of these things.

From the definite historical utterances of the prophets themselves, and in the light of analogies among other nations, we may attempt to describe the *inner development* which took place in the souls of these men to produce this consciousness.

Among the various nations of the world we find instances in which we are able to observe how certain persons, popularly regarded as a special type of men, distinct from their fellows, pass into ecstatic states, and in them make peculiar observations. Generally these experiences come to them during worship, or whilst they offer fervent prayer, or during some other powerful religious occupation of the mind. They get into a condition in which they are in a peculiar sense cut off from the world, but in which their souls are all the more active, and respond readily to influences which have no effect upon a man in his ordinary waking life. In this condition they see visions and hear voices and words, the significance of which is unknown to the ordinary man. This condition is, as we have already said, one of ecstasy, a kind of semi-consciousness, at times accompanied by a strange excitement brought about by strong external stimuli which easily affect the mind in such a state of prostration. Outwardly the man seems to be insane. Since mental abnormality was regarded in antiquity as the direct result of the presence of a powerful deity in the affected person, these men seem to their fellows to be of necessity, and in a special sense, inspired by God. They themselves know no other explanation than that what they hear are the words of a deity, and that what they see are *visions* which God Himself gives to them.

A man of this kind was Balaam, of whom the Mosaic tradition reports that he had been summoned from a distant country by the enemies of Israel to curse the Israelites, and thus to stay their advance, but that—against his own will—he was inspired by Jahwe and compelled to bless where he had intended to curse. In this story of Balaam we probably have a description of an ancient seer. Even though the story may not be historical in all its details, the figure of Balaam is still a true type of such a seer of the olden times. The description of his appearance should be read:

> The oracle of Balaam, the son of Beor,
> And the oracle of the man whose eye was closed.
> The oracle of him who heareth the words of God,
> Who knoweth the counsel of the Most High;
> Who seeth the face of the Almighty—
> Fallen down and having his eyes opened.

Here the ecstatic state is clearly described. The outward eye closed, physically unconscious, the seer lies there and utters his oracle. But his inner eye is opened that he may see the face of the Almighty, his ear uncovered that he may hear His words and counsel.

Something similar is the report which we have of Mohammed. It is said that during devotional exercises he suddenly heard voices and saw a vision, an experience which was over and over repeated in the course of his life. Whilst he was in this state his senses seemed to be stupefied, as though he was unconscious; but when he recovered from the trance he was able to describe what he had seen and heard. To accuse Mohammed of imposture is unjust, although such is the general opinion concerning him. It would be more correct to describe him as a man who possessed a morbid "hysterical" disposition. But we must not forget that it does not necessarily follow that nervous weakness and abnormal dispositions are to be classed with weak-mindedness. Men afflicted by the former may be capable of the highest mental capacity and intellectual accomplishments.

As a third example of such ecstatic persons we may refer to a man who dwelt in Canaan somewhere about the time of Saul and David. An Egyptian papyrus, the so-called Papyrus Golěnischeff, mentions a man from Bylos, in Syria, who lived about 1100 B.C., who was suddenly seized by the god to whom he was sacrificing, and became mad or ecstatic, and gave utterance to all manner of things, which seem to have been regarded as messages from the deity, as oracles.

In each of these cases we have clear analogies to the prophetical state as represented in the Old Testament, and they also provide us with the natural basis of what we observe in the prophets of Israel since the time of Samuel: first in the earlier period and in purely popular forms, still considerably influenced by the Canaanitish religion; then in Elijah, who has advanced to a clearer and more spiritual conception of God, and has a higher and nobler religious ideal; and lastly in the great classics of prophecy, the so-called canonical prophets, who have attained a still higher moral and spiritual plane, until the climax is reached in men like Hosea, Isaiah, and Jeremiah, in whom the passivity of the mind during the reception of God's revelation has been changed into a clear, conscious activity.

But even at its highest stage of development, Israelitic prophecy has many affinities with the non-Israelitic phenomena of a like kind, and the connection with natural causes is still clearly seen—a clear proof that the highest religious experiences are always connected with natural historical and psychic conditions and circumstances. They do not necessarily depend upon these latter, but, in order to be historically and psychologically understood, they cannot dispense with them.

It is in this way that we must explain the accounts of the *calling* of the prophets to their great work, which is described most vividly to us, in which the prophets themselves tell us how they became conscious that God was near to them, and put words into their mouths. Isaiah (see vi. 1 ff.) stood or reclined in the court of the Temple in deep meditation, and before he was aware of it he was transported in the spirit from his earthly surroundings into the heavenly sanctuary itself. With eyes opened by the Spirit of God he saw before him the heavenly Temple in the place of the earthly one; the heavenly altar and fire at which the celestial angelic beings worshipped in the place of the earthly altar served by human priests; and instead of the earthly throne of God upon which was placed the ancient Ark of the Covenant under the wings of the cherubim as representatives of Jahwe, he saw the heavenly throne upon which Jahwe Himself sat, clothed in royal raiment, and hovering around Him were celestial spirits who proclaimed His glory and majesty. He heard Jahwe speaking and calling to him to take up the prophetic office. When he recovered consciousness he was a prophet, and from that time he experienced again and again the same or similar experiences, which gave him the right to proclaim his sayings and speeches as having been revealed to him by Jahwe. Somewhat similar was the manner in which Amos, Jeremiah, and Ezekiel received their call, and perhaps all the other prophets.

Nor is it a mere manner of speaking, an imaginative, poetic expression of the fact that Isaiah or the others resolved one day to become prophets, that these accounts represent. These "calls" have often been explained as though they were meant to be figuratively interpreted, that they are legendary glorifications or fantastic imaginative accounts of the circumstances which induced these men to adopt the calling of prophets.

Nothing of the kind. Generally speaking, they are accounts of *real experiences*. Naturally, there were previous events which formed a psychological basis to these great experiences. The "call" was preceded by self-preparation as well as by special experiences. The soul of the prophet was no *tabula rasa* before he heard the divine call. Meditation on the nature of God, and a resolution to offer themselves to His service, must have influenced their lives and inspired their souls long before God called them to their great task. At a certain definite moment the tension of their minds reached its highest point, and they felt themselves transported to the presence of their God, they heard His voice and received decisive commands to enter upon their life's work.

In what measure the prophets after Samuel —as is presupposed in the case of Moses and Samuel—felt themselves transported into the divine presence and were inspired independently of such passive conditions of the mind, is not quite clear. It is, however, quite probable that they were normally conscious of divine influences. This is at least clear— and that is the main consideration as far as we are concerned—that when they *spoke* their minds were perfectly clear and conscious, and that when they recounted their experiences in beautiful, artistic speeches they expressed themselves so clearly that every thought of their previous unconsciousness was obliterated from the minds of their hearers and readers. Indeed, it would be a great mistake to regard them as mere ecstatics. They were all men who possessed a clear insight — oftentimes more far-sighted than the leading politicians of their day.

The subjective *reality* of these accounts of specific prophetical experiences is therefore unquestionable. Here again, whilst we are seeking to establish the indubitable results of exact historical science, we may ignore the question of the *objective* reality and truth of these experiences, *i.e.* the question whether God really revealed Himself through the prophets. Since a knowledge of God can never be obtained by means of exact scientific methods, but only by personal experiences—which give us knowledge which is by no means inferior in certainty to that of the physical sciences,—neither is His activity in particular cases the object of exact conclusive science.

We have one more statement to add to what has already been said on this subject. We know that Jesus was greatly influenced by the prophetical writings of the Old Testament. He never tired of referring to them in His discourses, and when He had an opportunity to do so He read and expounded a passage from the prophetical books to the assembled community, which He significantly is unable to interpret in any other way than: "To-day hath this scripture been fulfilled in your ears" (Luke iv. 21).

What was the passage which Jesus read? A prophet of the ancient nation (Is. lxi. 1) said: "The spirit of the Lord God is upon me ... that I may proclaim liberty to the captives." So that Jesus Himself declared that this prophet was filled with the Spirit of God, and He recognised in him on that account and because of the nature of his declaration a type of Himself, and in his words a prophecy concerning Him. He declared Himself to be like that prophet, not in the sense that He was only a prophet, but that He was all that that prophet was. Therefore they who believe that the self-consciousness of Jesus is superior to that of other men, even to that of the most religious among them, will, after what Jesus said of these prophets, acknowledge that the prophetical writings reflect the same spirit which reveals itself in the life of our Lord and Saviour.

5. *The Hope of Israel*

We have already heard that the prophets, whilst they proclaimed the destruction of the nation, did not regard this as the ultimate fate of the people. They argued that, since their God was also the God of the whole world, the God of moral holiness and of holy love, and above all the God and the Father of Israel, who had ordained great blessings to His people, and through them to the whole world, He *must* find some means to make His people, despite the outward collapse of the State and the nation, what He had intended them to be, and through them to bless the world in the manner which He had foreordained.

That the prophets, as the spiritual leaders and the religious teachers of the nation, should argue in this way, and, despite everything that seemed to point to the contrary and the great forces they had to contend against, should build all their hopes thereon, was a natural consequence to their conception of Jahwe, and was the only possible conclusion they could arrive at in view of the conception of *religious belief* advocated by them, especially by Isaiah.

In his estimation the true faith is the sum-total of everything which he recognises to be religiously great and exalted. During periods of the greatest national peril, when the nation was in sore straits, and everybody except himself, including the king and the people, felt that the end was coming, Isaiah relied implicitly upon his religious faith and in his trust in God as the rock upon which his religion was founded, and standing before the king and his ministers he cried : " If ye will not believe, ye shall not be established" (Is. vii. 9). The courage of the prophet in thus proclaiming the infidelity of the nation is better appreciated when we remember that he uttered these words at a time when the nation was face to face with what seemed to be certain destruction. It is seen that Isaiah regarded politics from a religious point of view. His attitude towards the political affairs of his day was this, that in order to understand thoroughly the true nature of anything, it is necessary to regard it from the point of view of religion, as well as from other points of view, *i.e.* that a consideration as to what might be the will of God and the decrees of heaven, and of the fundamental and universal moral laws, cannot be ignored. He estimated the present and the future of the nation in the light of these two great central and fundamental principles—God and the moral law.

It was quite evident to Isaiah that God would *realise* His holy will and attain His end by establishing the moral government of the world, and by disseminating a true idea of His nature among all men, with the aid of men or opposed to them. Since He had in days gone by chosen Israel, and had blessed it above all people, and had appointed it as

His own special vineyard (Is. v. 1 ff.), Isaiah firmly believed that Jahwe could not permit Israel to be annihilated, even though He might let it suffer temporary destruction. For Jahwe had "laid in Zion for a foundation a stone, a tried stone, a precious corner stone of sure foundation" (Is. xxviii. 16). If the Israel of the present was unable to accomplish Jahwe's purpose, that would only affect the outward form of the Israelitic nation, but would in no way alter Jahwe's plan. Israel must be reformed in *spirit*, even though it meant that the nation must undergo the severest misfortunes, and even suffer destruction. A new generation must replace the old, a generation which would be more worthy of the divine mission.

The conception of the Messiah is a natural conclusion to such an argument. For the new generation of Israelites, which will be more spiritual than the older one, the generation which will be reformed in the spirit of moral purity and will possess a clearer knowledge of the attributes of God and of peace, will of necessity be represented, led and guided towards the consummation of its great task by a man after the heart of God, upon whom "the spirit of Jahwe shall rest, the spirit of wisdom and understanding, the spirit of counsel and might, the spirit of knowledge and the fear of Jahwe" (Is. xi. 2). Isaiah is in a special sense the creator of the Messianic idea.

It is scarcely necessary to say that Isaiah did not refer to the historical Jesus of Nazareth when he spoke of the Messiah. This is only the interpretation of the Christian Church. But it is quite probable that Isaiah associated the idea of a glorious future with his conception of the Messiah—an idea which was prevalent in Israel, as among other nations, long previous to the time of Isaiah—a future which was expected to be realised in the life of some descendant of the house of David. That Isaiah should associate this conception of a national revival with his conception of the Messiah is quite in accordance with his faith in the unchangeable God and His attachment to Israel and the house of David. The idea of a particular Messiah is a development from the general idea that God would at some time or other vindicate His chosen people before all the world. The expectation of a Saviour from the house of David, who would sit upon the throne of Israel, is comparatively late, and, as we said, a development from the older and more general conception.

It may be accepted as certain that some idea analogous to the general Messianic idea of the Old Testament existed from early times among other nations than Israel. Beyond this statement I am unwilling to commit myself, as the subject has not yet been fully discussed, the texts dealing thereon having only recently been published, so that new facts may come to light which will refute any theories that may now be proposed. But notwithstanding this reservation, I think we may confidently state that in the light of the latest discoveries in this field of investigation, the existence of a future hope was not confined to Israel. Thus, in ancient Egypt from the third to the second millennium B.C. people began to hope for a period of prosperity which would replace the present condition of wretchedness. This state of prosperity was to be brought about through the agency of some one person, who was conceived as a great king. The following passage reflects this hope:—

> The people will rejoice in the days of the Son of man and will perpetuate his name, because they will be far removed from misfortunes.

The peculiar expression "Son of man" means one who is high-born; here it seems to refer to the king who will bring about the expected state of blessedness, and the passage seems to refer to some special acts of grace on the part of the Son of man.

A similar conception seems to have been familiar to the Babylonians also. The more the existence of this expectation of a saviour-king among the Egyptians is confirmed, the more probable is the connection between certain allusions which we find expressed in Babylonian literature, which are otherwise obscure or ambiguous, and this personality. Among the Babylonians the hope of some future condition of prosperity centred itself primarily upon the god Marduk, but later upon the king as the one who represented the god on earth. But more significant than everything else is the fact that the Babylonians, like the Israelites and the Egyptians, looked forward to a time of peace and prosperity which would replace misery and wretchedness, and the one who is to bring it about is the king. These references remind us of the myths of the Golden Age well known to us from the literature of Greece and Rome, and which, so it was supposed, will come again at the end of time. We see, therefore, that this conception seems to have been the common heritage of many of the ancient civilised nations. The more certain we are of the facts referred to, the easier it becomes to understand the great *antiquity* of the Biblical tradition of similar conceptions familiar to the Israelites. But we must emphasise the fact that, even though it may not be possible to establish the historicity of these foreign witnesses to the existence of a definite future expectation — and we must always take possibility into consideration,—the age of the Biblical conception of a future hope is well established. It is true that some modern scholars have emphatically denied the great antiquity of this expectation, and have sought to prove that the Messianic passages in Isaiah and other early prophets are interpolations and belong to a comparatively late date, and they maintain that the Israelitic expectation of a future is nothing else than the creation of a declining or of a crushed nation. It was the destruction of the State, and that only—so we are told by some modern writers,—which inspired the conception of a revival of the nation; it was the fall of the monarchy that gave rise to the thought of its renovation. Hence there are many who support the view that the Israelites first conceived a new future kingdom whilst they were in exile, when they were no longer in possession of a visible kingdom.

It is a mistake to support such a view as this. It is only at the expense of great violence to the text of the Old Testament that it is possible to maintain that all these Messianic prophecies, or even the greater part of them, are the products of a late period. Certain presentations of this future expectation, such as "the holy remnant," "the day of the Lord," and others cannot be understood in any other sense than that they were familiar ideas to the earlier prophets and their followers. If we cease to regard this future expectation as peculiar to one people—as we really must do—then all seeming objections disappear. Moreover, it would be very strange if Israel, unlike its neighbours, had no share in this general hope of antiquity, a hope in accordance with its own special religion. But, as we have already intimated, a comparison with foreign parallels is unnecessary to establish the antiquity of the Israelitic conception.

Since we find intimations of the existence of such an expectation of some future deliverance in the older writings of the Old Testament belonging to the earliest periods of Israelitic history, we must accept their testimony as conclusive, unless we can bring forward very good reasons for denying their authenticity.

The assumption that the conception was first formed by the earlier prophets has no foundation in the Old Testament writings. It is by no means impossible that the remarkable words ascribed to Noah in Gen. v. 29, which, in their present context—where they seem to refer to the discovery of vine-culture,—are obscure, and afford only an unsatisfactory interpretation, viz. "this same shall comfort us for our work and for the toil of our hands, because of the ground which Jahwe hath cursed," had, at one time, a connection with this expectation of a saviour. If that is the case, then the true tradition is much older than the one found in the present narrative. (Some scholars would explain the names "deliverer," "saviour," so often applied to the judges in the book of Judges, as allusions to this hope; but personally — for philological reasons—I must admit that such an assumption is quite uncertain.)

However, we must, on the whole, confine ourselves to the literary monuments of the prevalence of this phenomenon, and the chronological order of their composition. We may regard the oracles of *Balaam*, already referred to, as the oldest extant literary witness. They are probably the product of the early monarchic period, perhaps of the reign of Saul or the early part of the reign of David, since Saul's victory over Agag seems to be still fresh in the memory of the writer, and not yet eclipsed by the greater conquests of David. The climax of the oracles of Balaam is reached where he predicts that a star shall come out of Jacob and a sceptre from Judah, which will arise and defeat the enemies of Israel. Apparently the reference is to the expected Saviour. It may be possible that the successful David is meant, but even in that case the figure has been borrowed from the general conception of a future saviour.

The next in chronological order is the so-called *Blessing of Jacob*, more precisely that part of it which refers to Judah. This was composed during the period immediately following David's first great victories. The manner in which conquest and prosperity are promised in this poem is well known to all of us, so that I need only point out how the composer looks beyond the near future to the later period of the Israelitic nation, and, in exactly the same way as Balaam, refers to the heroes of the future. Balaam, in Num. xxiv. 17, says:

> I see him, but not now;
> I behold him, but not nigh;
> There shall come forth a star out of Jacob,
> And a sceptre shall rise out of Judah.

Compare Gen. xlix. 10, where we find:

> The sceptre shall not depart out of Judah,
> Nor the ruler's staff from between his feet,
> Until he comes, for whom it is destined,[1]
> And unto him shall the obedience of the people be.

The one for whom the sceptre (or the lordship) is destined, or to whom it belongs—for we must translate and interpret this difficult text in this way,—is no other than the star referred to by Balaam, which will come forth out of Jacob, which may perhaps be explained as a star's son, some celestial man (*cf.* bar-Kochba = "son of a star," the name of the false Messiah of the reign of Hadrian). It may be noted also that, in both of the above quotations, we find similar modes of expression—I see "him"; until "he" comes. These expressions can only be understood if we assume that at the time when these poems were composed the figure of this future saviour was familiar to the Israelites of those days.

The examples cited reflect the popular idea

[1] Others read, "until his (rightful) governor comes."

which prevailed during the reign of Saul and the early years of David's reign. In the course of time the hope of Israel, particularly in Judah, became more and more clearly defined and exalted. The hope was a familiar conception from the very earliest period of Israel's history, so that it is not difficult to understand that, after the successes of the popular hero David, the expectation of a saviour should centre itself upon the house of this great king.

Indeed, the honour of vindicating Israel is assigned by *Nathan* to David and his dynasty, in the sense that one of David's descendants would establish an everlasting kingdom, and that Jahwe would be to David's successors as a father to his sons (2 Sam. vii. 12, 14). It does not necessarily follow, because the family of David were to be established for ever on the throne of Israel, that the coming saviour will be a son of David and a king of the family of David. But so great was the respect paid to the members of the house of David that they were called the sons of God, so that it is quite comprehensible how the two great ideals of the nation became fused, one into the other.

The uniting of these two national expectations gave rise to the Messianic hope in its narrower sense — the expectation of a king from the house of David, the vindicator of Israel, who would also be a king and lord of righteousness and of peace. Since the expectation of a saviour and of a great king was taken for granted, and in addition to this that of an enduring house of David, it was but a short step to the thought that the saviour-king would be a member of the great family of David. To elevate the whole ideal from the level of the naturalistic popular religion to a moral plane, to formulate what we call the Messianic idea in its peculiar sense, was, as we have already heard, the work of Isaiah.

But he only reaped where his predecessors had sown. The *Jahwist* (J), whose work we have assigned somewhere about the time of Elijah, has recorded an ancient tradition which proves that the evolution of the Messianic idea had been going on for generations prior to Isaiah's day. To the serpent as the tempter, and to the woman as the one who was unable to withstand the temptation, Jahwe spake as follows:—

> I will put enmity between thee and the woman,
> And between thy seed and her seed;
> It shall bruise thy head,
> And thou shalt bruise his heel.

These words have been called the first announcement of the Gospel, the Protevangelium—rightly and wrongly. They tell us first of all that eternal war has been declared between man and the powers of evil and temptation, a combat of life and death. This is the great moral struggle which can be traced throughout the history of the whole world as well as in the life-history of every individual. Not one of the combatants emerges from the fight unscathed; every individual soul as it develops passes through states of moral weakness and defeat. But it is not a hopeless struggle, for eventually the serpent will be destroyed—its head will be bruised—and humanity will gain the *victory*.

This passage, correctly translated, refers to mankind in general, not to *individual* human beings. But if we ask ourselves how and by whom this moral war is brought to victory, there remains only one answer—the answer of antiquity—that at some time in the history of the human race certain individuals or one individual will arise who will accomplish this end in the name and on behalf of the whole race. Closely connected with this idea is that of the saviour of the future, which is thus transferred from the naturalistic to the moral sphere.

The quotation is now a part of the Jahwist's book. We have already heard that this document contains a miscellany of traditions—some of its contents belonging to very early times. It has already been shown that the narratives of Paradise and the Fall have undergone considerable recensions. Since this is the case, the fact that we ascribe the Jahwist document to the time of Elijah does not enable us to make any statement concerning the age of the passage quoted above. It is quite possible that we ought to ascribe it to a much earlier date than the document itself, and that it is really the "first Gospel."

The manner in which Isaiah and the other literary prophets develop the conception of this hope of the future needs no further discussion. I need only refer you to the beautiful passages in the book of Isaiah (esp. ix. 1 ff., xi. 1 ff.) in which the prophet describes the majesty and holiness of the ruler of the new kingdom. His empire is one of righteousness and of peace; he himself is a prince of peace filled with the spirit of Jahwe, who, after he has conquered the godless ones, will inaugurate, with the aid of Jahwe, the Golden Age in the form of a moral kingdom of God.

The Messianic idea thus attained, in the main, that form in which it was familiar to Judaism, especially since the time of the

Maccabees, and prevalent among the contemporaries of Jesus—a kingdom of David, capable and ready to protect the weak and the oppressed, a menace to all evil-doers and oppressors of the poor. It naturally followed that, the more Israel felt itself, as in the days of Jesus, to be under the oppression of foreign rule, the more prominent became the characteristics of the brilliant conqueror in the conception of the Messiah.

And yet we know that Jesus Himself emphatically rejected these characteristics, and that He did everything He could to introduce a more spiritual Messianic conception. He did not describe the Messiah as a conquering king. His conception was that of the *suffering servant*. What is the origin of this idea?

The conception of the suffering servant of God, suffering not for his own sins but for those of the nation, is met with first in the writings of the exilic Isaiah, a man of kindred spirit with, and a follower of, the older Isaiah. The figure has been variously interpreted. Particularly favoured and general is the explanation that it refers to the nation of Israel itself, but to me this interpretation is far from being satisfactory. There is a great deal to be said against it. It is clear from the passages referring to the servant of Jahwe that either a small minority of the nation is meant, the pious Israelites, or, more correctly, an individual among these pious ones, their leader and champion.

In Isaiah liii. 5 it is said of him:

> The chastisement of our peace was upon him;
> And with his stripes we are healed.

We see from these words that some figure is conceived differing from both the earlier expectation and the later Messianic hope. For in the servant of Jahwe of Deutero-Isaiah we find no trace of the triumphant king. The outstanding characteristics of this personality are those of a meek and suffering martyr.

Still, there is something in this figure which connects it with that of the older Messianic conception. The connecting link is seen in the fact that both the servant and the king will bring *salvation* to the nation. Since in both the salvation of the masses is to be effected through the death of an individual, the connection between the older idea of the Saviour and Messiah and that of the suffering servant is established. The servant of Jahwe, on account of what he does, is also a saviour.

The connection between these two conceptions is not completely established in the Old

Testament—at least we have no direct proofs thereof. But Jesus, whilst He searched the prophetical writings and saw His work as Messiah foretold therein, and since He saw with increasing clearness the approach of His own death, could not fail to see that what He was destined to do and suffer had its parallel only in these accounts of the suffering servant, and that He in truth had been chosen as "the Lamb of God." The connection was re-established in His personality: the suffering servant is the Messiah, indeed is the true presentation of the Messiah, who will be realised in Him alone.

Thus the figure of a suffering Messiah prevails in Jesus over the older figure of a conquering king. The patient sufferer is to Him the true Saviour, whilst, from among the many characteristics of the triumphant king and conqueror, only those of a moral prince of peace and righteousness remain. Thus, to Him the suffering servant of Jahwe becomes also the conquering Messiah, a conqueror not by the sword but by the palm of peace and world-conquering suffering.

We have come to the end of our course of lectures. The attempt has of late been made to banish the Old Testament from the schools, deeming it to be advisable to confine religious instruction to the New Testament, as representing records which deal directly with Jesus and the Apostles.

I regret that such an attempt has been made, and I believe that it would be a serious mistake if the supporters of this movement succeeded in attaining their end. To understand the New Testament and the work of Jesus and His Apostles, we must understand the Old Testament as well. For in the latter Jesus and His Apostles lived. In it the most important conceptions and utterances of the men of the New Testament are found in their primary form; yes, even the Kingdom of God itself is founded upon it. To attempt to teach the Christian religion and the Christianity of the New Testament without founding it upon the Old Testament is to deprive the building of its foundation.

The fact that everything that is said in the Old Testament is not directly edifying or exemplary, need not prevent us from attaining a true conception of the book. Even where we find imperfect notions and immature ideas of God and of morality, we soon recognise their historical justification and even their necessity.

CONCLUSION

Even these imperfections will assist us onwards towards the correct understanding of Christianity—to understand the genesis of the perfect revelation of God in Christ—and will teach us to worship the wonderful dispensation of this divine philosophy of education.

SUPPLEMENT

SOME OF THE DISCUSSIONS AT THE CLOSE OF THE LECTURES

LECT. 1. CHAP. I., § 1.

Question 1.—In the discussions of teachers concerning religious instruction, it has often been said that the Biblical narratives of the Creation and the Fall are to be regarded as "sacred legends" of Israel. This opinion seems to be confirmed in these lectures. Would the lecturer be good enough to express his views on the question more definitely?

Answer.—I take it that the question refers not only to rightness or wrongness of the expression "sacred legend," but to the general character of these stories—whether they are historical or only legendary. As far as the first point is concerned, there is not much to be urged against the use of this expression and its application to the narratives in question

—that is to say, if the expression is rightly understood. Generally, however, it is not rightly understood. It is commonly supposed that a legend, as opposed to history, is an untrue story, and people are very apt to classify the legend with fairy tales, and oftentimes make no attempt to distinguish between them. To the masses both are fictitious narratives. In the lecture it was clearly stated that these early narratives do contain much of what is legendary in this popular sense. But to describe them as *fictitious* legends, inventions, even though they are admitted to be sacred, and as such are worthy of our veneration, is to do them an injustice.

Strictly speaking, what we understand by a legend, is that which a people has "to sing and to speak," its stories and its traditions handèd down from a time when the art of writing was unknown, and men were dependent upon oral reports of the great events of their days. The legend is not necessarily unhistorical, but can refer to historical personages and events; but because it is based upon popular oral tradition we cannot claim it to be historical in the strict sense. The historical nucleus of the legend must be searched for. Of such a kind are some of our patriarchal narratives, the stories of the Judges and others. To this class we must also assign many of the incidents related in the narrative of the Deluge, and others belonging to primitive times.

But if by legends we understand the contents of what was once orally current among a people, then, of course, the term may be applied to the Israelitic stories of the Creation, of Paradise and the Fall, as they were verbally known. In them we find conclusive evidence that they did exist in a primitive oral form, but as we now find them in Gen. i.–iii. they are legends only in a limited and conditional sense, so that I would rather avoid designating them by that name. As at present constituted, they represent the conclusions of a profound and sincere thinker, and should be regarded as *prophecies* rather than mere legends. They contain that which the *wise and holy or pious Israelites taught* concerning the Creation, etc.; *i.e.* what we now have are expositions of earlier legends.

The author of chs. ii. f., the Jahwist, is, as I shall show later,[1] anything but a recorder of popular legends, when he gives expression to his profoundest meditations; he is a

[1] See above, p. 91 f.

philosopher who tries to solve the great problems which engross the human mind, the religious and moral teacher of his nation, who has obtained a deeper insight into the human soul and has attained a fuller knowledge of God's nature than any of his predecessors. The same may be said of the author of Genesis i. He is least of all a narrator of popular legends, but is a philosopher, *a religious genius* of the first rank. If a prophet is a man who has revealed to us the nature of God more clearly than it was known before his time, and if revelation is the process whereby we are brought nearer to God, then both of these religious teachers of mankind were both true prophets of God and the revealers of His nature to the men of their days, and the narratives which we owe to them are not merely sacred legends, but—without being literally historical and without being free from fictitious characteristics—are *prophetical revelations* which are eternally true.

In my estimation, I do not see any objection—because it is in harmony with truth and religious experience—to tell the pupils who are in a position to understand—this is, of course, a necessary condition—quite frankly, that what is recorded in these stories is not strictly historical in all the details, but that they contain sacred *truths*, sacred thoughts implanted in the mind of the narrator by God Himself.

As far as the "general character" of the narratives, which was referred to in the lecture, is concerned, respecting their *strict historicity*, I shall limit myself to only a few examples. When we find duplicate narratives of the same events, as in the case of the Deluge, the Patriarchs, as well as the Creation, which differ from each other in important details— we shall have more to say on this point later, so that we shall here simply assume the fact of the occurrence—it follows of necessity that only one, if either, can be strictly historical, and further, that the other cannot be strictly authentic.

In the same way, if we find parallels to the Biblical stories in other literature than the Israelitic, and they are found to differ in details from the Old Testament narratives, one or the other of these duplicates, again, must be unauthentic. In this case we might feel inclined to decide always in favour of the Biblical accounts. But not only have we no conclusive proofs which will justify our unqualified support of the Old Testament, but what we have just admitted, viz. that the Bible can contain unhistorical details, warns us to be cautious.

These considerations show us that we will do well to disregard the demand for authentic historicity. Further considerations arising from the context of the narratives confirm this decision. Who was an eye-witness of the Creation? Certainly no human eye saw it. Therefore the only possible conclusion is that the narratives represent the ideas of a man deeply absorbed in thoughts of God's work, with which much that was fictitious was connected. Or in the case of the narratives of Paradise and the Fall, where God is said to have modelled a clod of earth and formed the woman from the man's rib, where the serpent is said to have spoken, and God Himself walked about in the garden searching for Adam and Eve—when reading such accounts, who will presume to speak of strictly authentic history, instead of exalted metaphors, expressed in beautiful language, reflecting purity and moral holiness?

From these and numerous other considerations the character of these primitive narratives, from *this* point of view, becomes at once clear. But we must not think that we have done justice to the narratives and have *fully* explained them when we dispute their historicity. On the contrary, they would be thoroughly misunderstood if we demanded this of them. It should never be forgotten that they have quite a different mission and quite another significance for us. Their information is *quite different* from historical details concerning persons and things—information not to be found in the same measure in any human documents.

Question 2.—The relation of the Biblical narrative of the Creation to the results of the *natural sciences* was only touched upon in the lecture. Would the lecturer express himself more explicitly on this matter?

Answer.—Whilst we are discussing the relation of the results of the natural sciences to the subject now under consideration, viz. the origin of the universe, the vegetable, animal, and human kingdoms, it may not be amiss to recall our remarks concerning the various grades of certainty of "authentic" results, which we made at the commencement of our first lecture. With certain modifications, the principles mentioned there can be applied to the natural sciences also. When we obtain results which are really authentic, I accept them unreservedly, and accept the testimony of those who are better able to judge than myself. But I think—and I am certain that the prudent representatives of the natural sciences will support me—that the task of these sciences is not to establish as their "results" philosophical or theological, atheistic or pantheistic, hypotheses or other speculations of a similar kind. When both these branches of science are conscious of their limitations and peacefully go their respective ways, there can be no conflict between theology and the natural sciences, even in the interpretation of the Biblical narrative of the Creation.

It must be maintained, in justice to the Old Testament, that this narrative, since it does not lay claims to be strictly historical, ought not to be regarded and treated as though it were a kind of compendium or catechism of a scientific account of the genesis of the world. This remark applies particularly to the six days, which must not be interpreted as though they represented six periods; nor yet, with due recognition of the metaphorical force of the expression "day"—for days presuppose the existence of the sun,—can we deprive the word day of its significance as a short interval of time, each one denoting a period of divine creative activity. But we are told by the natural scientists that the process of forming the world must have extended over long periods of time, and was not accomplished as the result of simple, brief words of command. (Perhaps the expression "day" did not form a part of the earliest tradition, but was introduced later, on account of the thought that God rested after He had completed His work of creating, which was imagined as a Sabbath.) This being the case, we should not shuffle and prevaricate, but, when necessary, should acknowledge, even to the masses and to children, if they are capable of apprehending what we mean, that the Biblical narrative of the Creation is the expression of a simple, childlike conception of nature, which does not set forth the truth as we now know it. In other words, as I said in my lecture, it is not the historicity of the details of the narrative which is important, but the *fact* of the divine creation and the great truths revealed concerning the manner in which He created the world and man. These latter are abiding truths and, rightly understood, constitute the divine elements in the narrative;

the details are transitory and temporal in character, and only represent the scientific explanations of primitive man.

But the position of the natural sciences is quite as untenable as that of the conservative students of the Old Testament. I have often remarked how unjust it would be to maintain that Genesis i. is a mere legend. The man who wrote it was a priest, one who was well versed in the knowledge of his day, who did not desire merely to transmit traditional legends, but recast the material at his disposal into a form corresponding to the scientific knowledge of his contemporaries and the results of his own observations of the nature of the world. I have already acknowledged him to be a *religious genius* of the first rank (see p. 259), and now I wish to acknowledge him as a philosopher and a scientist, who, I am confident, will always maintain a high position among the scientific geniuses of all ages.

In support of this statement I need only point out how closely related to the Kant-Laplace theory—which for many years was supported by all scholars—is his conception that light was created before everything else, even before the light-giving stars, and his thesis that the latter were created only at a comparatively later period in the course of the formation of the world. When I say this I do not, of course, mean to say that the two theories are one and the same in details. But the Biblical scientist divined the same principle as that which formed the basis of the modern theory. I may remind you, further, that the theory of *evolution*, the ascent from a lower to a higher stage of perfection, from the creation of the lower animals up to the creation of man, which latter marks the culminating point of the Creator's activity, is already familiar to him—a conception well known to the Babylonians also; but above all else I would ask you to note how, rising above the Babylonian parallel, he connects this conception of evolution with that of a *natural law* and natural *causality*. When he makes God say, "Let the earth put forth grass and herbs," he shows thereby that he is cognisant of the fact that there are forces in nature which are determined by fixed laws; he shows also that to him creation and evolution, natural law and Divine will, are no antitheses, but that God Himself has endowed nature with forces which enable it to develop itself in accordance with its own laws. In his account of the creation of the higher natures he shows us how nearly he conceived the relation between natural law and Divine will. There he describes God as saying, "*Let the waters bring forth* the moving creature that hath life . . . and God created great sea monsters" (*vv.* 20 f.); and again, "*Let the earth bring forth* the living creature after its kind . . . and God made the beast of the earth after its kind" (*vv.* 24 f.). Only the creation of man did God reserve exclusively for Himself.

The principle reflected here is perfectly clear. This gifted master of science and religion combines both in his account of the creation of the world. The existence and the activity of nature as determined by its own laws did not escape his observant eye; water and earth, *i.e.* the inorganic world, bring forth a living organic world, plants and animals of lower and higher forms. But just as the great Dubois Reymond warned his contemporaries of the "limitations of natural knowledge," and emphasised the deep gulf which separates the animate from the inanimate worlds, the conscious and unconscious life—a gulf which no science has yet been able to bridge over; so also does the philosopher-priest warn us in his own way, in the first chapter of Genesis. The *mystery of life*, although inanimate nature supplies the elements and conditions for its genesis out of itself, remains to him a miracle of the creating All-life, God, whilst the mystery of the human individual life, of the conscious and thinking self-determining *reason*, is to him a miracle of the highest reason, God. These are conceptions which, as far as I know, have not yet been surpassed by the science and worldly wisdom of our days. The natural conditions of life and of thought may be more clearly apprehended in these days, but life and thought themselves will always remain unravelled mysteries.

It signifies nothing that modern science traces the origin of life to another stage of the process of evolution, namely, to the vegetable kingdom (which Gen. i. looks upon as inanimate nature), and not to the animal kingdom. Nor does it matter that Gen. i. is silent concerning the manner in which God created man. The writer of Gen. ii. says: "And the Lord God formed man from the dust of the earth." The childlike mind of primitive man, which first conceived this narrative of the Creation, probably believed this statement recorded in Gen. ii. to be literally true. At a later date it was interpreted, as is evident from Gen. i., in a more spiritual sense. But however high or low the "moulded clay" from which God created man is to be conceived, however closely related these elements used by God may be to man, the moment at which natures of a higher order first became conscious that they were *men*, that they were self-determining personalities, bears witness to a mighty act of creation.

But however highly we may estimate the scientific, philosophical, and religious genius of the narrators of Gen. i.–iii., more important for us, and for the religious instruction of youth, is the fact that they were men who had surrendered themselves wholly to God and who had derived their knowledge from Him, *i.e.* that they were *men of God*, prophets.

Question 3.—How can the subject-matter of Lecture I. be *applied in the schools*?

Answer.—This question is a pedagogic one, and as such is not quite within my province, for although I was for some years engaged as a religious instructor in all the standards of the elementary and higher schools, I do not feel that I am qualified to advise in matters concerning educational methods, because I have been for many years a stranger to the schools, and therefore I am unable to gauge the mental capacity of children. My aim in these lectures is, as I have already stated, to make known to you the authentic results of Old Testament research, and the conclusions which I myself and other scholars have inferred from them. But if these lectures are to attain their end, we cannot overlook side issues which bear upon the practical utility of what we have heard. The question now under consideration gives us an admirable opportunity to consider these problems.

Speaking generally, I may take it that the *first* rule of education, particularly in that branch which deals with the question of religious instruction, is that the teacher must be prudent and tactful. Consequently he must, without departing from truth, always consider how far the results of scientific research can be *comprehended by the child.* It is absolutely necessary for the teacher to be in a position to answer satisfactorily any question he may set to the children. But it by no means follows that those questions which interest the teacher are likely to interest the children as well, or that the teacher should make known to his pupils *all* that he knows concerning a certain subject. I do not mean that the teacher should impress his class that he is in possession of some secret wisdom which he will impart gradually to his listeners. The object of instruction is to elucidate, not to confuse. Before a child attains a certain age of maturity, his mind is incapable of considering questions of the historical value of certain narratives, so that they are not likely to be asked by the pupils, nor, if set and answered by the teacher, will they be comprehended. Under these circumstances the narratives should be related simply without any comments; but if *questions* are asked by the children, then the teacher must enter into details, giving brief and prudent answers (p. 290). Or perhaps it would be well to reserve stories like that of the Creation until a stage of comparative maturity has been attained.

The *second* rule which seems important to note is that the child, even the more mature pupil, does not primarily seek reflection, and comprehensive teaching in religious instruction, but *religious* satisfaction and *moral* elevation. Naturally, knowledge and understanding must not be ignored, but these are not ends in themselves. Above all else, the teacher should abstain from introducing uncertain hypotheses into the subject of religious instruction. The subject is far too serious to experiment upon it. When being instructed in religious matters the pupil does not expect to hear discussions on abstruse problems as such. But whenever questions occur to the children as the result of what they have heard, they then expect an *answer*. Religious instruction must be *convincing*, not uncertain and unstable, not relative but absolute, not negative but positive.

Hence it follows that, even in the case of the more mature pupils, no questions should be suggested which cannot at once be answered; further, that the *religious* and *moral* contents of the narrative are always of the first importance, whilst questions relating to the historicity of these stories must always be treated as hypotheses.

I should like to lay down as a *third* rule to be observed by instructors of religion, that whenever historical and similar questions are asked by the pupils or are introduced by the teacher, the truth must certainly be told,[1] but the teacher must always insist upon a correct *comprehension of the principal truth* of the

---

[1] We do not mean by this statement that the truth should be withheld from the younger pupils. But these questions are not likely to offer themselves to the lower standards, where the simple narrative generally suffices.

narrative under consideration. Here, again, the object in view is to impart some positive knowledge, not negative. Although frankly acknowledging the truth, without any attempt to hide it, it is still the task of the religious instructor to establish the abiding *truth* and the religious *facts*. And the teacher must state the truth without seeking to make excuses, an "apology" on behalf of the Old Testament, as something founded on conviction. The *consequence* must, to cite an example, be to elevate the pupil to a higher religious plane, from which he is able to *ignore* the imperfections and the human elements in the narrative of the Creation, and to perceive the religious fact of the Creator and His magnificent creation. He will also be able to see the religious and moral *importance* of the narrative of the Fall over and above all else contained in it, its beauty and its elegance, as well as its other characteristics.[1] The task of the religious instructor is not to impart what is uncertain and transitory in these narratives (although he must not ignore these), and so make them the subject of his teaching. His main object must be to teach that which is of abiding and eternal religious and moral worth.

[1] See further, pp. 90–93.

Lec. 2. Chap. I., § 2.

Question.—The Mosaic legislation has been ascribed to Divine *revelation*. But Hammurabi claims that his laws are of Divine origin as well. Which of the two is right? or how are we to explain their respective claims?

Answer. — That the Mosaic legislation claims to be of Divine origin is well known. The Old Testament tells us that Jahwe gave the laws to Moses, and it even maintains that He wrote them on the tables with His own finger. The latter statement is probably only a poetic mode of expressing the Divine origin of the code. But the claim is quite as positive in the case of the Codex Hammurabi. Hammurabi says that Marduk, "in order that he might rule his subjects rightly and to make his country prosper," charged him to promulgate these laws. Again, when Hammurabi, at the commencement of his code, says that the gods summoned and "called him by name" (*cf.* Is. xlv. 1 ff.), he refers not only to his call to be the ruler of his people, but probably to the command to publish his code as well. The picture on the block upon which his code was written supports this view. It is generally interpreted — and I think rightly — as representing the sun-god in the act of delivering or dictating, *i.e.* "revealing," the laws to the king.

What then must our attitude towards these respective claims be?

We have already clearly established our attitude towards the claim of the Mosaic legislation to be divinely inspired (see pp. 222 ff., 232 f.), so that here I shall confine myself to the question whether the fact that Moses was inspired *excludes* the possibility of Hammurabi's claim. The answer to this question will be: No, decidedly.

In itself, apart from the Mosaic claim, it is quite comprehensible that Hammurabi should have maintained that his code was divinely inspired. It is unnecessary to speak of this claim as an example of priestly fraud, and to ascribe it to a desire to impose these laws upon the masses and to force the people to submit to them, although of course such motives are thinkable and possible. It is but just that we should form some other opinion of such a work as that of Hammurabi.

We have already heard that the legislation of Hammurabi was the product of a civilisation of the highest intellectual type. Whoever created this code must be acknowledged as one of the greatest geniuses the world has ever seen. That such a man should not claim to be the sole originator of these laws, but should feel that they were *inspired* by the gracious Deity, ought not to seem strange even in these days, to say nothing of the days in which Hammurabi lived. We do not wonder, therefore, that he claimed a Divine origin for his code, but acknowledge it to be quite natural.

But how must *we* judge this claim? What is its relation to that of Moses? This question can be extended to include other great religious leaders who felt that they were in direct communication with the Deity, at least who *claimed* to be inspired by God Himself.

Our answer must be the following:—If we recognise the hand of God directly guiding Moses and the prophets in the performance of their work, and acknowledge that they were influenced by the Spirit of God, there is no reason why we should not ascribe the same guidance to Hammurabi whilst he was formulating his code, or to the other great religious and moral reformers. The saying of Jesus, "The Spirit breatheth where it listeth," applies to these cases as in others. Although this Spirit manifested itself in a special degree in the history of Israel and in the lives of its prophets, its activity is universal and is manifested everywhere where men sincerely seek God. If we maintain that God does influence men, if we believe that God reveals Himself to those who seek Him, then we must also believe that God does not hide Himself from anyone who honestly seeks and desires His aid, but reveals Himself even to the heathen. Certainly the revelation afforded to the heathen is not comparable to that given to us, but only in accordance with their capacity to apprehend truth, and in relation to time, place, and circumstances, *i.e.* "in a mirror in a riddle."

LEC. 3. CHAP. II., §§ 1-4.

Question 1.—What is the relation between the *Babylonian penitential psalms* and those found in the Bible?

Answer.—This question has been considerably discussed in the past, because some scholars have sought to prove that the Babylonian system of religion was identical with the Biblical, some indeed maintaining that the former was superior to the latter. Of late, however, it has ceased to be seriously discussed, as all scholars agree that the Biblical religion shows a marked superiority over the Babylonian, as reflected in the parallels to the Old Testament psalms. A return to the calm and prudent point of view which formerly prevailed has been effected, so that I shall treat the subject quite briefly.

The relation between the Biblical and Babylonian psalms is no other than the relation between the Biblical and Babylonian *ideas of God*. It is here that we find the key to the whole problem. We cannot deny that some of the Babylonian penitential songs are such as stir our souls to their uttermost depths. They reflect a sincere consciousness of guilt towards the deity and a genuine desire for forgiveness. In this respect they approximate closely to the Biblical penitential psalms, even to the best of them. But we must not allow this fact to influence us unduly and to make us express false conclusions, to overestimate the Babylonian and to depreciate the Biblical psalms. The redeeming features of the former, and consequently the similarity between them and the latter, are really only formal. It is not the form but the contents which determine religion and decide how highly its precepts may be judged. What is the character of the deity prayed to? What is the character of the sins committed against it, and the repentance and penitence offered to it? These are the questions which decide the value of these psalms.

If we answer the first of these questions, we shall have answered all of them. We know what kind of Deity was worshipped in Israel, especially at the time when the nation had attained its highest religious level, the period of its prophets, its leading psalmists and kindred spirits. It was a species of moral monotheism. The One God ruled in accordance with moral principles.

The character of the Babylonian deity is quite as clearly known. Generally speaking, the Babylonians did not get beyond the most crude polytheism and the most uncouth forms of natural religion, despite the attempts, confined perhaps to the narrow limits of the priestly circle, to break away from it to a purer conception of God. The deity whose forgiveness is prayed for is one of many, one might almost say innumerable, deities, the most popular being Ishtar. These deities are not only innumerable, but each one of them is limited to a certain sphere of influence.

We are told in one of these psalms that these deities did not require pure hearts and morality from their worshippers, but "excellent fragrant sacrifices and an abundance of corn." The conception that the Deity does not desire sacrifices and burnt offerings, but a broken and contrite heart (Ps. li. 16 f.), which is so characteristic of the Israelitic religion at its highest point of development, is altogether wanting in the Babylonian psalms. The Babylonian religion remains a *natural religion*, possessing all the faults of such a religion, and is best characterised by the fact that the most popular deity was the same Ishtar whose worship was practised in the form of temple prostitution without its being declared (as was done in Israel) by prophets as shameful and unworthy of a deity; and further by the fact that, should the god not speedily respond, the priest must compel it to do so by means of *magical spells*, or the penitent one turns to other gods and implores their aid.

It is but natural, therefore, that the ideas of sin and guilt as well as of penitence and forgiveness are different in the Babylonian religion from what they are in a moral religion. After what has been said, this fact requires no further discussion. "Sin and guilt," "forgiveness and atonement," are words which have the same sound in the Babylonian psalms as in the Old Testament, but the meaning of these terms is much less exalted in the former than in the latter. Their connotation is as inferior in the one as the conception and the worship of Ishtar is inferior to the conception and the worship of Jahwe.

Question 2.—How do these results of literary criticism affect the value of Old Testament revelation? Is it not possible that some of them will lessen the religious worth of, and the reverence which is now paid to, the Old Testament?

Answer.—Before we proceed to answer this question it is necessary to warn ourselves not to overestimate the significance of these results, and not to misunderstand their character. They are of great importance to the historical examination of the Old Testament, in so far as we regard it as a literary production. But they afford us—as we have seen—only a conditional certainty, whilst they decide nothing concerning the religious value of the book — not, perhaps, because they occasionally disprove traditions, but because no historical examination *can* ever decide the religious value of a literary work. Even if it could be proved that all the Pentateuch was the work of Moses, and that all those seventy-three psalms which are ascribed to David did really come from his hand, this historical fact would by no means guarantee their value as revelations. It is the contents which establish their religious value. The question of the religious significance of the Old Testament is quite independent of the questions concerning the authorship and date of the various books. It would do no harm if people were more conscious of the fact that no hypothesis concerning the origin of the Biblical books can make the Old Testament or the Bible of no religious value.

Rather should it be emphasised again and again that it is not historical but *religious* judgments which will decide the religious worth of the Bible. The Old Testament is a witness of God's revelation to us as Christians, because it is connected with Christ and with the God of Christ. This is a pure decision of faith, it is a religious certainty, which has nothing to do with the traditions concerning its origin, which it neither confirms nor refutes. Every book in the Old Testament has—according to Luther's norm, which is the only proper one to adopt—its value as revelation in accordance with the measure in which it "reveals Christ" to us, *i.e.* in relation to its proximity to that centre of our religious belief.

What ought to be done in *practice* is obvious. As it is the object of the Bible to teach religion—practical religion—what is of primary importance is its value as a religious volume. The purely historical and literary problems should therefore be regarded as matters of secondary importance. These latter are valuable for the elucidation of the "human side" of the Bible, and as such must not be ignored. But they themselves do not emit religious life, warmth, and power. They neither enhance nor depreciate the value of the Bible as a religious volume—a fact which we must always keep in mind.

Lec. 4. Chap. III., §§ 1-3.

Question.—How are the imperfect moral conceptions and the uncertain historical character of the early narratives to be treated in the *instruction of the young*?

Answer.—This is one of the most vital questions of religious pedagogics of the present day. The fate of the religious instruction of the next generations depends to a large extent upon its being properly answered. On that account, and also because our purely scientific discussion of the subject has brought us so near to this question that it could hardly be overlooked, I shall not refuse to make an attempt to answer it, although, as I have already explained, I do not feel capable of giving expert advice. I shall take the two questions included in the above separately, and try to answer them.

(a) *The Moral Conceptions.*—Strictly speaking, the religious conceptions ought to be considered in conjunction with these, for they also, which perhaps is but natural, are in many respects inferior to those expressed in the New Testament.

A real objection to these primitive conceptions can only arise when we assume that the different parts of the Old Testament reflect the *same* degree of revelation as the New Testament. And we maintain that there can be no contradictions between the two covenants. Whosoever adopts this point of view forgets that the kingdom of God is like a cultivated field, whose growth progresses from stage to stage, "as if a man should cast seed upon the earth; and should sleep and rise night and day, and the seed should spring up and grow. . . . The earth yieldeth fruit of herself, first the *blade*, then the *ear*, then the full *corn* in the ear" (Mark iv. 27 f.). According to these words of Jesus, the Old Testament must contain imperfections, because it reflects only *preparatory revelation*.

If we consider the question seriously, we see at once that Jesus, and Paul also, regard the Old Testament throughout in this light. They did not regard the Old and the New Testaments as a unity in the sense that both represent *one and the same* degree of revelation, but in the sense that the same God is supreme in both covenants. That Jesus recognised the differences between the Old and the New Testaments, and was fully conscious of the imperfections of the former—which, however, were not imperfections at the time when they were revealed, but only became imperfect after the great revelation which was vouchsafed in Him,—is nowhere more clearly affirmed than in His, " Ye have heard that it was *said to them of old time*, An eye for an eye, etc. But I say unto you . . ." Who were the men "of old time"? They were the Israelites of Old Testament times. These men of old He regards as standing in a *preparatory* stage. This is the stage at which He places men like Samuel and Elijah, and in some respects the other prophets as well.

If we desire further proof, and wish to know the reasons why God permitted an inferior morality—and an inferior religious conception—to have a place in the old covenant, we have only to remember that Jesus Himself opposes certain Old Testament conditions and regulations which He declares to have been superseded. He does not wonder that certain practices, such as lax marriage customs, were suffered under the old dispensation. He does not blame God's tolerance, but seeks an explanation for it. And He finds it in God's educational wisdom, which permitted much in olden times, because of the "*hardness of heart*" of the men of those days, which at a more mature stage of development would not be tolerated. Along with this hardness of heart there was that other reason which we referred to in our lecture (see p. 199), viz. that at any stage in the development of civilisation and general knowledge other than a mature one, a conception of God or of morality higher than that found in the Old Testament would have been stone instead of bread to the Israelites.

Taking the figure of the corn-field and its gradual growth, and the attitude of Jesus

Himself, as our guide, I think the general public and the more mature children can be made to realise the true facts of the case. But both the teacher and his pupils must continually remind themselves that the revelation of the kingdom of God (from the point of view now under consideration) can be likened to nothing more appropriate than to human *education*. It is "the education of mankind" towards attaining the kingdom of God. No part of the work of the educator is more important than that he should observe a continuous strict *sequence of thought*, progressing from one stage to another more advanced stage. In other words, the pupil must not be taught *anything other than what he is able to comprehend*. The teacher must be able to speak to the child in the language of a child, and to adapt himself to the mental capacity of the young.

These facts are well known to you all, but they are important for our discussion, so that I need not make excuses for having mentioned them. In the Old Testament, and in the kingdom of God generally, *God* is the educator. If the principles of education which we have just referred to are true, then they must apply to God as the educator of the human race, more especially of the people of Israel. Therefore, when God wished to reveal Himself to men and to educate a nation to His service, and so to prepare the world for the coming of His kingdom, He found it necessary to adapt Himself to the mental and spiritual capacity of each consecutive generation. He was compelled—to make use of Jesus' parable—to let the field yield first the blade, then the ear, before He could expect it to bring forth corn, and He was obliged, because of the "hardness of heart" of the people, *i.e.* because of the imperfect state of development in civilisation, knowledge, and morals, to tolerate some things which a more mature period must learn to overcome.

It seems to me that if we regard the Old Testament from this point of view many of our scruples and misgivings will cease to be. If they adopt this view, the more mature pupils and the thinking public will at once understand that, although Jacob deceived his father and was dishonest to Laban, although the Israelites swindled the Egyptians, even though Samuel was cruel to captive enemies, and Elijah slew the pagan priests of Baal, and Elisha occasioned the death of the boys of Bethel, such acts are not to be regarded as *patterns* for Christians. That they are found recorded in the Bible does not mean that they are, on that account, good and worthy of *our* imitation. It o̶̶̶̶̶̶̶s that they represent a stage in the reli̶̶̶̶̶̶development of Israel; in other words, that God made use of even such instruments, who did not possess a full knowledge of His nature, nor fully expressed His will, to establish His kingdom among His people.

Speaking generally, we may say that it is wrong to expect the same religious and moral perfection among the ancient Israelites as in a Christian community. It was a mistake on the part of Delitzsch when he referred to the blood-vengeance and certain imprecatory psalms as proving the inferior character of Old Testament revelation. It is quite possible that the man who composed these psalms, and who was in this respect a child of his time, was, in other respects, a true messenger of God. The imperfections may perhaps represent only one side of his character, or reflect simply the knowledge of his time. Neither of these theories excludes the possibility that the man and the period in which he lived represented a stage in the development of the divine plan.

(*b*) *The Uncertain Historical Character of*

the Narratives.—I presume that this question refers mainly to the antediluvian, patriarchal, and Mosaic histories, concerning which we have admitted that we possess no means of verifying their historical claims, and which we have acknowledged to be unhistorical in their details.

Whilst we are considering this subject, it is well to remember that the historicity of these primitive narratives does not concern children and those of limited knowledge in the least. A real *child* and simple-minded adults are quite incapable of comprehending the force of this question, and its introduction tends to confuse rather than help them. Such people are in danger of losing, without gaining anything in return, by an examination of such problems. In cases such as this, the simple narratives should be related without any comment. An exception can be made only when the pupil has become acquainted with some of the questions concerning the historical character of the narratives, and asks definite questions. In this case the teacher should give brief and true answers.

When dealing with more mature pupils and adults the case is different. But even here criticism ought never to be exercised for its own sake. It should never be made the end of religious education, in schools or in churches. The true end of such education should be *religious edification* and *moral development* (see p. 271). These narratives should be used for this and no other purpose. Their religious and moral teaching must be presented to the pupils, and the teacher must show that, although they are not, strictly speaking, historical, although they depend to a large extent upon legends which may have absolutely no foundation in fact, they contain a great deal of truth.

A more mature pupil or an average man can easily recognise that the narrative which represents Jahwe as appearing to Adam or Abraham, and conversing with them as man to man, walking with them and eating in their company, is not real history, but only a representation of the childlike conception of primitive man of God's relation to man. Although unhistorical, this popular conception emphasises the high religious value of an active personal communion with God, of a close, intimate acquaintance with Him. Even though these narratives declare that Jacob saw a ladder which reached from heaven to the earth, upon which the angels of God were descending and ascending, or that he fought with the Deity himself in order to secure His blessing, and we grant that these stories are poetical rather than historical, yet no one will deny the edifying force of the idea that God has established a bond between heaven and earth, and has thus made communion with Him possible, or the thought that His blessing can only be obtained after a strenuous struggle in prayer. It is not enough to speak of Abraham's readiness to sacrifice his only son Isaac as a relic of the Canaanitish practice of child-sacrifice. We can only do justice to this narrative when we point out the very high degree of faith which the narrator ascribes to Abraham, a faith which will always remain the ideal to be aimed at by Christians whenever God demands a great sacrifice at our hands. Something similar may be said of the narrative of Joseph, the great religious value of which is established, were it only for that one verse: "And as for you, ye meant evil against me, but God meant it for good" (Gen. l. 20), and of some narratives of Deuteronomic origin, concerning which see see p. 112 above.

In these and numerous other narratives of a like kind it will not be found difficult to bring what is religiously and morally valuable in them to light; their importance in this respect is abiding, even though they are not historical records in the strict sense of the term. If we had to deal with narratives of uncertain moral contents, we would have to omit them from religious instruction, or at least reserve them until the pupils had attained the very last stage of elementary education.

In the case of some Old Testament stories, an emphasis upon their not being strictly historical *relieves* the mind rather than otherwise. I refer to such stories as that which recounts Elisha's cruelty to the boys of Bethel (2 Kings ii. 23 f.), or Elijah's treatment of the emissaries of the king of Israel (2 Kings i. 9–14), or the apparently mythical story of Samuel's anger against Saul (1 Sam. xiii. 8–15; *cf.* 2 Sam. xv.).

Index

Abraham, history of—parallels in Hammurabi, 27: historical character, 149-162: "Field of Abraham," 157.
Adapa myth, 14 f.: introduced to Palestine, 26, 43.
Ahab, only blamed in Old Testament, 112.
Amarna period, 27.
Amarna tablets, 4-43, 47.
Amenophis, Pharaoh, 41.
Amos, position as prophet, 211 ff.: how he became a prophet, 225.
Asher, tribe of, 160: remained in Canaan, 161, 168.
Asherah, symbol of Astarte, 51: symbol of Jahwe, 181.
Assyria, *see also* Babylonia: at the time of the prophets, 206 ff.
Astarte, chief deity of the Canaanites, 53.
Astruc, physician-in-ordinary to Louis XIV., 71.
Authentic results, what is meant by, 1-8.
Authenticity of scientific results, grades of, 1-8.

Baal, chief deity of the Canaanites, 51: worship of, 51-56: no images of, 52 f.: influence of his worship upon Israel, 176 ff.
Babylonia, supreme in Palestine, 26: Babylonian parallels to the Biblical narratives, 9-24: Babylonian legislation in Palestine, 26-28: Babylonian myths current in Palestine, 26, 43: Babylonian civilisation in Palestine, 32, 42 f.: Babylonian expectation of a future Saviour, 241: Babylonian penitential psalms, 130, 277 ff.
Balaam, the seer, 227 f.: his oracles, 244 f.
Bēs, Egyptian deity worshipped in Palestine, 52.
Book of the Covenant, 28-40: authorship and date, 37-40: relation to Hammurabi, 29 f.
Bronze used in Palestine, 35, 48, 51.

INDEX

Canaan, *see* Palestine: the Canaanite civilisation, 50 f.: the Canaanite religion, 51 ff.: pre-Israelitic settlement of the land of Canaan, 54–59: influence of the Canaanitish religion on the Israelites, 176 ff.: Canaanitish religious orgies, 180.

Canticles, 126 f.

Causality in Gen. i., 266.

Child-sacrifice practised by the Canaanites, 54: condemned in Israel, 181 ff.

Chronicles, historical value of, 114 f.

Civilisation, conditions of, reflected in the Book of the Covenant, 34–36: in pre-Israelitic times (*see* Stone, Bronze, Iron), 54: fortifications, 48: Babylonian influences, 32, 42 f.: Egyptian influences, 42 f.

Conquest of Canaan gradually brought about, 177.

Creation, the, narratives of, in Babylonian writings as well as in the Bible, 10–14, 19: religious value of the Biblical narrative, 13 f., 23 f., 261: its relation to natural science, 262 ff.: is it a legend? 256 ff.: work of a religious and scientific genius, 259, 265: its application in religious instruction, 269 ff.: duplicate narratives of the Creation in the Bible, 66: comparatively early date of the narrative, 86, 250.

Criticism, legitimate, limited, 60 f.: literary criticism of the Old Testament, 60 ff.: Pentateuch criticism, 61–93: attitude towards revelation, 276.

Cup-marks, relics of a primitive pre-Semitic religion, 58.

D = Deuteronomium.

David, composer of a lamentation over Saul and Jonathan, 95 f., 112, 134, 137: his history, 112 f.: author of Psalms? 133 ff.: his character as a man and as a religious genius estimated, 134 ff., 188 f.: his census, 185: his position in the future hope, 247 f.

Deborah, Song of, 95: as a historical document, 112, 165.

Decalogue, *see* Ten Commandments.

Delitzsch, Professor Friedr., 9, 289.

Deuteronomium (D), 73: relation to P, 79: discovery of, 79 ff.: authorship and date, 81 ff.: D a unity? 85: D the point of departure of P? 85.

Dhutmes III., Pharaoh, mentions Jacob, 160.

INDEX

Documents, significance of, 1-8: in the Pentateuch, 71 ff.: the antediluvian narratives not documents in the strict sense, 23, 259 ff.: or the patriarchal and the Mosaic narratives, 163, 164.
Dolmen, 55.
Dt. = Deuteronomic recension, *see* Recensions.
Dubois-Reymond, 267.

E = Elohist.
Egypt exercises overlordship in Palestine, 27, 42: influence of Egyptian civilisation upon Canaan, 43: Egyptian temple laws, 84: Egyptian accounts of the early history of Israel, 157: Israel in Egypt, 167 ff.: the plagues, 166.
Elementary schools, *see* School.
Elijah, 191, 196, 222: his influence, 109.
Elohist (E)—discovery of E, 72, 73: relation to P, 78: sources of, 100 f., 158 f.: idea of God, 192 f.
Excavations, 9-59: in Palestine, 43-59.
Ezra and Nehemiah, 115.

Fall, the—foreign parallels to the Biblical narrative, 14 f.: religious significance, 24: in what sense is it a historical fact? 24: sources of the narrative, 88 f., 250: is it a legend? 256 ff.
Flood—parallel narratives in the Bible and Babylonian records, 16 ff.: its presence in the Bible explained, 17 ff.: an historical event, 20: literary form of the Biblical narrative, 67.
Future expectation, 235-253: among people other than Israelites, 240 ff.: antiquity of the hope, 242 f.: its development, 245 ff.: the "Servant of Jahwe," 251.

Gezer, excavations at, 43-46: child-sacrifices at, 54.
Golenischeff papyrus, 229.
Graf's hypothesis, 74, 79, 85.

H = Law of Holiness.
Hadad, Syrian god, 51.
Hammurabi, Babylonian king, 25: his code of laws, 26-30: its relation to the Mosaic code, 28 ff.: its claim to be of Divine origin, 274 ff.
Heroic period of Israel, 95 ff.: poems of this period, 101, 107.
Hexateuch, 62.
High places as sanctuaries, 104, 180.
Hilkiah, high priest, discoverer of D, 79, 84: not the author of D, 81 ff.

INDEX

Historical books and their composition, 93–115: present form not original, 99: incomplete, 100: their recension, 101 ff.: their historical value, 112 ff.: important historical records in Old Testament, 112 f.
Holiness, Law of (H), 73, 78: parts of it very old, 85 f.
Hope of Israel, *see* Future expectation.
Hypothesis, its value in research, 5, 6: in Pentateuch criticism, 77.

Idea of God, *see* Jahwe, Revelation, and Popular religion.
Ilgen, rector of Schulpforta, 72.
Imageless worship, 39: among the Canaanites, 52 f.
Images among the Israelites, 39: among the Canaanites, 52.
Imprecatory psalms, 143, 195, 289.
Iron in Palestine, 35 f., 48, 51.
Isaac, *see* Patriarchs: how to interpret the sacrifice of Isaac, 181 f.: how to be used in the schools, 290 ff.
Isaiah, his "call," 231 f.: goes barefoot and half naked, 118: his attitude towards worship, 217: his attitude towards social wrongs, 219 f.: his conception of religion, 236 f.: his expectation of a Saviour, 237 f.: Deutero-Isaiah, 122, 251 ff.
Ishtar, Babylonian goddess, 279, 281: worshipped in Palestine, 52.
Ishtarwashur, king of Taanach, 46 f.
Isis, Egyptian goddess, worshipped in Palestine, 52.

J = Jahwist.
Jahwe—the name used to signify a document, 72: revealed through Moses, 174: a Kenite god? 175: conceptions of, obscured under the influence of Baal, 176 ff.: regarded as a national God, 183: other limitations of, 184: state worship of, 187 f.: His worship in the days of the earlier prophets, 191: His attitude towards morality, 193 ff.: is Jahwe our God? 196 ff.: moral monotheism, 214 ff.
Jahwist (J), discovery of the, 72: his attitude towards primitive history, 20 ff.: his relation to P, 78: not a mere "school," but an individual, 87 f.: his literary and religious characteristics, 90–93: sources of

the, 93-98 : his idea of God, 192 f. : his hope, 248 f.
Jensen, 153.
Jeroboam, king of Israel, and his royal seal, 49 : his great deeds but briefly mentioned in Old Testament, 112.
Jesus on the Pentateuch, 64 : on Isaiah, 64 : compared to the prophets, 217 f., 231 f. : His relation to the Messianic idea, 239, 251 ff.
Joseph, history of, its literary form, 67 : its historical value, 168 f. : its religious value, 292.
Josiah, king of Judah, 79 : his reforms, 80.
Judges' period the heroic age of Israel, 98.

Kings, books of, 102 ff. : their historical value, 112 ff.

Lamentations, 127.
Law, *see* Pentateuch : the law of Hammurabi, 25-31 : its relation to the Mosaic, 28-30 : the Mosaic law in its present form not derived from Moses, 61 ff., 64 ff. : the underlying principles are Mosaic, 33-37, 84 : Temple rules, 84 ff. : authorship and date of the law, 28 ff., 85 ff. : *see further under* Moses.

Legends, meaning of, 257 f. : in the Old Testament, 23 f., 258 f. : their presence does not depreciate the value of Old Testament, 259 ff. : place in religious instruction, 281 f.
Levites and priests in D, 81 f. ; Levi as the tribe of Moses, 189.
Luther resembled the prophets, 216 : had not in some respects advanced beyond the religious conceptions of the Old Testament, 197 : his estimation of the Psalter, 144.
Lyric—antiquity of the religious lyric, 128 ff. : the profane lyric, 125 ff.

Massebah, or stone pillar, its religious significance, 51 : at Gezer, 45 : in Israel, 181.
Megiddo, excavations at, 48 f. : child-sacrifice at, 54 f.
Meremptah, Pharaoh, mentions Israel, 160.
Messiah, *see* Future expectation.
Minstrels, their position among the Israelites, 96.
Morality and moral conceptions in the Israelitic popular religion, 193 f. : in the higher religious circles, 194, 211 ff. : relation to Christian conceptions,

193 f.: attitude of religious instructors, 283 ff.

Moses, not the author of the modern Pentateuch, 64 ff.: Pentateuch probably based upon his teaching, 31-37, 84: a historical person, 170: his historical significance, 172 f.: his religious significance, 174 ff.: literary form of the traditions concerning him, 65 ff.: historical, 164 ff.: use in the schools, 290 ff.: Moses as prophet, 176, 221, 233.

Muhammed as an ecstatic, 228.

Myths, Babylonian, 17: current in Palestine, 27, 43: Israelitic myths, 20, 92: *see further under* Legends.

Nathan, the prophet of David's reign, 190, 222, 247.

Natural law in Gen. i. 266.

Natural religion in Israel, 215 f.: in Babylonia, 280.

Natural science and theology, 262 ff.

P = Priestly Code.

Palestine, under Babylonian and Egyptian rule, 26 f., 42 f.: under the influence of Babylonian civilisation, 32, 42 f.: under the influence of Egyptian civilisation, 42 f., 51: the oldest inhabitants Aryan? 56-58.

Patriarchs, whether gods, tribes, or individuals, 149-158: traditions of the patriarchs have a historical nucleus, 158-161: traditions not strictly historical, 162 f.: use of the narratives in the schools, 283 ff.

Pentateuch, 61 f.: criticism of the, 61-93: authentic results of Pentateuch criticism, 78: future problems of Pentateuch criticism, 79 ff.

Plagues in Egypt, how to explain them, 166.

Priestly Code (P or PC), its separation from J and E, 72 f.: P in the antediluvian narratives, 20 ff.: age of P, 73 ff.: relation to D, 78 f.: not a unity, 85: some parts very old, 85 f.

Primitive history in Bible, 9-24: not records in strict sense of term, 23 f., 256 ff.: *see also under* Creation and Fall.

Popular religion of Israel under Canaanitish influences, 179 ff.: idea of God, 183 f.: orgies in public worship, 185 f.: attitude of the prophets towards it, 209 ff.: a form of natural religion, 216.

Prophets—the great canonical prophets, 200-235: their characteristics, 221 ff.:

their significance, 202 ff., 223 f.: their one-sidedness, 108 f.: their attitude towards Assyria and Aram, 205-209: their conception of patriotism, 210, 223 f.: their conception of religion, 210 ff.: their conception of a moral monotheism, 214 ff.: their attitude towards public worship, 215 ff.: towards social questions, 219 f.: their history, 221 f.: their inspiration, 224 ff.: their calling, 229 ff.: their optimism, 235 ff.: prophetic literature, 115-125: the prophets as orators and poets, 115-119: as writers, 119 ff.

Protevangelium, 248 f.

Psalms, age of, 128-133: titles no criterion, 133 f.: did David compose some of the psalms? 134 ff.: primitive psalms, 137 ff.: late psalms, 139 f.: the subject of the psalms, 140: whether collective or individual? 140 ff.: their religious significance, 142-147: Biblical and Babylonian penitential psalms, 277 ff.

R = Redactor.

Rameses II., Pharaoh, mentions Asher, 160.

Ramman, a Syrian god, 51.

Redactions of the historical books of the Old Testament, 101: plan adopted, 102 f.: spirit of these recensions, 104: their significance in the preservation of the Holy Scriptures, 107 f.: and of the Israelitic nation, 108 ff.: value for church and school, 111: historical value of, 112 ff.

Revelation, to Moses, 174 f., 274 f.: to the prophets, 224 f., 232 ff.: in antediluvian history, 264 f.: grades of revelation, 194 ff., 256 ff., 281 ff.

Revelation and criticism, 281: revelation as education, 284 ff.

Sacred and heroic songs the basis of historical writings, 94 f.: ancient songs, 125 f.: and song-books, 100 f.: religious poetry and its origin, 128 ff.: elegies and love poems, 127 f. *See* Lyric.

Samuel as prophet, 188, 196 f., 221 f., 233: books of Samuel, 112-115.

School, its claim to the Old Testament generally, 253 ff.: to authentic results, 7 f.: to discuss these results, 269 ff.: significance of the Dt. recensions to religious instruction, 111: treatment of the imperfect

moral conceptions of Old Testament in the school, 283 ff.
Sellin, Professor, 46.
Seti, Pharaoh, mentions Asher, 160.
Shema's seal, 49.
Stone Age in Palestine, 35, 48, 54–58: stone circles, 55.
Syria, wars with Israel, 206 ff.: Elisha and Hazael, 207.

Taanach, excavations at, 46 ff.
Temple of Jerusalem, its ancient rules, 83 f.: centralisation of worship, 80, 84.
Ten Commandments of Moses, 31, 38–40: the theory of the two Decalogues, 38 f.

Wellhausen and his school on the Decalogue and the Book of the Covenant, 32, 38 ff.: on P and the Pentateuch, 74 ff., 85 f.: on the Psalms, 128 f.
Winckler, Hugo, 153.

Zorah, altar of, 190.

A Catalogue

of

Williams & Norgate's

Publications

Divisions of the Catalogue

		PAGE
I.	THEOLOGY	2
II.	PHILOSOPHY, PSYCHOLOGY	28
III.	ORIENTAL LANGUAGES, LITERATURE, AND HISTORY	33
IV.	PHILOLOGY, MODERN LANGUAGES	38
V.	SCIENCE, MEDICINE, CHEMISTRY, ETC.	43
VI.	BIOGRAPHY, ARCHÆOLOGY, LITERATURE, MISCELLANEOUS	51
	GENERAL INDEX UNDER AUTHORS AND TITLES	57

For Full List and Particulars of Educational Works, see separate Catalogue.

London
Williams & Norgate
14 Henrietta Street, Covent Garden, W.C.

I. Theology and Religion.

THEOLOGICAL TRANSLATION LIBRARY.
New Series.

A Series of Translations by which the best results of recent Theological Investigations on the Continent, conducted without reference to doctrinal considerations, and with the sole purpose of arriving at the truth, are placed within reach of English readers.

Vols. I.-XII. were edited by the Rev. T. K. Cheyne, M.A., D.D., late Oriel Professor of Interpretation in the University of Oxford, and the late Rev. A. B. Bruce, D.D., late Professor of Apologetics, Free Church College, Glasgow.

Vol. XIII. was edited by Rev. Allan Menzies, D.D., Professor of Divinity and Biblical Criticism in the University, St Andrews.

Vols. XV., XVII., XVIII., and XXI.-XXVI. are edited by Rev. W. D. Morrison, M.A., LL.D.

Vols. XIX. and XX. are edited by Rev. James Moffatt, B.D., D.D., St Andrews.

The Price of Vols. I.-XXI. is 10s. 6d.;
Vol. XXII. and after, 10s. 6d. net.

Subscribers to the Series obtain three volumes for 22s. 6d. carriage free, payable before publication, which only applies to the current year's volumes, viz., XXV.-XXVII., which are as follows.

In Active Preparation.

THE OLD TESTAMENT IN THE LIGHT OF THE EAST. By Alfred Jeremias, Professor of Old Testament History in the University of Leipzig. The translation will be edited by Professor C. H. W. Johns of Cambridge. The work will be profusely illustrated.

Vol. XXV. Ready. 10s. 6d. net.
ETHICS OF THE CHRISTIAN LIFE. By Theodor Haering, Professor of New Testament Dogmatics and Ethics at Tübingen.

Vol. XXVI.
PRIMITIVE CHRISTIANITY: Its Writings and Teachings in their Historical Connections. By Otto Pfleiderer, of Berlin. Vol. II. The Historical Books.

Vol. XXII. Ready. 10s. 6d. net.
PRIMITIVE CHRISTIANITY, Vol. I.: Its Writings and Teachings in their Historical Connections. By Otto Pfleiderer, Professor of Practical Theology in the University of Berlin.

14 Henrietta Street, Covent Garden, London, W.C.

CATALOGUE OF PUBLICATIONS.

THEOLOGICAL TRANSLATION LIBRARY—Continued.

Vol. XXIII. Ready. 10s. 6d. net.
THE INTRODUCTION TO THE CANONICAL BOOKS OF THE OLD TESTAMENT. By Carl Cornill, Professor of Old Testament Theology at the University of Breslau.

Vol. XXIV. Ready. 10s. 6d. net.
HISTORY OF THE CHURCH. By Hans von Schubert, Professor of Church History at Kiel. Translated from the Second German Edition. By arrangement with the author, an Additional Chapter has been added on "Religious Movements in England in the Nineteenth Century," by Miss Alice Gardner, Lecturer and Associate of Newnham College, Cambridge.

The following Volumes are published at 10s. 6d. per Volume, excepting Vols. XIX. and XX.

Vol. XXI.
ST. PAUL: The Man and his Work. By Prof. H. Weinel of the University of Jena. Translated by Rev. G. A. Bienemann, M.A. Edited by Rev. W. D. Morrison, M.A., LL.D.

"Prof. Weinel may be described as the Dean Farrar of Germany; the work is quite equal to Dean Farrar's work on the same subject. In some respects it is better."—*Daily News.*

Vols. XIX. and XX.
THE MISSION AND EXPANSION OF CHRISTIANITY IN THE FIRST THREE CENTURIES. By Adolf Harnack, Ordinary Professor of Church History in the University, and Fellow of the Royal Academy of the Sciences, Berlin. Second, revised and much enlarged edition, 25s. net.

Vol. XVIII.
CHRISTIAN LIFE IN THE PRIMITIVE CHURCH. By Ernst von Dobschütz, D.D., Professor of New Testament Theology in the University of Strassburg. Translated by Rev. G. Bremner, and edited by the Rev. W. D. Morrison, LL.D.

"It is only in the very best English work that we meet with the scientific thoroughness and all-round competency of which this volume is a good specimen; while such splendid historical veracity and outspokenness would hardly be possible in the present or would-be holder of an English theological chair."—Dr RASHDALL in *The Speaker.*

Vol. XVI.
THE RELIGIONS OF AUTHORITY AND THE RELIGION OF THE SPIRIT. By the late Auguste Sabatier, Professor of the University of Paris, Dean of the Protestant Theological Faculty.

"Without any exaggeration, this is to be described as a great book, the finest legacy of the author to the Protestant Church of France and to the theological thought of the age."—*Glasgow Herald.*

14 Henrietta Street, Covent Garden, London, W.C.

WILLIAMS & NORGATE'S

THEOLOGICAL TRANSLATION LIBRARY—Continued.

Vols. XV. and XVII.

THE BEGINNINGS OF CHRISTIANITY. By Paul Wernle, Professor Extraordinary of Modern Church History at the University of Basel. Revised by the Author, and translated by the Rev. G. A. Bienemann, M.A., and edited, with an Introduction, by the Rev. W. D. Morrison, LL.D.

Vol. I. The Rise of the Religion.
Vol. II. The Development of the Church.

> Dr. Marcus Dods in the *British Weekly*—"We cannot recall any work by a foreign theologian which is likely to have a more powerful influence on the thought of this country than Wernle's *Beginnings of Christianity*. It is well written and well translated; it is earnest, clear, and persuasive, and above all it is well adapted to catch the large class of thinking men who are at present seeking some non-miraculous explanation of Christianity."

The Earlier Works included in the Library are:—

HISTORY OF DOGMA. By Adolf Harnack, Berlin. Translated from the Third German Edition. Edited by the Rev. Prof. A. B. Bruce, D.D. 7 vols. (New Series, Vols. II., VII., VIII., IX., X., XI., XII.) 8vo, cloth, each 10s. 6d.; half-leather, suitable for presentation, 12s. 6d.

ABBREVIATED LIST OF CONTENTS :—Vol. I.: INTRODUCTORY DIVISION :—I. Prolegomena to the Study of the History of Dogma. II. The Presuppositions of the History of Dogma. DIVISION I.—The Genesis of Ecclesiastical Dogma, or the Genesis of the Catholic Apostolic Dogmatic Theology, and the first Scientific Ecclesiastical System of Doctrine. BOOK I. :— *The Preparation.* Vol. II.: DIVISION I. BOOK II. :—*The Laying of the Foundation.*—I. Historical Survey.—*I. Fixing and gradual Secularising of Christianity as a Church.—II. Fixing and gradual Hellenising of Christianity as a System of Doctrine.* Vol. III.: DIVISION I. BOOK II.:—*The Laying of the Foundation—* continued. DIVISION II.—The Development of Ecclesiastical Dogma. BOOK I. :—*The History of the Development of Dogma as the Doctrine of the God-man on the basis of Natural Theology. A. Presuppositions of Doctrine of Redemption or Natural Theology. B. The Doctrine of Redemption in the Person of the God-man in its historical development.* Vol. IV.: DIVISION II. BOOK I. :— *The History of the Development of Dogma as the Doctrine of the God-man on the basis of Natural Theology*—continued. Vol. V.: DIVISION II. BOOK II. :—*Expansion and Remodelling of Dogma into a Doctrine of Sin, Grace, and Means of Grace on the basis of the Church.* Vol. VI.: DIVISION II. BOOK II. :—*Expansion and Remodelling of Dogma into a Doctrine of Sin, Grace, and*

---

14 Henrietta Street, Covent Garden, London, W.C.

THEOLOGICAL TRANSLATION LIBRARY—Continued.

Means of Grace on the basis of the Church—continued. Vol. VII.: DIVISION II. BOOK III. :—*The Threefold Issue of the History of Dogma.*—Full Index.

"No work on Church history in recent times has had the influence of Prof. Harnack's *History of Dogma.*"—*Times.*

"A book which is admitted to be one of the most important theological works of the time."—*Daily News.*

WHAT IS CHRISTIANITY? Sixteen Lectures delivered in the University of Berlin during the Winter Term, 1899–1900. By Adolf Harnack. Translated by Thomas Bailey Saunders. (New Series, Vol. XIV.) Demy 8vo, cloth, 10s. 6d.; can only be supplied when complete set of the New Series is ordered.

Prof. W. Sanday of Oxford, in the examination of the work, says :—" I may assume that Harnack's book, which has attracted a good deal of attention in this country as in Germany, is by this time well known, and that its merits are recognised—its fresh and vivid descriptions, its breadth of view and skilful selection of points, its frankness, its genuine enthusiasm, its persistent effort to get at the living realities of religion."

"Seldom has a treatise of the sort been at once so suggestive and so stimulating. Seldom have the results of so much learning been brought to bear on the religious problems which address themselves to the modern mind."—*Pilot.*

"In many respects this is the most notable work of Prof. Harnack.... These lectures are most remarkable, both for the historical insight they display and for their elevation of tone and purpose."—*Literature.*

THE COMMUNION OF THE CHRISTIAN WITH GOD: A Discussion in Agreement with the View of Luther. By W. Herrmann, Dr. Theol., Professor of Dogmatic Theology in the University of Marburg. Translated from the Second thoroughly revised Edition, with Special Annotations by the Author, by J. Sandys Stanyon, M.A. (New Series, Vol. IV.) 8vo, cloth. 10s. 6d.

"It will be seen from what has been said that this book is a very important one.... The translation is also exceedingly well done."—*Critical Review.*

"We trust the book will be widely read, and should advise those who read it to do so twice."—*Primitive Methodist Quarterly.*

"Instinct with genuine religious feeling; ... exceedingly interesting and suggestive."—*Glasgow Herald.*

A HISTORY OF THE HEBREWS. By R. Kittel, Ordinary Professor of Theology in the University of Breslau. In 2 vols. (New Series, Vols. III. and VI.) 8vo, cloth. Each volume, 10s. 6d.

Vol. I. **Sources of Information and History of the Period up to the Death of Joshua.** Translated by John Taylor, D. Lit., M.A.

THEOLOGICAL TRANSLATION LIBRARY—Continued.

Vol. II. **Sources of Information and History of the Period down to the Babylonian Exile.** Translated by Hope W. Hogg, B.D., and E. B. Speirs, D.D.

"It is a sober and earnest reconstruction, for which every earnest student of the Old Testament should be grateful."—*Christian World.*

"It will be a happy day for pulpit and pew when a well-thumbed copy of the *History of the Hebrews* is to be found in every manse and parsonage."—*Literary World.*

"It is a work which cannot fail to attract the attention of thoughtful people in this country."—*Pall Mall Gazette.*

AN INTRODUCTION TO THE TEXTUAL CRITICISM OF THE GREEK NEW TESTAMENT. By Professor Eberhard Nestle, of Maulbronn. Translated from the Second Edition, with Corrections and Additions by the Author, by William Edie, B.D., and edited, with a Preface, by Allan Menzies, D.D., Professor of Divinity and Biblical Criticism in the University of St. Andrews. (New Series, Vol. XIII.) With eleven reproductions of Texts. Demy 8vo, 10s. 6d.; half-leather, 12s. 6d.

"We have no living scholar more capable of accomplishing the fascinating task of preparing a complete introduction on the new and acknowledged principles than Prof. Nestle. This book will stand the most rigorous scrutiny; it will surpass the highest expectation."—*Expository Times.*

"Nothing could be better than Dr. Nestle's account of the materials which New Testament textual criticism has to deal with."—*Spectator.*

"We know of no book of its size which can be recommended more cordially to the student, alike for general interest and for the clearness of its arrangement. . . . In smoothness of rendering, the translation is one of the best we have come across for a considerable time."—*Manchester Guardian.*

THE APOSTOLIC AGE. By Prof. Carl von Weizsäcker. Translated by James Millar, B.D. 2 vols. (New Series, Vols. I. and V.) Demy 8vo, cloth. Each 10s. 6d.

"Weizsäcker is an authority of the very first rank. The present work marks an epoch in New Testament criticism. The English reader is fortunate in having a masterpiece of this kind rendered accessible to him."—*Expository Times.*

". . . No student of theology or of the early history of Christianity can afford to leave Weizsäcker's great book unread."—*Manchester Guardian.*

"In every direction in this work we find the mark of the independent thinker and investigator . . . this remarkable volume . . . this able and learned work. . . ."—*Christian World.*

"The book itself . . . is of great interest, and the work of the translation has been done in a most satisfactory way."—*Critical Review.*

14 Henrietta Street, Covent Garden, London, W.C.

THEOLOGICAL TRANSLATION FUND LIBRARY.
Old Series.
Uniform Price per Volume, 6s.

BAUR (F. C.). CHURCH HISTORY OF THE FIRST THREE CENTURIES. Translated from the Third German Edition. Edited by Rev. Allan Menzies. 2 vols. 8vo, cloth. 12s.

—— **PAUL, THE APOSTLE OF JESUS CHRIST, HIS LIFE AND WORK, HIS EPISTLES AND DOCTRINE.** A Contribution to a Critical History of Primitive Christianity. Edited by Rev. Allan Menzies. 2nd Edition. 2 vols. 8vo, cloth. 12s.

BLEEK (F.). LECTURES ON THE APOCALYPSE. Translated. Edited by the Rev. Dr. S. Davidson. 8vo, cloth. 6s.

EWALD'S (Dr. H.) COMMENTARY ON THE PROPHETS OF THE OLD TESTAMENT. Translated by the Rev. J. F. Smith. [Vol. I. General Introduction, Yoel, Amos, Hosea, and Zakharya 9-11. Vol. II. Yesaya, Obadya, and Mikah. Vol. III. Nahûm, Ssephanya, Habaqqûq, Zakhârya, Yéremya. Vol. IV. Hezekiel, Yesaya xl.-lxvi. Vol. V. Haggai, Zakharya, Malaki, Jona, Baruc, Daniel, Appendix and Index.] 5 vols. 8vo, cloth. 30s.

—— **COMMENTARY ON THE PSALMS.** Translated by the Rev. E. Johnson, M.A. 2 vols. 8vo, cloth. 12s.

—— **COMMENTARY ON THE BOOK OF JOB, with Translation.** Translated from the German by the Rev. J. Frederick Smith. 8vo, cloth. 6s.

HAUSRATH (Prof. A.). HISTORY OF THE NEW TESTAMENT TIMES. The Time of Jesus. Translated by the Revs. C. T. Poynting and P. Quenzer. 2 vols. 8vo, cloth. 12s.

The second portion of this work, "The Times of the Apostles," was issued apart from the Library, but in uniform volumes; *see* p. 18.

KEIM'S HISTORY OF JESUS OF NAZARA: Considered in its connection with the National Life of Israel, and related in detail. Translated from the German by Arthur Ransom and the Rev. E. M. Geldart. [Vol. I. Second Edition. Introduction, Survey of Sources, Sacred and Political Groundwork. Religious Groundwork. Vol. II. The Sacred Youth, Self-recognition, Decision. Vol. III. The First Preaching, the Works of

14 Henrietta Street, Covent Garden, London, W.C.

WILLIAMS & NORGATE'S

THEOLOGICAL TRANSLATION FUND LIBRARY—Continued.

Jesus, the Disciples, and Apostolic Mission. Vol. IV. Conflicts and Disillusions, Strengthened Self-confidence, Last Efforts in Galilee, Signs of the Approaching Fall, Recognition of the Messiah. Vol. V. The Messianic Progress to Jerusalem, the Entry into Jerusalem, the Decisive Struggle, the Farewell, the Last Supper. Vol. VI. The Messianic Death at Jerusalem. Arrest and Pseudo-Trial, the Death on the Cross, Burial and Resurrection, the Messiah's Place in History, Indices.] Complete in 6 vols. 8vo. 36s.

(Vol. I. only to be had when a complete set of the work is ordered.)

KUENEN (Dr. A.). THE RELIGION OF ISRAEL TO THE FALL OF THE JEWISH STATE. By Dr. A. Kuenen, Professor of Theology at the University, Leiden. Translated from the Dutch by A. H. May. 3 vols. 8vo, cloth. 18s.

PFLEIDERER (O.). PAULINISM: A Contribution to the History of Primitive Christian Theology. Translated by E. Peters. 2nd Edition. 2 vols. 8vo, cloth. 12s.

—— PHILOSOPHY OF RELIGION ON THE BASIS OF ITS HISTORY. (Vols. I. II. History of the Philosophy of Religion from Spinoza to the Present Day; Vols. III. IV. Genetic-Speculative Philosophy of Religion.) Translated by Prof. Allan Menzies and the Rev. Alex. Stewart. 4 vols. 8vo, cloth. 24s.

RÉVILLE (Dr. A.). PROLEGOMENA OF THE HISTORY OF RELIGIONS. With an Introduction by Prof. F. Max Müller. 8vo, cloth. 6s.

PROTESTANT COMMENTARY ON THE NEW TESTAMENT. With General and Special Introductions. Edited by Profs. P. W. Schmidt and F. von Holzendorff. Translated from the Third German Edition by the Rev. F. H. Jones, B.A. 3 vols. 8vo, cloth. 18s.

SCHRADER (Prof. E.). THE CUNEIFORM INSCRIPTIONS AND THE OLD TESTAMENT. Translated from the Second Enlarged Edition, with Additions by the Author, and an Introduction by the Rev. Owen C. Whitehouse, M.A. 2 vols. (Vol. I. not sold separately.) With a Map. 8vo, cloth. 12s.

ZELLER (Dr. E.). THE CONTENTS AND ORIGIN OF THE ACTS OF THE APOSTLES CRITICALLY INVESTIGATED. Preceded by Dr. Fr. Overbeck's Introduction to the Acts of the Apostles from De Wette's Handbook. Translated by Joseph Dare. 2 vols. 8vo, cloth. 12s.

14 Henrietta Street, Covent Garden, London, W.C.

THE CROWN THEOLOGICAL LIBRARY.

The volumes are uniform in size (crown octavo) and binding, but the price varies according to the size and importance of the work.

Vol. I. **BABEL AND BIBLE.** By Dr. Friedrich Delitzsch, Professor of Assyriology in the University of Berlin. Authorised Translation. Edited, with an Introduction, by Rev. C. H. W. Johns. Crown 8vo, with 77 illustrations, cloth. 5s.

Vol. II. **THE VIRGIN BIRTH OF CHRIST: An Historical and Critical Essay.** By Paul Lobstein, Professor of Dogmatics in the University of Strassburg. Translated by Victor Leuliette, A.K.C., B.-ès-L., Paris. Edited, with an Introduction, by Rev. W. D. Morrison, LL.D. Crown 8vo. 3s.

Vol. III. **MY STRUGGLE FOR LIGHT: Confessions of a Preacher.** By R. Wimmer, Pastor of Weisweil-am-Rhein in Baden. Crown 8vo, cloth. 3s. 6d.

Vol. IV. **LIBERAL CHRISTIANITY: Its Origin, Nature, and Mission.** By Jean Réville, Professeur adjoint à la Faculté de Théologie Protestante de l'Université de Paris. Translated and edited by Victor Leuliette, A.K.C., B.-ès-L. Crown 8vo, cloth. 4s.

Vol. V. **WHAT IS CHRISTIANITY?** By Adolf Harnack, Professor of Church History in the University, Berlin. Translated by Thomas Bailey Saunders. Third and Revised Edition. Crown 8vo. 5s.

Vol. VI. **FAITH AND MORALS.** By W. Herrmann, Professor of Systematic Theology at the University of Marburg; Author of "The Communion of the Christian with God." Crown 8vo, cloth. 5s.

Vol. VII. **EARLY HEBREW STORY.** A Study of the Origin, the Value, and the Historical Background of the Legends of Israel. By John P. Peters, D.D., Rector of St. Michael's Church, New York; author of "Nippur, or Explorations and Adventures on the Euphrates." Crown 8vo, cloth. 5s.

Vol. VIII. **BIBLE PROBLEMS AND THE NEW MATERIAL FOR THEIR SOLUTION.** A Plea for Thoroughness of Investigation, addressed to Churchmen and Scholars. By the Rev. T. K. Cheyne, D.Litt., D.D., Fellow of the British Academy; Oriel Professor of Interpretation in the University of Oxford, and Canon of Rochester. Crown 8vo. 5s.

---

14 Henrietta Street, Covent Garden, London, W.C.

THE CROWN THEOLOGICAL LIBRARY—Continued.

Vol. IX. THE DOCTRINE OF THE ATONEMENT AND ITS HISTORICAL EVOLUTION; and RELIGION AND MODERN CULTURE. By the late Auguste Sabatier, Professor in the University of Paris. Translated by Victor Leuliette, A.K.C., B.-ès-L. Crown 8vo. 4s. 6d.

Vol. X. THE EARLY CHRISTIAN CONCEPTION OF CHRIST: Its Value and Significance in the History of Religion. By Otto Pfleiderer, D.D., Professor of Practical Theology in the University, Berlin. Crown 8vo. 3s. 6d.

Vol. XI. THE CHILD AND RELIGION. Eleven Essays. By Prof. Henry Jones, M.A., LL.D., University of Glasgow; C. F. G. Masterman, M.A.; Prof. George T. Ladd, D.D., LL.D., University of Yale; Rev. F. R. Tennant, M.A., B.Sc., Hulsean Lecturer; Rev. J. Cynddylan Jones, D.D.; Rev. Canon Hensley Henson, M.A.; Rev. Robert F. Horton, M.A., D.D.; Rev. G. Hill, M.A., D.D.; Rev. J. J. Thornton; Rev. Rabbi A. A. Green; Prof. Joseph Agar Beet, D.D. Edited by Thomas Stephens, B.A. Crown 8vo. 6s.

"No fresher and more instructive book on this question has been issued for years, and the study of its pages will often prove a godsend to many perplexed minds in the church and in the Christian home."—*British Weekly*.

Vol. XII. THE EVOLUTION OF RELIGION: An Anthropological Study. By L. R. Farnell, D.Litt., Fellow and Tutor of Exeter College, Oxford; University Lecturer in Classical Archæology, etc., etc. Crown 8vo, cloth. 5s.

Vol. XIII. THE BOOKS OF THE NEW TESTAMENT. By H. von Soden, D.D., Professor of Theology in the University of Berlin. Translated by the Rev. J. R. Wilkinson, and edited by Rev. W. D. Morrison, LL.D. Crown 8vo, cloth. 5s.

Vol. XIV. JESUS. By Wilhelm Bousset, Professor of Theology in Göttingen. Translated by Janet Penrose Trevelyan, and edited by Rev. W. D. Morrison, LL.D. Crown 8vo. 4s.

"It is true the writers, von Soden and Bousset, have in the course of their papers said things that I regard as as nothing less than admirable. I very much doubt whether we have anything so admirable in English."—Rev. Dr. Sanday in the *Guardian*.

Vol. XV. THE COMMUNION OF THE CHRISTIAN WITH GOD. By Prof. Wilhelm Herrmann. Translated from the new German Edition by Rev. J. S. Stanyon, M.A., and Rev. R. W. Stewart, B.D., B.Sc. Crown 8vo, cloth. 5s.

14 Henrietta Street, Covent Garden, London, W.C.

CATALOGUE OF PUBLICATIONS.

THE CROWN THEOLOGICAL LIBRARY—Continued.

Vol. XVI. HEBREW RELIGION TO THE ESTABLISHMENT OF JUDAISM UNDER EZRA. By W. E. Addis, M.A. Crown 8vo, cloth. 5s.

Vol. XVII. NATURALISM AND RELIGION. By Rudolf Otto, Professor of Theology in the University of Göttingen. Translated by J. Arthur Thomson, Professor of Natural History in the University of Aberdeen, and Margaret R. Thomson. Edited with an Introduction by Rev. W. D. Morrison, LL.D. Crown 8vo. 6s.

". . . A valuable survey, and a critical estimate of scientific theory and kindred ideas as they concern the religious view of the world. ; . . It is well written, clear, and even eloquent."—*Expository Times*.

Vol. XVIII. ESSAYS ON THE SOCIAL GOSPEL. By Professor Adolf Harnack, of Berlin, and Professor W. Herrmann, of Marburg. Crown 8vo, cloth. 4s. 6d.

Vol. XIX. THE RELIGION OF THE OLD TESTAMENT: Its Place among the Religions of the Nearer East. By Karl Marti, Professor of Old Testament Exegesis, Bern. Crown 8vo, cloth. 4s. 6d.

In a leading review *The Spectator* says:—"It is a valuable contribution to a great theme by one who has devoted his life to its study. Not only the general reader, for whom it is specially intended, but the theologian will learn not a little from its pages."

Vol. XX. LUKE, THE PHYSICIAN. By Adolf Harnack, D.D. Translated by the Rev. J. R. Wilkinson, M.A. Crown 8vo, cloth. 6s.

"What is new and interesting and valuable is the ratiocination, the theorising, and the personal point of view in the book under review. We study it to understand Professor Harnack, not to understand Luke; and the study is well worth the time and work. Personally, I feel specially interested in the question of Luke's nationality. On this the author has some admirable and suggestive pages."—Prof. Sir W. M. Ramsay in *The Expositor*.

Vol. XXI. THE HISTORICAL EVIDENCE FOR THE RESURRECTION OF JESUS CHRIST. By Kirsopp Lake, Professor of New Testament Exegesis in the University of Leiden, Holland. Crown 8vo, cloth. 5s.

Vol. XXII. THE APOLOGETIC OF THE NEW TESTAMENT. By E. F. Scott, M.A., author of "The Fourth Gospel: Its Purpose and Theology." Crown 8vo, cloth. 5s.

14 Henrietta Street, Covent Garden, London, W.C.

WILLIAMS & NORGATE'S

THE CROWN THEOLOGICAL LIBRARY—Continued.

Vol. XXIII. **THE SAYINGS OF JESUS.** By Adolf Harnack, D.D. Being Vol. II. of Dr Harnack's New Testament Studies. Crown 8vo, cloth. 6s.

Vol. XXIV. **ANGLICAN LIBERALISM.** By Twelve Churchmen. Rev. Hubert Handley, Prof. F. C. Burkitt, M.A., D.D., Rev. J. R. Wilkinson, M.A., Rev. C. R. Shaw Stewart, M.A., Rev. Hastings Rashdall, D.Litt., D.C.L., Prof. Percy Gardner, Litt.D., LL.D., Sir C. T. Dyke Acland, Rev. A. J. Carlyle, M.A., Rev. H. G. Woods, D.D., Rev. A. Caldecott, D.Litt., D.D., Rev. W. D. Morrison, LL.D., Rev. A. L. Lilley, M.A. Crown 8vo, cloth. 5s.

"This is a stimulating volume, and we are glad to see an able body of writers uniting to claim the free atmosphere as the condition of spiritual progress."—*Westminster Gazette.*

Vol. XXV. **THE FUNDAMENTAL TRUTHS OF THE CHRISTIAN RELIGION.** By R. Seeberg, Professor of Systematic Theology in Berlin. Sixteen Lectures delivered before the Students of all Faculties in the University of Berlin. Crown 8vo, 350 pp. 5s.

Vol. XXVI. **THE ACTS OF THE APOSTLES.** By Adolf Harnack, D.D. Being Vol. III. of Dr Harnack's New Testament Studies. Crown 8vo, cloth. 6s.

Vol. XXVII. **THE LIFE OF THE SPIRIT.** By Rudolf Eucken, Professor of Philosophy in Jena. Second Edition. 8vo, cloth. 5s.

Vol. XXVIII. **MONASTICISM: Its Ideals and History; and THE CONFESSIONS OF ST. AUGUSTINE.** Two Lectures by Adolf Harnack, D.D. Translated into English by E. E. Kellett, M.A., and F. H. Marseille, Ph.D. Crown 8vo, cloth. 4s.

"One might read all the ponderous works of Montalembert without obtaining so clear a view or so rare a judgment of this immense subject as are offered in these luminous pages."—*Christian World.*

Vol. XXIX. **MODERNITY AND THE CHURCHES.** By Prof. Percy Gardner, Litt.D., of Oxford. Crown 8vo, cloth. 5s.

Vol. XXX. **THE OLD EGYPTIAN FAITH.** By Edouard Naville, Hon. LL.D., Ph.D., Litt.D., Fellow of King's College, London, Professor of Egyptology at the University of Geneva. Translated by Colin Campbell, M.A., D.D. Illustrated.

14 Henrietta Street, Covent Garden, London, W.C.

THE HIBBERT LECTURES.

Library Edition, demy 8vo, 10s. 6d. per volume. Cheap Popular Edition, 3s. 6d. per volume.

ALVIELLA (Count GOBLET D'). LECTURES ON THE ORIGIN AND THE GROWTH OF THE CONCEPTION OF GOD AS ILLUSTRATED BY ANTHROPOLOGY AND HISTORY. Translated by the Rev. P. H. Wicksteed. (Hibbert Lectures, 1891.) Cloth. 10s. 6d. Cheap Edition, 3s. 6d.

BEARD (Rev. Dr. C.). LECTURES ON THE REFORMATION OF THE SIXTEENTH CENTURY IN ITS RELATION TO MODERN THOUGHT AND KNOWLEDGE. (Hibbert Lectures, 1883.) 8vo, cloth. 10s. 6d. Cheap Edition, 3rd Edition, 3s. 6d.

DAVIDS (T. W. RHYS). LECTURES ON SOME POINTS IN THE HISTORY OF INDIAN BUDDHISM. (Hib. Lec., 1881.) 2nd Ed. 8vo, cloth. 10s. 6d. Cheap Ed., 3s. 6d.

DRUMMOND (Dr.) VIA, VERITAS, VITA. Lectures on Christianity in its most Simple and Intelligible Form. (The Hibbert Lectures, 1894.) 10s. 6d. Cheap Edition, 3s. 6d.

HATCH (Rev. Dr.). LECTURES ON THE INFLUENCE OF GREEK IDEAS AND USAGES UPON THE CHRISTIAN CHURCH. Edited by Dr. Fairbairn. (Hibbert Lectures, 1888.) 3rd Edition. 8vo, cloth. 10s. 6d. Cheap Edition, 3s. 6d.

KUENEN (Dr. A.). LECTURES ON NATIONAL RELIGIONS AND UNIVERSAL RELIGION. (The Hibbert Lectures, 1882.) 8vo, cloth. 10s. 6d. Cheap Edition, 3s. 6d.

MONTEFIORE (C. G.). ORIGIN AND GROWTH OF RELIGION AS ILLUSTRATED BY THE RELIGION OF THE ANCIENT HEBREWS. (The Hibbert Lectures, 1892.) 2nd Edition. 8vo, cloth. 10s. 6d. Cheap Edition, 3s. 6d.

PFLEIDERER (Dr. O.). LECTURES ON THE INFLUENCE OF THE APOSTLE PAUL ON THE DEVELOPMENT OF CHRISTIANITY. Translated by the Rev. J. Frederick Smith. (Hibbert Lectures, 1885.) 2nd Edition. 8vo, cloth. 10s. 6d. Cheap Edition, 3s. 6d.

RENAN (E.). ON THE INFLUENCE OF THE INSTITUTIONS, THOUGHT, AND CULTURE OF ROME ON CHRISTIANITY AND THE DEVELOPMENT OF THE CATHOLIC CHURCH. Translated by the Rev. Charles Beard. (Hibbert Lectures, 1880.) 8vo, cloth. 10s. 6d. Cheap Edition, 3rd Edition, 3s. 6d.

14 Henrietta Street, Covent Garden, London, W.C.

WILLIAMS & NORGATE'S

THE HIBBERT LECTURES—Continued.

RENOUF (P. LE PAGE). ON THE RELIGION OF ANCIENT EGYPT. (Hibbert Lectures, 1879.) 3rd Edition. 8vo, cloth. 10s. 6d. Cheap Edition, 3s. 6d.

RHYS (Prof. J.). ON THE ORIGIN AND GROWTH OF RELIGION AS ILLUSTRATED BY CELTIC HEATHENDOM. (Hibbert Lectures, 1886.) 8vo, cloth. 10s. 6d. Cheap Edition, 3s. 6d.

RÉVILLE (Dr. A.). ON THE NATIVE RELIGIONS OF MEXICO AND PERU. Translated by the Rev. P. H. Wicksteed. (Hibbert Lectures, 1884.) 8vo, cloth. 10s. 6d. Cheap Edition, 3s. 6d.

SAYCE (Prof. A. H.). ON THE RELIGION OF ANCIENT ASSYRIA AND BABYLONIA. 4th Edition. (Hibbert Lectures, 1887.) 8vo, cloth. 10s. 6d. Cheap Ed., 3s. 6d.

UPTON (Rev. C. B.). ON THE BASES OF RELIGIOUS BELIEF. (Hibbert Lectures, 1893.) Demy 8vo, cloth. 10s. 6d. Cheap Edition, 3s. 6d.

ALPHABETICAL LIST.

ADDIS (W. E.). HEBREW RELIGION. 5s. *See* Crown Theological Library, p. 11.

ALLIN (Rev. THOS.). UNIVERSALISM ASSERTED AS THE HOPE OF THE GOSPEL ON THE AUTHORITY OF REASON, THE FATHERS, AND HOLY SCRIPTURE. With a Preface by Edna Lyall, and a Letter from Canon Wilberforce. Crown 8vo, cloth. 2s. 6d. net.

ALVIELLA (Count GOBLET D'). THE CONTEMPORARY EVOLUTION OF RELIGIOUS THOUGHT IN ENGLAND, AMERICA, AND INDIA. Translated from the French by the Rev. J. Moden. 8vo, cloth. 10s. 6d.

—— **EVOLUTION OF THE IDEA OF GOD.** *See* The Hibbert Lectures, p. 13.

ANGLICAN LIBERALISM. By Twelve Churchmen. 5s. *See* Crown Theological Library, p. 12.

BAUR (F. C.). CHURCH HISTORY OF THE FIRST THREE CENTURIES. 2 vols., 12s. *See* Theological Translation Library, Old Series, p. 7.

—— **PAUL, THE APOSTLE OF JESUS CHRIST.** 2 vols., 12s. *See* Theological Translation Library, Old Series, p. 7.

BEARD (Rev. Dr. C.). THE UNIVERSAL CHRIST. AND OTHER SERMONS. Crown 8vo, cloth. 7s. 6d.

14 Henrietta Street, Covent Garden, London, W.C.

CATALOGUE OF PUBLICATIONS.

ALPHABETICAL LIST—Continued.

BEARD (Rev. Dr. C.). LECTURES ON THE REFORMATION OF THE SIXTEENTH CENTURY IN ITS RELATION TO MODERN THOUGHT AND KNOWLEDGE. *See* The Hibbert Lectures, p. 13.

BEEBY (Rev. C. E., B.D., Author of "Creed and Life"). **DOCTRINE AND PRINCIPLES.** Popular Lectures on Primary Questions. Demy 8vo, cloth. 4s. 6d.

BEVAN (Rev. J. O., M.A., F.G.S., F.S.A., etc., Rector of Chillenden, Dover). **THE GENESIS AND EVOLUTION OF THE INDIVIDUAL SOUL SCIENTIFICALLY TREATED.** Including also Problems relating to Science and Immortality. Crown 8vo, cloth. 2s. 6d. net.

"Meets the much debated questions which are raised by the more thoughtful, and perhaps able, opponents of belief in a second life, and is a work of great value, and one that is opportune in its publication, and besides, *per se*, emphatically interesting reading."—*Manchester Courier*.

BIBLE. Translated by Samuel Sharpe, being a Revision of the Authorised English Version. 6th Edition of the Old, 10th Edition of the New Testament. 8vo, roan. 5s. *See also* Testament.

BLEEK (F.). LECTURES ON THE APOCALYPSE. *See* Theological Translation Library, Old Series, p. 7.

BREMOND (HENRI). THE MYSTERY OF NEWMAN. With an Introduction by Rev. George Tyrrell, M.A. Medium 8vo, cloth. 10s. 6d. net.

"From France comes a remarkable volume, excellently translated, which endeavours to probe the mystery; to realise, as it were, the soul of Newman, to describe to us justly and truthfully the personality of the man."—*Daily Chronicle*.

"No subsequent work can deprive M. Bremond's book of its great psychological interest; it is a work that, unlike many books on Newman and the Tractarians, no student of modern Christianity can afford to miss."—*Pall Mall Gazette*.

CAMPBELL (Rev. Canon COLIN, M.A., D.D.,). FIRST THREE GOSPELS IN GREEK. 3s. 6d. net. *See* Testament, New, p. 26.

CAMPBELL (Rev. R. J., M.A.). NEW THEOLOGY SERMONS. Crown 8vo, cloth. 6s.

CHANNING'S COMPLETE WORKS. Including "The Perfect Life," with a Memoir. Centennial Edition. 4to Edition. Cloth. 7s. 6d.

CHEYNE (Prof. T. K.). BIBLE PROBLEMS AND THE NEW MATERIAL FOR THEIR SOLUTION. 5s. *See* Crown Theological Library, p. 9.

CHILD AND RELIGION. Edited by Thomas Stephens, B.A. 6s. *See* Crown Theological Library, p. 10.

CHRISTIAN CREED (OUR). 2nd and greatly Revised Edition. Crown 8vo, cloth. 3s. 6d.

---

14 Henrietta Street, Covent Garden, London, W.C.

ALPHABETICAL LIST—Continued.

COIT (STANTON, Ph.D.). NATIONAL IDEALISM AND A STATE CHURCH.
"No one reading this book could miss its interest and ability.... Criticises existing Christianity along lines almost literally opposite to those of Herbert Spencer and the majority of the critics.... Great clearness and eloquence."—G. K. CHESTERTON in *The Nation*.

—— **NATIONAL IDEALISM AND THE BOOK OF COMMON PRAYER.** An Essay in Re-Interpretation and Revision. Demy 8vo, cloth. 10s. 6d. net.

COMMON PRAYER FOR CHRISTIAN WORSHIP: in Ten Services for Morning and Evening. 32mo, cloth. 1s. 6d. Also in 8vo, cloth. 3s.

CONWAY (MONCURE D.). CENTENARY HISTORY OF THE SOUTH PLACE ETHICAL SOCIETY. With numerous Portraits, a facsimile of the original MS. of the hymn, "Nearer, my God, to Thee," and Appendices. Crown 8vo, half vellum, paper sides. 5s.

CORNILL (Prof. CARL). INTRODUCTION TO THE CANONICAL BOOKS OF THE OLD TESTAMENT. Demy 8vo, cloth. 10s. 6d. net. See Theological Translation Library, New Series, p. 3.

DAVIDS (T. W. RHYS). LECTURES ON SOME POINTS IN THE HISTORY OF INDIAN BUDDHISM. See The Hibbert Lectures, p. 13.

DELITZSCH (F.). BABEL AND BIBLE. Two Lectures delivered before the Deutsche Orient-Gesellschaft in the presence of the German Emperor. 5s. See Crown Theological Library, p. 9. See also Harnack, A., "Letter to *Preuss. Jahrbücher*," p. 18.

DOBSCHÜTZ (E. VON). CHRISTIAN LIFE IN THE PRIMITIVE CHURCH. Demy 8vo. 10s. 6d. See Theological Translation Library, New Series, p. 3.

DOLE (CHARLES F.). THE ETHICS OF PROGRESS, or the Theory and the Practice by which Civilisation proceeds. Small demy 8vo, cloth. 6s. net.

DRIVER (S. R.). See Mosheh ben Shesheth, p. 22.

DRUMMOND (JAMES, M.A., LL.D., Hon. Litt.D., late Principal of Manchester College, Oxford). AN INQUIRY INTO THE CHARACTER AND AUTHORSHIP OF THE FOURTH GOSPEL. *New Edition in Preparation.*
"The book is not only learned, but also reverent and spiritual in tone, and ought to find its way into the libraries of students of all shades of belief, as a very notable attempt to solve one of the most important of New Testament problems."—*Christian World*.

—— **VIA, VERITAS, VITA.** See The Hibbert Lectures, p. 13.

—— **PHILO JUDÆUS.** See p. 28.

14 Henrietta Street, Covent Garden, London, W.C.

CATALOGUE OF PUBLICATIONS.

ALPHABETICAL LIST—Continued.

ECHOES OF HOLY THOUGHTS: Arranged as Private Meditations before a First Communion. 2nd Edition, with a Preface by Rev. J. Hamilton Thom. Printed with red lines. Fcap. 8vo, cloth. 1s.

EUCKEN (Prof. RUDOLF). THE LIFE OF THE SPIRIT. 5s. See page 12.

EWALD (H.). COMMENTARY ON THE PROPHETS OF THE OLD TESTAMENT. See Theological Translation Library, Old Series, p. 7.

—— **COMMENTARY ON THE PSALMS.** See Theological Translation Library, Old Series, p. 7.

EWALD (H.). COMMENTARY ON THE BOOK OF JOB. See Theological Translation Library, Old Series, p. 7.

FARNELL (L. R.). THE EVOLUTION OF RELIGION. An Anthropological Study. By L. R. Farnell, D.Litt., Fellow and Tutor of Exeter College, Oxford. 5s. See Crown Theological Library, p. 10.

FIGG (E. G.). ANALYSIS OF THEOLOGY, NATURAL AND REVEALED. Crown 8vo, cloth. 6s.

FORMBY (Rev. C. W.). RE-CREATION: A New Aspect of Evolution. Large Crown 8vo, cloth. 5s.

FOUR GOSPELS (THE) AS HISTORICAL RECORDS. 8vo, cloth. 15s.

GILL (C.). THE EVOLUTION OF CHRISTIANITY. By Charles Gill. 2nd Edition. With Dissertations in answer to Criticism. 8vo, cloth. 12s.

—— **THE BOOK OF ENOCH THE PROPHET.** Translated from an Ethiopic MS. in the Bodleian Library, by the late Richard Laurence, LL.D., Archbishop of Cashel. The Text corrected from his latest Notes by Charles Gill. Re-issue, 8vo, cloth. 5s.

HARNACK (ADOLF). ACTS OF THE APOSTLES. 6s. See Crown Theological Library, p. 12.

—— **MONASTICISM: Its Ideals and History; and THE CONFESSIONS OF ST. AUGUSTINE.** Two Lectures by Adolf Harnack. Translated into English by E. E. Kellett, M.A., and F. H. Marseille, Ph.D., M.A. Crown 8vo, cloth. 4s.

"The lectures impart to these old subjects a new and vivid interest which cannot but win this faithful version many admiring readers."—*Scotsman*.

"One might read all the ponderous volumes of Montalembert without obtaining so clear a view or so rare a judgment of this immense subject as are offered in these luminous pages.... The translation is excellent, and gives us Harnack in pure and vigorous English."—*Christian World*.

14 Henrietta Street, Covent Garden, London, W.C.

WILLIAMS & NORGATE'S

ALPHABETICAL LIST—Continued.

HARNACK (ADOLF). LETTER to the "Preussische Jahrbücher" on the German Emperor's Criticism of Prof. Delitzsch's Lectures on "Babel and Bible." Translated into English by Thomas Bailey Saunders. 6d. net.

—— LUKE, THE PHYSICIAN. 6s. *See* Crown Theological Library, p. 11.

—— HISTORY OF DOGMA. 7 vols., 10s. 6d. each. *See* Theological Translation Library, New Series, p. 4.

—— THE SAYINGS OF JESUS. 6s. *See* Crown Theological Library, p. 12.

—— WHAT IS CHRISTIANITY? *See* Theological Translation Library, New Series, p. 5. *Also* Crown Theological Library, p. 10. 5s. *See* Saunders (T. B.), "Professor Harnack and his Oxford Critics," p. 24.

—— MISSION AND EXPANSION OF CHRISTIANITY IN THE FIRST THREE CENTURIES. By Adolf Harnack, D.D., Berlin. Entirely new edition, re-written, with numerous additions and maps. 2 vols. demy 8vo, cloth. 25s. net.

—— and HERRMANN (Dr. WILHELM). ESSAYS ON THE SOCIAL GOSPEL. 4s. 6d. Translation edited by Maurice A. Canney, M.A. *See* Crown Theological Library, p. 11

HATCH (Rev. Dr.). LECTURES ON THE INFLUENCE OF GREEK IDEAS AND USAGES UPON THE CHRISTIAN CHURCH. *See* The Hibbert Lectures, p. 13.

HAUSRATH (Prof. A.). HISTORY OF THE NEW TESTAMENT TIMES. The Time of the Apostles. Translated by Leonard Huxley. With a Preface by Mrs Humphry Ward. 4 vols. 8vo, cloth. 42s. (Uniform with the Theological Translation Library, Old Series.)

—— NEW TESTAMENT TIMES. The Times of Jesus. 2 vols. 12s. *See* Theological Translation Library, Old Series, p. 7.

HEBREW TEXTS, in large type for Classes:
    Genesis. 2nd Edition. 16mo, cloth. 1s. 6d.
    Psalms. 16mo, cloth. 1s.
    Isaiah. 16mo, cloth. 1s.
    Job. 16mo, cloth. 1s.

HENSLOW (Rev. G.). THE ARGUMENT OF ADAPTATION; or, Natural Theology reconsidered. 8vo, cloth. 1s.

—— SPIRITUAL TEACHINGS OF BIBLE PLANTS; or, The Garden of God. 8vo, cloth. 1s.

—— THE AT-ONE-MENT; or, The Gospel of Reconciliation. 8vo, cloth. 1s.

14 Henrietta Street, Covent Garden, London, W.C.

CATALOGUE OF PUBLICATIONS.

ALPHABETICAL LIST—Continued.

HENSLOW (Rev. G.). THE SPIRITUAL TEACHING OF CHRIST'S LIFE. 8vo, cloth. 5s. net.

—— **CHRIST NO PRODUCT OF EVOLUTION.** 8vo, cloth. 1s.

—— **VULGATE, THE: The Source of False Doctrines.** A work specially applicable to the Clergy, Bible Teachers, and other exponents of the Gospel of Christ. Crown 8vo, cloth. 2s. 6d. net.

HERFORD (R. TRAVERS, B.A.). CHRISTIANITY IN TALMUD AND MIDRASH. Demy 8vo, cloth. 18s. net.
CONTENTS:—Introduction. Division I. Passages from the Rabbinical Literature: A. Passages relating to Jesus. B. Passages relating to Minim, Minuth. Division II. General Results. Appendix containing the Original Texts of the Passages translated. Indices.
"It is no exaggeration to say that it will prove indispensable not only to scholars interested in Talmudic literature, but to all who study the subject of the evangelical tradition. It will introduce the reader into a new world—that of Jewish thought in the centuries after Christ."—*Cambridge Review*.

HERRMANN (W.). THE COMMUNION OF THE CHRISTIAN WITH GOD. 5s. *See* Theological Translation Library, New Series, p. 5.

—— **FAITH AND MORALS.** 5s. *See* Crown Theological Library, p. 9.

—— and **HARNACK (ADOLF.). ESSAYS ON THE SOCIAL GOSPEL.** 4s. 6d. *See* Crown Theological Library, p. 11.

HIBBERT JOURNAL: A Quarterly Review of Religion, Theology, and Philosophy. Edited by L. P. Jacks and G. Dawes Hicks. Vol. I. Royal 8vo, 856 pp. Vol. II., 864 pp. Vol. III., 869 pp. Vols. IV., V., VI., and VII., 960 pp. Cloth. Each 12s. 6d. net. Annual Subscription, 10s. post free.

HIBBERT JOURNAL SUPPLEMENT, 1909, entitled JESUS OR CHRIST? Containing Essays by the following writers:—The late Rev. George Tyrrell, The Bishop of Southwark, Professor H. Weinel, Professor Percy Gardner, Professor P. Schmiedel, Professor Henry Jones, The Rev. Richard Morris, B.D., Sir Oliver Lodge, Canon H. Scott Holland, The Rev. Father Joseph Rickaby, S.J., Professor Nathan Söderblom (Upsala)., Rev. Principal A. E. Garvie, D.D., The Rev. R. J. Campbell, M.A., The Rev. James Drummond, D.D., Professor B. W. Bacon, D.D., Rev. Principal J. E. Carpenter, D.D., Mr James Collier, The Rev. R. Roberts. Super-royal 8vo, cloth. 5s. net.

HOERNING (Dr. R.). THE KARAITE MSS., BRITISH MUSEUM. The Karaite Exodus (i. to viii. 5) in Forty-two Autotype Facsimiles, with a Transcription in ordinary Arabic type. Together with Descriptions and Collation of that and five other MSS. of portions of the Hebrew Bible in Arabic characters in the same Collection. Royal 4to, cloth, gilt top. 20s.

14 Henrietta Street, Covent Garden, London, W.C.

ALPHABETICAL LIST—Continued.

HUNTER (Rev. J., D.D.). DE PROFUNDIS CLAMAVI, and Other Sermons. Large Crown 8vo, cloth. 5s. net.

—— **THE COMING CHURCH.** A Plea for a Church simply Christian. Cloth. 1s. 6d. net.

JOHNSON (EDWIN, M.A.). THE RISE OF CHRISTENDOM. Demy 8vo, cloth. 7s. 6d.

JOHNSON (EDWIN, M.A.). ANTIQUA MATER: A Study of Christian Origins. Crown 8vo, cloth. 2s. 6d.

—— **THE RISE OF ENGLISH CULTURE.** Demy 8vo, cloth. 15s. net.

JONES (Rev. R. CROMPTON). HYMNS OF DUTY AND FAITH. Selected and Arranged. 247 pp. Fcap. 8vo, cloth. 2nd Edition. 3s. 6d.

—— **CHANTS, PSALMS, AND CANTICLES.** Selected and Pointed for Chanting. 18mo, cloth. 1s. 6d.

—— **ANTHEMS.** With Indexes and References to the Music. 18mo, cloth. 1s. 3d.

—— **THE CHANTS AND ANTHEMS.** Together in 1 vol., cloth. 2s.

—— **A BOOK OF PRAYER.** In Thirty Orders of Worship, with Additional Prayers and Thanksgivings. 18mo, cloth. 2s. 6d. With Chants, in 1 vol. 18mo, cloth. 3s.

KAUTZSCH (E.). AN OUTLINE OF THE HISTORY OF THE LITERATURE OF THE OLD TESTAMENT. With Chronological Tables for the History of the Israelites, and other Aids to the Explanation of the Old Testament. Reprinted from the "Supplement to the Translation of the Old Testament." By E. Kautzsch, Professor of Theology at the University of Halle. Edited by the Author. Translated by John Taylor, D.Lit., M.A., etc. Demy 8vo, cloth. 6s. 6d.

"This English translation . . . is likely to prove very acceptable to all those students who desire to see for themselves the view taken by the 'higher critics' of the growth of the Old Testament."—*The Guardian.*

"Dr. Taylor has rendered a great service to the English readers by his excellent translation of this important work."—*British Weekly.*

KEIM'S HISTORY OF JESUS OF NAZARA. 6 vols. 6s. each. *See* Theological Translation Library, Old Series, p. 7.

KENNEDY (Rev. JAS.). BIBLICAL HEBREW. 12s. *See* p. 34.

KITTEL (R.). HISTORY OF THE HEBREWS. 2 vols. 10s. 6d. each. *See* Theological Translation Library, New Series, p. 5.

KUENEN (Dr. A.). LECTURES ON NATIONAL AND UNIVERSAL RELIGIONS. *See* The Hibbert Lectures, p. 13.

14 Henrietta Street, Covent Garden, London, W.C.

ALPHABETICAL LIST—Continued.

KUENEN (Dr. A.). THE RELIGION OF ISRAEL TO THE FALL OF THE JEWISH STATE. 3 vols. 18s. *See* Theological Translation Library, Old Series, p. 8.

LAKE (Professor KIRSOPP). THE HISTORICAL EVIDENCE FOR THE RESURRECTION OF JESUS CHRIST. 5s. *See* Crown Theological Library, p. 11.

LEA (HENRY CHARLES, LL.D.). HISTORY OF SACERDOTAL CELIBACY IN THE CHRISTIAN CHURCH. Third Edition. Thoroughly Revised and Reset. 2 vols. Medium 8vo, cloth. 21s. net.

LOBSTEIN (P.). THE DOGMA OF THE VIRGIN BIRTH OF CHRIST. 3s. *See* Crown Theological Library, p. 9.

LODGE (Sir O.). LIFE AND MATTER. An Exposition of Part of the Philosophy of Science, with Special References to the Influence of Professor Haeckel. Second Edition, with an Appendix of Definitions and Explanations. Crown 8vo, cloth. 2s. 6d. net. Popular Edition. Paper cover. 6d. net.

MACAN (R. W.). THE RESURRECTION OF JESUS CHRIST. An Essay in Three Chapters. 8vo, cloth. 5s.

MACFIE, (RONALD C., M.A., M.B.). SCIENCE, MATTER, AND IMMORTALITY. Crown 8vo, cloth. 5s. net.

MACKAY (R. W.). SKETCH OF THE RISE AND PROGRESS OF CHRISTIANITY. 8vo, cloth. 6s.

MARCHANT (JAMES). THEORIES OF THE RESURRECTION OF JESUS CHRIST. Crown 8vo, stiff covers, 2s. net; superior cloth binding, 3s.

MARTI (KARL). RELIGION OF THE OLD TESTAMENT. 4s. 6d. *See* Crown Theological Library, p. 11.

MARTINEAU (Rev. Dr. JAMES). THE RELATION BETWEEN ETHICS AND RELIGION. An Address. 8vo, sewed. 1s.

—— **MODERN MATERIALISM: ITS ATTITUDE TOWARDS THEOLOGY.** A Critique and Defence. 8vo, sewed. 2s. 6d.

MÉNÉGOZ (E.). RELIGION AND THEOLOGY. By E. Ménégoz, Professor of the Faculty of Protestant Theology, Paris. Stiff boards. 1s. net.

MERCER (Right Rev. J. EDWARD, D.D.). THE SOUL OF PROGRESS. Being the Moorhouse Lectures for 1907. Crown 8vo, cloth. 6s. For Moorhouse Lectures *vide* also Stephen, page 25.

"To be congratulated on an effective and freshly thought out exposure of the familiar failure of materialism to account for evolution, humanity or progress in any intelligible sense."—*The Christian World*.

14 Henrietta Street, Covent Garden, London, W.C.

WILLIAMS & NORGATE'S

ALPHABETICAL LIST—Continued.

MITCHELL (Rev. A. F.). HOW TO TEACH THE BIBLE. 2nd Edition, thoroughly revised and reset. Crown 8vo, cloth. 2s. 6d.

"The lectures are marked by much insight and moderation. The book is notable also for its gracious and cultured note, and for the quiet persuasiveness with which a revolutionary reform is advocated."—*Sunday School Chronicle.*

MONTEFIORE (C. G.). ORIGIN AND GROWTH OF RELIGION AS ILLUSTRATED BY THE RELIGION OF THE ANCIENT HEBREWS. *See* The Hibbert Lectures, p. 13.

MOSHEH BEN SHESHETH'S COMMENTARY ON JEREMIAH AND EZEKIEL. Edited from a Bodleian MS., with a Translation and Notes, by S. R. Driver. 8vo, sewed. 3s.

MÜNSTERBERG (Prof. HUGO). THE AMERICANS. 12s. 6d. net. *See* p. 29.

NESTLE (E.). INTRODUCTION TO THE TEXTUAL CRITICISM OF THE GREEK NEW TESTAMENT. *See* Theological Translation Library, New Series, p. 6.

OTTO (R.). NATURALISM AND RELIGION. 6s. *See* Crown Theological Library, p. 11.

PERCIVAL (G. H.). THE INCARNATE PURPOSE. Essays on the Spiritual Unity of Life. Crown 8vo, cloth. 2s. 6d. net.

PERRIN (R. S.). THE EVOLUTION OF KNOWLEDGE. A Review of Philosophy. Crown 8vo, cloth. 6s.

PERSONAL AND FAMILY PRAYERS. 8vo, buckram. 1s. net.

PETERS (JOHN P.). EARLY HEBREW STORY. A Study of the Origin, the Value, and the Historical Background of the Legends of Israel. 5s. *See* Crown Theological Library, p. 10.

PFLEIDERER (Dr. O.). LECTURES ON THE INFLUENCE OF THE APOSTLE PAUL ON THE DEVELOPMENT OF CHRISTIANITY. *See* The Hibbert Lectures, p. 13.

—— **PAULINISM: A Contribution to the History of Primitive Christianity.** 2 vols. 12s. *See* Theological Translation Library, Old Series, p. 8.

—— **PHILOSOPHY OF RELIGION ON THE BASIS OF ITS HISTORY.** 4 vols. 24s. *See* Theological Translation Library, Old Series, p. 8.

14 Henrietta Street, Covent Garden, London, W.C.

ALPHABETICAL LIST—Continued.

PFLEIDERER (Dr. O.). THE EARLY CHRISTIAN CONCEPTION OF CHRIST: Its Significance and Value in the History of Religion. 3s. 6d. *See* Crown Theological Library, p. 10.

—— PRIMITIVE CHRISTIANITY. Vols. I. and II. Demy 8vo, cloth. 10s. 6d. net each. *See* Theological Translation Library, New Series, p. 2.

PICTON, (J. ALLANSON, M.A., Lond.). MAN AND THE BIBLE. A Review of the Place of the Bible in Human History. Demy 8vo, cloth. 6s. net.

POOLE (REG. LANE). ILLUSTRATIONS OF THE HISTORY OF MEDIÆVAL THOUGHT IN THE DEPARTMENTS OF THEOLOGY AND ECCLESIASTICAL POLITICS. 8vo, cloth. 10s. 6d.

PROTESTANT COMMENTARY ON THE NEW TESTAMENT. 3 vols. 18s. *See* Theological Translation Library, Old Series, p. 8.

RENAN (E.). ON THE INFLUENCE OF THE INSTITUTIONS, THOUGHT, AND CULTURE OF ROME ON CHRISTIANITY AND THE DEVELOPMENT OF THE CATHOLIC CHURCH. *See* Hibbert Lectures, p. 13.

RENOUF (P. LE PAGE). ON THE RELIGION OF ANCIENT EGYPT. *See* Hibbert Lectures, p. 14.

RÉVILLE (A.). THE SONG OF SONGS, Commonly called the Song of Solomon, or the Canticle. Translated from the French. Crown 8vo, cloth. 1s. 6d.

—— ON NATIVE RELIGIONS OF MEXICO AND PERU. *See* Hibbert Lectures, p. 14.

—— PROLEGOMENA OF THE HISTORY OF RELIGIONS. 6s. *See* Theological Translation Library, Old Series, p. 8.

RÉVILLE (JEAN). LIBERAL CHRISTIANITY. 4s. *See* Crown Theological Library, p. 10.

RIX (HERBERT). TENT AND TESTAMENT. A Camping Tour in Palestine, with some Notes on Scripture Sites. With 61 Illustrations, Frontispiece, and Maps. Demy 8vo, cloth. 8s. 6d. net.

"His narrative of travel is that of an intelligent and well-informed traveller who went without prepossessions and was both able and willing to weigh evidence. . . . Mr. Rix's contribution is one that must be taken into account." —*Spectator*.

"The result is a thoughtful, well-written, even learned work, far from the vain outpourings of the tourist. The narrative, though heavily charged with information, is wonderfully unembarrassed, and the word-pictures which abound are true to life."—*Athenæum*.

14 Henrietta Street, Covent Garden, London, W.C.

ALPHABETICAL LIST—Continued.

RIX (HERBERT). A DAWNING FAITH. Crown 8vo, cloth. 5s.

ROBINSON (ALEX., M.A., B.D.). A STUDY OF THE SAVIOUR IN THE NEWER LIGHT. 2nd Edition. Revised and partly re-written. Demy 8vo, cloth. 5s. net

—— OLD AND NEW CERTAINTY OF THE GOSPEL: A Sketch. Crown 8vo, cloth. 2s. 6d.

SABATIER (AUGUSTE). THE RELIGIONS OF AUTHORITY AND THE RELIGION OF THE SPIRIT. With a Memoir by Professor J. Réville. 10s. 6d. See Theological Translation Library, New Series, p. 3.

—— THE DOCTRINE OF THE ATONEMENT AND ITS HISTORICAL EVOLUTION; and RELIGION AND MODERN CULTURE. 4s. 6d. See Crown Theological Library, p. 10.

SADLER (Rev. Dr.). PRAYERS FOR CHRISTIAN WORSHIP. Crown 8vo, cloth. 3s. 6d.

—— CLOSET PRAYERS, Original and Compiled. 18mo, cloth. 1s. 6d.

SAUNDERS (T. BAILEY). PROFESSOR HARNACK AND HIS OXFORD CRITICS. Crown 8vo, cloth. 1s. 6d. net.

"It gives thoughtful and acutely reasoned support to the great historical student of Christianity who represents Berlin in theology against the pigtailed opposition which Oxford has offered to his learning. A spirited piece of controversial writing, it cannot but prove stimulating to readers interested in modern divinity, no matter to which side of the debate their private prepossessions incline them."—*Scotsman.*

"Mr. Saunders writes with sobriety and with a knowledge of the points at issue. Readers of 'Harnack and his Critics' will do well to read his comments."—*Sheffield Daily Telegraph.*

SAVAGE (M. J.). BELIEFS ABOUT THE BIBLE. 8vo, cloth. 7s. 6d.

SAYCE (A. H.). ON THE RELIGION OF ANCIENT ASSYRIA AND BABYLONIA. See Hibbert Lectures, p. 14.

SCHRADER (E.). CUNEIFORM INSCRIPTIONS AND THE OLD TESTAMENT. 2 vols. 12s. See Theological Translation Library, Old Series, p. 8.

SCHUBERT (HANS VON). OUTLINES OF CHURCH HISTORY. See Theological Translation Library, New Series, p. 3.

CATALOGUE OF PUBLICATIONS.

ALPHABETICAL LIST—Continued.

SCOTT (Rev. E. F., M.A.). THE APOLOGETIC OF THE NEW TESTAMENT. 5s. *See* Crown Theological Library, p. 11.

SCULLARD (Rev. Prof. H. H., M.A., D.D.). EARLY CHRISTIAN ETHICS IN THE WEST, FROM CLEMENT TO AMBROSE. Large crown 8vo, cloth. 6s.

SEEBERG (R.). THE FUNDAMENTAL TRUTHS OF THE CHRISTIAN RELIGION. By R. Seeberg, Professor of Systematic Theology in Berlin. 5s. *See* Crown Theological Library, p. 12.

SEVERUS (Patriarch of Antioch). THE SIXTH BOOK OF THE SELECT LETTERS OF SEVERUS, PATRIARCH OF ANTIOCH, in the Syriac Version of Athanasius of Nisibis. Edited and translated by E. W. Brooks. Vol. I. (Text), Part 1, and Vol. II. (Translation), Part 1. 2 vols. 8vo, cloth. 42s. net. Vol. I. (Text), Part 2, and Vol. II. (Translation), Part 2. 2 vols. 8vo, cloth. 42s. net. *See* Text and Translation Society, p. 37.

SHARPE (SAMUEL). CRITICAL NOTES ON THE AUTHORISED ENGLISH VERSION OF THE NEW TESTAMENT. 2nd Edition. 12mo, cloth. 1s. 6d.

SODEN (H. von, D.D.). THE BOOKS OF THE NEW TESTAMENT. 5s. *See* Crown Theological Library, p. 10.

STEPHEN (Rev. Canon REGINALD, M.A.). DEMOCRACY AND CHARACTER. Being the Moorhouse Lectures for 1908. Crown 8vo, cloth. 5s.

"Canon Stephen's book is much too clear and thoughtful to be neglected in this country. Within the narrow limits of seven lectures he has discussed some important issues of politics in a democratic country with strong practical common sense and the right kind of theoretical learning."—*Athenæum.*

THE STATUTES OF THE APOSTLES. The hitherto unedited Ethiopic and Arabic Texts. Edited, with an Introduction and Translations of the Ethiopic, Arabic, and Coptic Texts, by Rev. G. Horner, M.A. With an Appendix—a recently discovered variant of the Coptic Text. 18s. net.

TAYLER (Rev. JOHN JAMES). AN ATTEMPT TO ASCERTAIN THE CHARACTER OF THE FOURTH GOSPEL, especially in its Relation to the First Three. 2nd Edition. 8vo, cloth. 5s.

TAYLOR (Rev. C.). THE DIRGE OF COHELETH IN ECCLES. XII. DISCUSSED AND LITERALLY INTERPRETED. 8vo, cloth. 3s.

14 Henrietta Street, Covent Garden, London, W.C.

ALPHABETICAL LIST—Continued.

TAYLOR (Rev. Dr. J.). THE MASSORETIC TEXT AND THE ANCIENT VERSIONS OF THE BOOK OF MICAH. Crown 8vo, cloth. 5s.

—— *See also* Kautzsch, "Outline," p. 20.

TEN SERVICES OF PUBLIC PRAYER, with Special Collects. 8vo, cloth, 3s.; or 32mo, cloth, 1s. 6d.

—— **PSALMS AND CANTICLES.** 8vo, cloth. 1s. 6d.

—— **PSALMS AND CANTICLES, with Anthems.** 8vo, cloth. 2s.

TEN SERVICES OF PUBLIC PRAYER, taken in Substance from the Common Prayer for Christian Worship, with a few additional Prayers for particular Days. 8vo, cloth, 2s. 6d.; or 32mo, cloth, 1s.

TESTAMENT, THE NEW. TISCHENDORF (C.). NOVUM TESTAMENTUM GRÆCE. 3 vols. 8vo. 70s. net.

—— **CAMPBELL (Rev. Canon COLIN, M.A., D.D.). THE FIRST THREE GOSPELS IN GREEK.** Arranged in parallel columns. 2nd Edition, Revised. Crown 8vo, cloth. 3s. 6d. net.

THOMAS (Rev. J. M. LLOYD). A FREE CATHOLIC CHURCH. Crown 8vo, cloth. 1s. 6d. net.

UPTON (C. B.). ON THE BASES OF RELIGIOUS BELIEF. *See* Hibbert Lectures, p. 14.

WEIR (T. H., B.D.). A SHORT HISTORY OF THE HEBREW TEXT OF THE OLD TESTAMENT. By Thomas H. Weir, Assistant to the Professor of Oriental Languages in the University of Glasgow. 2nd Edition, with Additions. Crown 8vo, cloth. 6s.

WEIZSÄCKER (C. von). THE APOSTOLIC AGE. 2 vols. Demy 8vo. 21s. *See* Theological Translation Library, New Series, p. 6.

WERNLE (PAUL). THE BEGINNINGS OF CHRISTIANITY. 2 vols. 8vo. 21s. *See* Theological Translation Library, New Series, p. 4.

WICKSTEED (Rev. P. H.). THE ECCLESIASTICAL INSTITUTIONS OF HOLLAND, treated with Special Reference to the Position and Prospects of the Modern School of Theology. A Report presented to the Hibbert Trustees, and published by their direction. 8vo, sewed. 1s.

14 Henrietta Street, Covent Garden, London, W.C.

CATALOGUE OF PUBLICATIONS.

ALPHABETICAL LIST—Continued.

WIMMER (R.). MY STRUGGLE FOR LIGHT: Confessions of a Preacher. 3s. 6d. *See* Crown Theological Library, p. 9.

WOODS (C. E.) THE GOSPEL OF RIGHTNESS. A Study in Pauline Philosophy. 300 pages, cloth. 5s. net.

> The chief purpose in the author's mind has been to present a book to a class of thinkers and readers who are not so widely catered for as might be, and by whom the writings of the great Apostle have been shelved as no longer in keeping with the liberal thought of to-day. The attempt is made to present the Apostle in a somewhat new light as a philosopher who develops a remarkable scheme of spiritual thought from one or two very simple and self-evident principles.

WRIGHT (Rev. C. H. H.). BOOK OF GENESIS IN HEBREW TEXT. With a critically revised Text, various Readings, and Grammatical and Critical Notes. Demy 8vo. 3s. 6d.

—— **BOOK OF RUTH IN HEBREW TEXT.** With a critically revised Text, various Readings, including a new Collation of Twenty-eight Hebrew MSS., and a Grammatical and Critical Commentary; to which is appended the Chaldee Targum. Demy 8vo. 7s. 6d.

—— **DANIEL AND HIS PROPHECIES.** Demy 8vo, cloth. 7s. 6d.

—— **DANIEL AND ITS CRITICS.** A Critical and Grammatical Commentary with Appendix. Demy 8vo, cloth. 7s. 6d.

—— **LIGHT FROM EGYPTIAN PAPYRI ON JEWISH HISTORY BEFORE CHRIST.** Crown 8vo, cloth. 3s. net.

WRIGHT (G. H. BATESON). THE BOOK OF JOB. A new critically revised Translation, with Essays on Scansion, Date, etc. 8vo, cloth. 6s.

—— **WAS ISRAEL EVER IN EGYPT? or, A Lost Tradition.** By G. H. Bateson Wright, D.D., Queen's College, Oxford; Headmaster Queen's College, Hong-Kong; Author of "A Critical Revised Translation of the Book of Job." 8vo, art linen. 7s. 6d.

WRIGHT (W. ALDIS), Edited by, and Dr S. A. HIRSCH. A COMMENTARY ON THE BOOK OF JOB. From a Hebrew MS. in the University Library, Cambridge. Med. 8vo, cloth. 21s. net.

ZELLER (E.). CONTENTS AND ORIGIN OF THE ACTS OF THE APOSTLES. *See* Theological Translation Library, Old Series, p. 8.

---

14 Henrietta Street, Covent Garden, London, W.C.

II. Philosophy, Psychology.

BACON (ROGER), THE "OPUS MAJUS" OF. Edited, with Introduction and Analytical Table, by John Henry Bridges, Fellow of Royal College of Physicians, sometime Fellow of Oriel College. Complete in 3 vols., 31s. 6d. ; Vol. III. sold separately, 7s. 6d.

BREWSTER (H. B.). THE THEORIES OF ANARCHY AND OF LAW. A Midnight Debate. Crown 8vo, parchment. 5s.

—— **THE PRISON.** A Dialogue. Crown 8vo, parchment. 5s.

—— **THE STATUETTE AND THE BACKGROUND.** Crown 8vo, parchment. 4s.

COLLINS (F. H.). AN EPITOME OF THE SYNTHETIC PHILOSOPHY. By F. Howard Collins. With a Preface by Herbert Spencer. 5th Edition. The Synthetic Philosophy Completed. 8vo, cloth. 21s.

DRUMMOND (Dr.). PHILO JUDÆUS; or, The Jewish Alexandrian Philosophy in its Development and Completion. By James Drummond, LL.D., late Principal of Manchester New College, Oxford. 2 vols. 8vo, cloth. 21s.

HODGSON (S. H.). PHILOSOPHY AND EXPERIENCE. An Address delivered before the Aristotelian Society. 8vo, sewed. 2s.

—— **THE REORGANISATION OF PHILOSOPHY.** Address. 8vo, sewed. 1s.

JORDAN (HUMFREY R., B.A.). BLAISE PASCAL. A Study in Religious Psychology. Crown 8vo, cloth. 4s. 6d. net.

JESUS OR CHRIST? The Hibbert Journal Supplement for 1909. Containing Essays by the following writers :—The late Rev. George Tyrrell, the Bishop of Southwark, Professor H. Weinel, Professor Percy Gardner, Professor P. Schmiedel, Professor Henry Jones, The Rev. Richard Morris, B.D., Sir Oliver Lodge, Canon H. Scott Holland, The Rev. Father Joseph Rickaby, S.J., Professor Nathan Soderblom (Upsala), Rev. Principal A. E. Garvie, D.D., The Rev. R. J. Campbell, M.A., The Rev. James Drummond, D.D., Professor B. W. Bacon, D.D., Rev. Principal J. E. Carpenter, D.D., Mr. James Collier, The Rev. R. Roberts. Super-royal 8vo, cloth. 5s. net.

14 Henrietta Street, Covent Garden, London, W.C.

LAURIE (Professor SIMON). ETHICA: or, The Ethics of Reason. By Scotus Novanticus. 2nd Edition. 8vo, cloth. 6s.

—— **METAPHYSICA NOVA ET VETUSTA: A Return to Dualism.** 2nd Edition. Crown 8vo, cloth. 6s.

LODGE (Sir O.). LIFE AND MATTER. 2s. 6d. net. *See* Religion, p. 21.

MACCOLL (HUGH). MAN'S ORIGIN, DESTINY, AND DUTY. Crown 8vo, cloth. 4s. 6d. net.

> Professor A. E. Taylor in *Mind*:—"On the main issues involved the writer of the present notice must avow himself entirely on the author's side, and would unreservedly express his admiration for the skill and luminosity with which the chief points are made, and the happiness of the illustrations.
> "Would that some public-minded society would provide the funds for circulating a book like the present in a sixpenny edition as a counterblast to the sorry stuff which the secularist press is providing as spiritual pabulum for the inquiring artisan.
> "The tenth essay, on the 'fallacies of Haeckel,' in particular, is a most admirable piece of work, at once clear, untechnical, and unanswerable."

MÜNSTERBERG (HUGO, Professor of Psychology at Harvard University). THE AMERICANS. Translated by Edwin B. Holt, Ph.D., Instructor at Harvard University. Royal 8vo, cloth. 12s. 6d. net.

PERRIN (R. S.). EVOLUTION OF KNOWLEDGE, THE. A Review of Philosophy. 6s. *See* Religion, p. 22.

PIKLER (JUL.). THE PSYCHOLOGY OF THE BELIEF IN OBJECTIVE EXISTENCE. Part I. 8vo, cloth. 4s. 6d.

PROCEEDINGS OF THE ARISTOTELIAN SOCIETY FOR THE SYSTEMATIC STUDY OF PHILOSOPHY. Proceedings. Vol. I., 4 Nos., 1890-91. 8vo, 12s. Discontinued after Vol. III. Part 2. Or each Part separately. Vol. I. No. 1, 2s. 6d.; No. 2, 2s. 6d.; No. 3, Part 1, 1s. 6d.; Part 2, 2s.; No. 4, Part 1, 1s. 6d.; Part 2, 2s. Vol. II. No. 1, Part 1, 1s. 6d.; Part 2, 2s.; No. 2, Part 1, 1s. 6d.; Part 2, 2s.; No. 3, Part 1, 2s.; Part 2, 2s. Vol. III. Part 1, 2s. 6d.; Part 2, 2s. NEW SERIES, Vols. I.-IX. Demy 8vo, buckram, each 10s. 6d. net.

SALEEBY (C. W., M.D., F.R.S.). INDIVIDUALISM AND COLLECTIVISM. Crown 8vo, cloth. 2s.

SCHURMAN (J. GOULD). KANTIAN ETHICS AND THE ETHICS OF EVOLUTION. 8vo, cloth. 5s.

—— **THE ETHICAL IMPORT OF DARWINISM.** Crown 8vo, cloth. 5s.

---

14 Henrietta Street, Covent Garden, London, W.C.

SCRIPTURE (EDWARD W., Ph.D.). STUDIES FROM THE YALE PSYCHOLOGICAL LABORATORY. Vols. I.-VI., each 4s. 2d. net.

SCULLARD (Rev. Prof. H.H., M.A., D.D.). EARLY CHRISTIAN ETHICS IN THE WEST, FROM CLEMENT TO AMBROSE. Large crown 8vo, cloth. 6s.

SHEARMAN (A. T., M.A.). THE DEVELOPMENT OF SYMBOLIC LOGIC. A Critical Historical Study of the Logical Calculus. Crown 8vo, cloth. 5s. net.

From the Contents.

Symbols as representing Terms and as representing Propositions—Symbols of Operation—The Process of Solution—Concerning a Calculus Based on Intension—The Doctrines of Jevons and of Mr. MacColl—Later Logical Doctrines—The Utility of Symbolic Logic.

"Its style is smooth, pleasant, and lucid."—*Athenæum.*

SPENCER (HERBERT). AN AUTOBIOGRAPHY. 2 vols. demy 8vo. With Portraits. Popular Edition, 12s. 6d. net. Library Edition, 28s. net.

"It is not too much to say that we close this book, the most interesting, and certainly one of the most important we have ever opened, feeling better, wiser, and humbler for having thus hastily read it."—*Academy.*

"It is a book for all men and for all time. In its pages the thinker may trace, step by step, the synthesis of synthetic philosophy. Here the poet will find not only a worthy inspiration, but a possibly surprising vein of sympathy. The statesman, the inventor, the litterateur, the man of theory, and the man of practice will find alike, within the covers of these two massive volumes, an almost inexhaustible treasury of interest and constructive thought. There is suggestion and instruction for all the world, and an almost indefinable fascination—whether it be due to the mere intrinsic beauty of the picture itself, or to the dignity of its execution, or to the sense of its almost laborious faithfulness, or to the combined attraction of all three."—*St. James's Gazette.*

—— **A SYSTEM OF SYNTHETIC PHILOSOPHY—**

Vol. I. **First Principles.** With an Appendix and a Portrait. Finally revised. New Edition, large crown 8vo, cloth. 7s. 6d.

Vols. II. and III. **The Principles of Biology.** 6th Thousand. 8vo, cloth. Revised and greatly enlarged. Vols. I. and II. 18s. each.

Vols. IV. and V. **The Principles of Psychology.** 5th Thousand. 2 vols. 8vo, cloth. 36s.

Vol. VI. **The Principles of Sociology.** Vol. I. Part 1, The Data of Sociology; Part 2, The Inductions of Sociology; Part 3, Domestic Institutions. 4th Thousand, revised and enlarged. 8vo, cloth. 21s.

---

14 Henrietta Street, Covent Garden, London, W.C.

A SYSTEM OF SYNTHETIC PHILOSOPHY—Continued.

Vol. VII. **The Principles of Sociology.** Vol. II. Part 4, Ceremonial Institutions; Part 5, Political Institutions. 3rd Thousand. 8vo, cloth. 18s.

Vol. VIII. **The Principles of Sociology.** Vol. III. Part 6, Ecclesiastical Institutions; Part 7, Professional Institutions; Part 8, Industrial Institutions. 2nd Thousand. 8vo, cloth. 16s.

Vol. IX. **The Principles of Ethics.** Vol. I. Part 1, The Data of Ethics; Part 2, The Inductions of Ethics; Part 3, The Ethics of Individual Life. 2nd Thousand. 8vo, cloth. 15s.

Vol. X. **The Principles of Ethics.** Vol. II. Part 4, Justice; Part 5, Negative Beneficence; Part 6, Positive Beneficence; Appendices. Demy 8vo, cloth. 12s. 6d.

Also to be had separately:

SPENCER (HERBERT). **DATA OF ETHICS.** Reset uniform with popular edition of "First Principles." Sewed, 2s. 6d. net; cloth, 3s. net.

—— **JUSTICE.** Being Part 4 of the Principles of Ethics. 2nd Thousand. 8vo, cloth. 6s.

Other Works.

—— **THE STUDY OF SOCIOLOGY.** Library Edition (21st Thousand), with a Postscript. 8vo, cloth. 10s. 6d.

—— **EDUCATION: Intellectual, Moral, and Physical.** Cheap Edition. Entirely reset. 46th Thousand. Crown 8vo, cloth. 2s. 6d.

—— **ESSAYS: Scientific, Political, and Speculative.** A new Edition, rearranged, with additional Essays. 3 vols. 8vo, cloth. (Each 10s.) 30s.

—— **SOCIAL STATICS.** Abridged and revised, together with "The Man v. The State." 8vo, cloth. 10s.

—— **VARIOUS FRAGMENTS.** Uniform in Library binding. Demy 8vo, cloth. Enlarged Edition. 6s.

—— **FACTS AND COMMENTS.** Demy 8vo, cloth. 6s.

—— **THE MAN *versus* THE STATE.** 14th Thousand. Sewed. 1s.

—— **A REJOINDER TO PROFESSOR WEISMANN.** Sewed. 6d.

14 Henrietta Street, Covent Garden, London, W.C.

SPENCER (HERBERT). REASONS FOR DISSENTING FROM THE PHILOSOPHY OF M. COMTE. Sewed. 6d.

—— **DESCRIPTIVE SOCIOLOGY; or, Groups of Sociological Facts.** Compiled and abstracted by Professor D. Duncan of Madras, Dr. Richard Scheppig, and James Collier. Folio, boards.

    No. 1. **English.** 18s.
    No. 2. **Ancient American Races.** 16s.
    No. 3. **Lowest Races, Negritto Races, Polynesians.** 18s.
    No. 4. **African Races.** 16s.
    No. 5. **Asiatic Races.** 18s.
    No. 6. **American Races.** 18s.
    No. 7. **Hebrews and Phœnicians.** 21s.
    No. 8. **The French Civilisation.** 30s.

In Preparation.

Edited by Henry R. Tedder, Secretary and Librarian of the Athenæum Club.

    Chinese. Compiled and abstracted by E. T. C. Werner, H.M.'s Consular Service, China.
    Ancient Egyptians.
    Hellenic Greeks. By Rev. Dr J. P. Mahaffy, and Professor W. A. Goligher, Trinity College, Dublin.
    Hellenistic Greeks. By the same.
    Romans. By Mr E. H. Alton, F.T.C.D., and Professor W. A. Goligher.

—— **COLLINS (F. H.). AN EPITOME OF THE SYNTHETIC PHILOSOPHY.** By F. Howard Collins. Being a Digest of Mr. Herbert Spencer's Works. 5th Edition, the Synthetic Philosophy Completed. With a Preface by Herbert Spencer. 8vo, cloth. 21s.

SPINOZA: Four Essays. By Professors Land, Van Vloten, and Kuno Fischer, and by E. Renan. Edited by Professor Knight, of St. Andrews. Crown 8vo, cloth. 5s.

STUDIES FROM THE YALE PSYCHOLOGICAL LABORATORY. Edited by Professor E. W. Scripture. With many Illustrations. 8vo, sewed. 4s. 2d. each net. Vol. I. 1892–93, 100 pages. Vol. II. 1894, 124 pages. Vol. III. 1895, 110 pages. Vol. IV. 1896, 141 pages. Vol. V. 1897, 105 pages. Vol. VI. 1898, 105 pages.

WUNDT (WILHELM). OUTLINES OF PSYCHOLOGY. Translated, with the co-operation of the Author, by Charles Hubbard Judd, Ph.D., Instructor in the Wesleyan University. 3rd Enlarged Edition Demy 8vo, cloth. 8s. net.

14 Henrietta Street, Covent Garden, London, W.C.

III. Oriental Languages, Literature, and History.

ABHIDHANARATNAMALA (THE) OF HALAYUDHA. A Sanskrit Vocabulary (120 pp.). Edited, with a Sanskrit-English Glossary (180 pp.), by Dr. T. Aufrecht. 8vo, cloth. (Published at 18s.) 10s.

AVESTI, PAHLAVI, and ANCIENT PERSIAN STUDIES in Honour of the late SHAMS-UL-ULAMA DASTUR PESHOTANJI BEHRAMJI SANJANA, M.A., Ph.D. Paper cover, 12s. 6d. net; cloth, 13s. 6d. net.

BERNSTEIN and KIRSCH. SYRIAC CHRESTOMATHY AND LEXICON (Chrestomathia Syriaca cum Lexico). 2 vols. in 1. 8vo, cloth boards. 7s. 6d. I. Chrestomathia, separately. Sewed. 3s.

DAVIDS (T. W. RHYS). LECTURES ON SOME POINTS IN THE HISTORY OF INDIAN BUDDHISM. See The Hibbert Lectures, p. 13.

DELITZSCH (Prof. F.). ASSYRIAN GRAMMAR. With Paradigms, Exercises, Glossary, and Bibliography. Translated by the Rev. Prof. A. R. S. Kennedy. Crown 8vo, cloth. 15s.

—— **THE HEBREW LANGUAGE VIEWED IN THE LIGHT OF ASSYRIAN RESEARCH.** Demy 8vo, cloth. 4s.

—— **BABEL AND BIBLE.** 5s. See Crown Theological Library, p. 9.

DILLMANN (A.). ETHIOPIC GRAMMAR. Translated from C. Bezold's Second German Edition. By Rev. J. A. Crichton, D.D., with Index of Passages, Philological Tables, etc. 1 vol., Royal 8vo. 25s. net.

DÎPAVAMSA (THE): A Buddhist Historical Record in the Pali Language. Edited, with an English Translation, by Dr. H. Oldenberg. 8vo, cloth. 21s.

<small>The "Dipavamsa" is the most ancient historical work of the Ceylonese; it contains an account of the ecclesiastical history of the Buddhist Church, of the conversion of the Ceylonese to the Buddhist faith, and of the ancient history of Ceylon.</small>

ERMAN'S EGYPTIAN GRAMMAR. Translated, under Professor Erman's supervision, by J. H. Breasted, Professor of Egyptology in the University of Chicago. Crown 8vo, cloth. 18s.

EVANS (GEORGE). AN ESSAY ON ASSYRIOLOGY. With 4to Tables of Assyrian Inscriptions. 8vo, cloth. 5s.

FAIZULLAH-BHAI (Shaikh, B.D.). A MOSLEM PRESENT. Part I., containing the famous poem of Al-Busaree. With an English Version and Notes. 8vo, cloth. 4s.

—— **AN ESSAY ON THE PRE-ISLAMITIC ARABIC POETRY**, with special reference to the Seven Suspended Poems. 8vo, sewed. 4d.

FLINDERS PETRIE PAPYRI. See Cunningham Memoirs, pp. 43, 44.

FRANKFURTER (Dr. O.). HANDBOOK OF PALI: Being an Elementary Grammar, a Chrestomathy, and a Glossary. 8vo, cloth. 16s.

FUERST (Dr. JUL.). HEBREW AND CHALDEE LEXICON TO THE OLD TESTAMENT. 5th Edition, improved and enlarged. Translated by Rev. Dr. Samuel Davidson. Royal 8vo, cloth. 21s.

HEBREW TEXTS. Large type. 16mo, cloth.
> Genesis. (2nd Edition. Baer and Delitzsch's Text.) 1s. 6d.
> Psalms. 1s.
> Job. 1s.
> Isaiah. 1s.

KENNEDY (Rev. JAS.). INTRODUCTION TO BIBLICAL HEBREW, presenting Graduated Instruction in the Language of the Old Testament. By James Kennedy, B.D., Acting Librarian in the New College, and one of the additional Examiners in Divinity at the University, Edinburgh. 8vo, cloth. 12s.

—— **STUDIES IN HEBREW SYNONYMS.** Demy 8vo, cloth. 5s.

LYALL (C. J., M.A., K.C.I.E.). ANCIENT ARABIAN POETRY, CHIEFLY PRÆ-ISLAMIC. Translations, with an Introduction and Notes. Fcap. 4to, cloth. 10s. 6d.

MACHBEROTH ITHIEL. By Yehuda ben Shelomoh Alcharizi. Edited from the MS. in the Bodleian Library, by Thomas Chenery, M.A. 8vo, cloth. 3s.

MILANDA PANHO, THE: Being Dialogues between King Milanda and the Buddhist Sage Nāgasena. The Pali Text, edited by V. Trenckner. 440 pp. 8vo, sewed. 21s. *See also* "Pali Miscellany."

MOSHEH BEN SHESHETH'S COMMENTARY ON JEREMIAH AND EZEKIEL. *See* p. 22.

MUSS-ARNOLT (W.). A CONCISE DICTIONARY OF THE ASSYRIAN LANGUAGE (Assyrian—English—German). By W. Muss-Arnolt. Completed in 19 parts. Each 5s. net.; or bound in 2 vols., £5 net.

NEW HEBREW SCHOOL of POETS of the SPANISH-ARABIAN EPOCH. Selected Texts with Introduction, Notes, and Dictionary. Edited by H. Brody, Ph.D., Rabbi in Nachod (Bohemia), and K. Albrecht, Ph.D., Professor in Oldenburg (Grand Duchy). English translation of the Introduction, etc., by Mrs Karl Albrecht. Cloth. 7s. 6d. net.

NOLDEKE (THEODOR, Professor of Oriental Languages in the University of Strassburg). **COMPENDIOUS SYRIAC GRAMMAR.** With a Table of Characters by Julius Euting. Translated (with the sanction of the author) from the second and improved German Edition by Rev. James A. Crichton, D.D. Royal 8vo. 18s. net.

—— **DELECTUS VETERUM CARMINUM ARABICORUM GLOSSARIUM CONFECIT A. MULLER.** Crown 8vo, cloth. 7s. 6d.

NORRIS (E.). ASSYRIAN DICTIONARY. Intended to further the Study of the Cuneiform Inscriptions of Assyria and Babylonia. Vols. I. to III. 4to, cloth. Each 28s.

OLDENBERG (Prof. H.). BUDDHA: His Life, his Doctrine, his Order. By Dr. Hermann Oldenberg, Professor at the University of Berlin. Translated by W. Hoey, M.A. 8vo, cloth gilt. 18s.

PALI MISCELLANY. By V. Trenckner. Part I. The Introductory Part of the Milanda Panho, with an English Translation and Notes. 8vo, sewed. 4s.

14 Henrietta Street, Covent Garden, London, W.C.

WILLIAMS & NORGATE'S

PLATTS (J. T.). A GRAMMAR OF THE PERSIAN LANGUAGE. By John T. Platts, Hon. M.A. (Oxon.), Teacher of Persian in the University of Oxford; late Inspector of Schools in the Central Provinces of India. Part I. Accidence. Broad crown 8vo. 10s. 6d.

RENOUF (P. LE PAGE). LECTURES ON THE RELIGION OF ANCIENT EGYPT. See Hibbert Lectures, p. 14.

SADI. THE GULISTAN (ROSE GARDEN) OF SHAIK SADI OF SHIRAZ. A new Edition of the Persian Text, with a Vocabulary, by F. Johnson. Square royal 8vo, cloth. 15s.

SAYCE (Prof. A. H.). LECTURES ON THE RELIGIONS OF ANCIENT BABYLONIA AND SYRIA. See the Hibbert Lectures, p. 14.

SCHRADER (E.). THE CUNEIFORM INSCRIPTIONS AND THE OLD TESTAMENT. 2 vols. 12s. See Theological Translation Library, Old Series, p. 8.

SHIHAB AL DIN. FUTŪH AL-HABASHAH; or, The Conquest of Abyssinia. By Shināb al Din Ahmad B. 'Abd al Kādir B. Sālim B. 'Uthman. Edited, from an Arabic MS., by S. Arthur Strong. Part I. 8vo, sewed. 3s. net.

SÖRENSEN (S., Ph.D.), Compiled by. AN INDEX TO THE NAMES IN THE MAHABHARATA. With short explanations. Royal 4to, in twelve parts, which are not sold separately, at 7s. 6d. per part net. Parts I. and V. now ready.

STATUTES, THE, OF THE APOSTLES. The hitherto unedited Ethiopic and Arabic Texts, with translations of Ethiopic, Arabic, and Coptic Texts, by G. Horner, M.A. See p. 25.

TEXT AND TRANSLATION SOCIETY. *Established for the purpose of editing and translating Oriental Texts chiefly preserved in the British Museum.*

THE SIXTH BOOK OF THE SELECT LETTERS OF SEVERUS, PATRIARCH OF ANTIOCH, in the Syriac Version of Athanasius of Nisibis. Edited and translated by E. W. Brooks, M.A. Vol. I. Text, Parts I. and II. Vol. II. Translation, Parts I. and II. 84s. net.

THE CANONS OF ATHANASIUS OF ALEXANDRIA, in Arabic, Ethiopic, and Coptic. Edited and Translated by Prof. W. Riedel (Griefswald) and W. E. Crum. 21s. net.

CATALOGUE OF PUBLICATIONS.

TEXT AND TRANSLATION SOCIETY—continued.

Volumes already issued—

A RABBINIC COMMENTARY ON THE BOOK OF JOB, contained in a unique MS. at Cambridge. Edited, with Translation and Commentary, by W. Aldis Wright, LL.D. 21s. net.

AN ANCIENT ARMENIAN VERSION OF THE APOCALYPSE OF ST JOHN; also **THE ARMENIAN TEXTS OF CYRIL OF ALEXANDRIA, SCHOLIA DE INCARNATIONE** and **EPISTLE TO THEODOSIUS UPON EASTER**, the former incompletely preserved in Greek, the latter unknown in Greek or Latin. All edited, with English versions, etc., by F. C. Conybeare, formerly Fellow of University College, Oxford.

REMNANTS OF THE LATER SYRIAC VERSIONS OF THE BIBLE. Part I. (Sixth Century). The Four Minor Catholic Epistles. Reconstructed Text, with Apparatus Criticus. Part II. (Seventh Century). Extracts, hitherto unedited, from the Syro-Hexaplar Text of Chronicles, Nehemiah, etc. All edited, with Greek versions, etc., by John Gwynn, D.D., Regius Professor of Divinity, Dublin.

In the Press.

THE REFUTATION OF MANI, MARCION, AND BARDAISAN OF ST EPHRAIM. Edited by the Rev. C. W. Mitchell.

TURPIE (Dr. D. McC.). MANUAL OF THE CHALDEE LANGUAGE. Containing Grammar of the Biblical Chaldee and of the Targums, and a Chrestomathy, with a Vocabulary. Square 8vo, cloth. 7s.

VINAYA PITAKAM: One of the Principal Buddhist Holy Scriptures. Edited in Pali by Dr. H. Oldenberg. 5 vols. 8vo, cloth. Each 21s.

WALLIS (H. W.). THE COSMOLOGY OF THE RIG-VEDA: An Essay. 8vo, cloth. 5s.

---

14 Henrietta Street, Covent Garden, London, W.C.

IV. Modern Languages & Literature.

A complete list of Messrs. Williams & Norgate's Educational Publications on Modern Languages may be had on application.

ARMY SERIES OF FRENCH AND GERMAN NOVELS.
Edited, with short Notes, by J. T. W. Perowne, M.A.

This series is equally well adapted for general reading, and for those preparing for the Army, Oxford and Cambridge Certificates, and other Examinations—in fact, for all who wish to keep up or improve their French and German. The notes are as concise as possible, with an occasional etymology or illustration to assist the memory. The books selected being by recent or living authors, are adapted for the study of most modern French and German.

LE COUP DE PISTOLET, etc. Prosper Merimée. 2s. 6d.

"A book more admirably suited to its purpose could not be desired. The Editors deserve to be congratulated."—*National Observer*.

VAILLANTE. Jacques Vincent. 2s. 6d.

"The books are well got up, and in *Vaillante* an excellent choice has been made."—*Guardian*.

AUF VERLORNEM POSTEN AND NAZZARENA DANTI. Johannes v. Dewall. 3s.

"Well printed, well bound, and annotated just sufficiently to make the reading of them sure as well as easy."—*Educational Times*.

CONTES MILITAIRES. A. Daudet. 2s. 6d.

"These stories are mainly culled from a series called *Contes du Lundi*, originally contributed by their author to the *Figaro*. Written at fever heat immediately after the great 1870 war, they show Daudet's power in many ways at its highest. . . . We therefore do more than recommend—we urge all readers of French to get the stories in some form, and the present one is both good and cheap."—*The Schoolmaster*.

ERZÄHLUNGEN. E. Höfer. 3s.

"The series has brought fascinating examples of fiction under the eyes of English readers in a neat and handy form. Besides having the military flavour, they are models of style."—*Scotsman*.

BAYLDON (Rev. G.). ICELANDIC GRAMMAR. An Elementary Grammar of the Old Norse or Icelandic Language. 8vo, cloth. 7s. 6d.

14 Henrietta Street, Covent Garden, London, W.C.

CATALOGUE OF PUBLICATIONS. 39

BOÏELLE (JAS.). FRENCH COMPOSITION THROUGH LORD MACAULAY'S ENGLISH. Edited, with Notes, Hints, and Introduction, by the late James Boïelle, B.A. (Univ. Gall.), Officier d'Académie, Senior French Master, Dulwich College, etc., etc. Crown 8vo, cloth. Vol. I. Frederick the Great. 3s. Vol. II. Warren Hastings. 3s. Vol. III. Lord Clive. 3s.

—— *See* Victor Hugo, "Les Misérables" and "Notre Dame."

DELBOS (L.). NAUTICAL TERMS IN ENGLISH AND FRENCH AND FRENCH AND ENGLISH. With Notes and Tables. For the use of Naval Officers and Naval Cadets. By Leon Delbos, M.A., of H.M.S. *Britannia*, Dartmouth. 4th Edition, thoroughly revised and considerably enlarged, with additional Plates. Crown 8vo, cloth. 7s. 6d. net.

—— **THE STUDENT'S GRADUATED FRENCH READER.** Remodelled and rewritten. Edited, with Notes and a Complete Vocabulary. First Year—Part I. Anecdotes, Tales, and Exercises. Part II. Tales, Historical Pieces, and Exercises. 1s. 6d. each. Second Year—Parts I. and II. in the Press.

EUGENE'S STUDENT'S COMPARATIVE GRAMMAR OF THE FRENCH LANGUAGE, with an Historical Sketch of the Formation of French. For the use of Public Schools. With Exercises. By G. Eugène-Fasnacht, late French Master, Westminster School. 23rd Edition, thoroughly revised. Square crown 8vo, cloth, 5s.; or separately, Grammar, 3s.; Exercises, 2s. 6d.

GOETHE (W. v.). ANNOTATED TEXTS. *See* Educational Catalogue.

HAGMANN (J.G., Ph.D.). REFORM IN PRIMARY EDUCATION. Translated from Second German Edition by R. H. Hoar, Ph.D., and Richmond Barker, M.A. Cr. 8vo, cl., 2s. 6d. net.

HUGO (VICTOR). LES MISÉRABLES: Les Principaux Episodes. Edited, with Life and Notes, by the late J. Boïelle. 2 vols. 6th Edition. Crown 8vo, cloth. Each 3s. 6d.

—— **NOTRE DAME DE PARIS.** Adapted for the use of Schools and Colleges. By the late J. Boïelle. 2 vols. 2nd Edition. Crown 8vo, cloth. Each 3s.

KYRIAKIDES (A.). MODERN GREEK-ENGLISH DICTIONARY. With a Cypriote Vocabulary. 2nd Edition, revised throughout. Medium 8vo. 920 pages. Cloth. 15s. net.

14 Henrietta Street, Covent Garden, London, W.C.

LEABHAR BREAC. The "Speckled Book," otherwise styled, "The Great Book of Dun Doighre": a Collection of Pieces in Irish and Latin, transcribed towards the close of the Fourteenth Century. "The oldest and best Irish MS. relating to Church History now preserved" (*G. Petrie*). Now first published, from the original MS. in the Royal Irish Academy's Library. In imperial folio, on toned paper. In one vol., half-calf, £4, 4s. (200 copies only printed.)

LEABHAR NA H-UIDHRI. A Collection of Pieces in Prose and Verse, in the Irish Language, transcribed about A.D. 1100; the oldest volume now known entirely in the Irish language, and one of the chief surviving native literary monuments—not ecclesiastical—of ancient Ireland; now for the first time published, from the original in the Library of the Royal Irish Academy, with account of the Manuscript, description of its contents, index, and facsimiles in colours. In folio on toned paper, half-calf. £3, 3s. (200 copies only printed.)

LILJA (The Lily). An Icelandic Religious Poem. By Eystein Asgrimson. Edited, with Translation, Notes, and Glossary, by E. Magnusson. Crown 8vo, cloth extra. 10s. 6d.

LODGE (Sir O.). SCHOOL TEACHING AND SCHOOL REFORM. A Course of Four Lectures on School Curricula and Methods, delivered to Secondary Teachers and Teachers in Training at Birmingham during February 1905. 3s.

"The work of a sensible iconoclast, who does not pull down for the sake of mere destruction, but is anxious to set up something more worthy in place of the mediævalism he attacks."—*Outlook*.

"Let me commend this wise volume not only to teachers but to all concerned in national education. And especially to the politician. Half an hour with Sir Oliver Lodge would make him realise that there are problems on the inner side of the school door not dreamt of in his philosophy—would make him feel that the more he knows of these the better will he be able wisely to handle those others about which he is glibly talking every day."—Dr MACNAMARA in the *Daily Chronicle*.

MAORI. NEW AND COMPLETE MANUAL OF MAORI CONVERSATIONS. Containing Phrases and Dialogues on a variety of Topics, together with a few general rules of Grammar, and a comprehensive Vocabulary. 4s. net. *See also* Williams.

MARKHAM (Sir CLEMENTS, K.C.B.). VOCABULARIES OF THE GENERAL LANGUAGE OF THE INCAS OF PERU. Crown 8vo, cloth. 7s. 6d. net.

NIBELUNGENLIED. "The Fall of the Nibelungens," otherwise "The Book of Kriemhild." An English Translation by W. N. Lettsom. 5th Edition. 8vo, cloth. 5s.

CATALOGUE OF PUBLICATIONS. 41

O'GRADY (STANDISH H.). SILVA GADELICA (I.-XXXI.). A Collection of Tales in Irish, with Extracts illustrating Persons and Places. Edited from MSS. and translated. 2 vols. royal 8vo, cloth. 42s. Or separately, Vol. I., Irish Text; and Vol. II., Translation and Notes. Each vol. 21s.

OORDT (J. F. VAN, B.A.). CAPE DUTCH. Phrases and Dialogues, with Translations, preceded by short Grammatical Notes. Crown 8vo, cloth. 2s. 6d. net.

PHILLIPPS (V., B.A.). A SHORT SKETCH OF GERMAN LITERATURE, for Schools. By Vivian Phillipps, B.A., Assistant Master at Fettes College, Edinburgh. 2nd Edition, revised. Pott 8vo, cloth. 1s.

ROGET (F. F.). AN INTRODUCTION TO OLD FRENCH. History, Grammar, Chrestomathy, and Glossary. 2nd Edition. Crown 8vo, cloth. 6s.

—— **FIRST STEPS IN FRENCH HISTORY, LITERATURE, AND PHILOLOGY.** For Candidates for the Scotch Leaving Certificate Examinations, the various Universities Local Examinations, and the Army Examinations. 4th Edition. Crown 8vo, cloth. 5s.

ROSING (S.). ENGLISH-DANISH DICTIONARY. New Edition. Large 8vo, strongly bound, half-roan. 11s. 6d.

SCHILLER (F. VON). ANNOTATED TEXTS. See Educational Catalogue.

SULLIVAN (W. K.). CELTIC STUDIES FROM THE GERMAN OF EBEL. With an Introduction on the Roots, Stems, and Derivatives, and on Case-endings of Nouns in the Indo-European Languages. 8vo, cloth. 10s.

VELASQUEZ. LARGER SPANISH DICTIONARY. Composed from the Dictionaries of the Spanish Academy, Terreros and Salva. Spanish-English and English-Spanish. 1279 pp., triple columns. 2 vols. in 1. Imp. 8vo, cloth. 24s.

VIGA GLUMS SAGA. Translated from the Icelandic, with Notes and an Introduction, by Sir Edmund Head, Bart. Fcap. 8vo, cloth. 5s.

WEISSE (T. H.). ELEMENTS OF GERMAN. With a Course of Exercises instructing in Simpler Composition. Crown 8vo, cloth. 3s.

14 Henrietta Street, Covent Garden, London, W.C.

WEISSE (T. H.). SYSTEMATIC CONVERSATIONAL EXERCISES FOR TRANSLATING INTO GERMAN, adapted to his Grammar. New Edition. Crown 8vo, cloth. (Key, 5*s.* net.) 3*s.* 6*d.*

—— **A SHORT GUIDE TO GERMAN IDIOMS**: being a Collection of the Idioms most in use. With Examination Papers. 3rd Edition. Cloth. 2*s.*

WERNER'S ELEMENTARY LESSONS IN CAPE DUTCH (AFRIKANDER TAAL). By A. Werner and G. Hunt. 16mo, cloth. 1*s.* 6*d.*

"We most cordially recommend this book to anyone going out to settle in South Africa. ... The dialogues and exercises are admirably planned."—*Reformer.*

"To those outward bound such a book is sure to be useful."—*Practical Teacher.*

WILLIAMS (The Right Rev. W. L., D.C.L.). A DICTIONARY OF THE NEW ZEALAND LANGUAGE. 4th Edition. Edited by the Right Rev. Bishop W. L. Williams, with numerous additions and corrections. Demy 8vo, cloth. 12*s.* 6*d.*

—— **LESSONS IN MAORI.** 3rd Edition. Fcap. 8vo, cloth. 3*s.*

YELLOW BOOK OF LECAN. A Collection of Pieces (Prose and Verse) in the Irish Language, in part compiled at the end of the Fourteenth Century; now for the first time published from the original Manuscript in the Library of Trinity College, Dublin, by the Royal Irish Academy. With Introduction, Analysis of Contents, and Index, by Robert Atkinson. 30 and 468 pp. (Royal Irish Academy's Irish facsimiles.) Large post folio, 1896, half-roan, Roxburghe, cloth sides. £4, 4*s.*

ZOEGA (G. T.) ENGLISH-ICELANDIC DICTIONARY. 8vo, cloth. 6*s.* net.

ZOMPOLIDES (Dr. D.). A COURSE OF MODERN GREEK; or, The Greek Language of the Present Day. I. The Elementary Method. Crown 8vo, cloth. 5*s.*

14 Henrietta Street, Covent Garden, London, W.C.

V. Science.

MEDICINE—CHEMISTRY—BOTANY—ZOOLOGY—MATHEMATICS.

BASTIAN (H. CHARLTON, M.A., M.D., F.R.S.). STUDIES IN HETEROGENESIS. With 825 Illustrations from Photomicrographs. Royal 8vo, cloth. 31s. 6d.

BENEDICT (F. E., Ph.D.). ELEMENTARY ORGANIC ANALYSIS. Small 8vo. Pages vi + 82. 15 Illustrations. 4s. 6d. net.

BERGEY (D. G.). HANDBOOK OF PRACTICAL HYGIENE. Small 8vo. Pages v + 164. 6s. 6d. net.

BILTZ (HENRY). THE PRACTICAL METHODS OF DETERMINING MOLECULAR WEIGHTS. Translated by Jones. Small 8vo. Pages viii + 245. 44 Illustrations. 8s. 6d. net.

BOLTON. HISTORY OF THE THERMOMETER. 12mo. 96 pages. 6 Illustrations. 4s. 6d. net.

BRUCE (ALEX., M.A., M.D., F.R.C.P.E., F.R.S.E.). A TOPOGRAPHICAL ATLAS OF THE SPINAL CORD. Fcap. folio, half-leather. £2, 2s. net.

COLBY (ALBERT LADD). REINFORCED CONCRETE IN EUROPE. Demy 8vo, cloth. 14s. 6d. net.

CREIGHTON (CHAS., M.D.). CANCER AND OTHER TUMOURS OF THE BREAST. Researches showing their true seat and cause. With 24 Lithographic Plates containing 138 figures from the Author's drawings. Royal 8vo, cloth. 12s. 6d. net.

—— **CONTRIBUTIONS TO THE PHYSIOLOGICAL THEORY OF TUBERCULOSIS.** By Charles Creighton, M.D., sometime Demonstrator of Anatomy, Cambridge Medical School, author of "Bovine Tuberculosis in Man," etc. Royal 8vo, cloth. 12s. 6d. net.

CUNNINGHAM MEMOIRS—

1. **Cubic Transformations.** By John Casey, LL.D. 4to, sewed. 2s. 6d.
2. **On the Lumbar Curve in Man and the Apes.** By D. J. Cunningham, M.D. 13 Plates. 4to, sewed. 5s.
3. **New Researches on Sun-heat, Terrestrial Radiation, etc.** By Rev. Samuel Haughton, M.A., M.D. 9 Plates. 4to, sewed. 1s. 6d.
4. **Dynamics and Modern Geometry.** A New Chapter in the Theory of Screws. By Sir Robert S. Ball, LL.D. 4to, sewed. 2s.

---

14 Henrietta Street, Covent Garden, London, W.C.

CUNNINGHAM MEMOIRS—Continued.

   5. **The Red Stars.** Observations and Catalogue. New Edition. Edited by Rev. T. Espin, M.A. 4to, sewed. 3s. 6d.
   6. **On the Morphology of the Duck Tribe and the Auk Tribe.** By W. K. Parker, F.R.S. 9 Plates. 4to, sewed. 3s. 6d.
   7. **Contribution to the Surface Anatomy of the Cerebral Hemispheres.** By D. J. Cunningham, M.D. With a Chapter upon Cranio-Cerebral Topography by Victor Horsley, M.B., F.R.S. 4to, sewed. 8s. 6d.
   8. **On the Flinders Petrie Papyri.** Part I. Out of Print.
   9. **On the Flinders Petrie Papyri.** Part II. With 18 Autotypes. 4to, sewed. 42s. net. Appendix to 8 and 9. 5s. net.
   10. **The Decorative Art of British New Guinea.** A Study in Papuan Ethnography. By Alfred C. Haddon, M.A. With 12 Plates, and numerous other Illustrations. 4to, sewed. 14s. net.
   11. **On the Flinders Petrie Papyri.** With Transcriptions, Commentaries, and Index. By John P. Mahaffy, D.D., and Prof. J. Gilbert Smyly. With 7 Autotypes. 4to, sewed. 42s. net.

EMERY (F. B., M.A.). ELEMENTARY CHEMISTRY. With numerous Illustrations. 8s. 6d. net.

ENGELHARDT (V.). THE ELECTROLYSIS OF WATER. 8vo. Pages x + 140. 90 Illustrations. 5s. net.

FISCHER (Prof. EMIL, of Berlin University). INTRODUCTION TO THE PREPARATION OF ORGANIC COMPOUNDS. Translated with the author's sanction from the new German edition by R. V. Stanford, B.Sc., Ph.D. With figures in the text. Crown 8vo, cloth. 4s. net.

HANTZSCH (A.). ELEMENTS OF STEREOCHEMISTRY. Translated by Wolf. 12mo. Pages viii + 206. 26 Figures. 6s. 6d. net.

HARDY. ELEMENTS OF ANALYTICAL GEOMETRY. 8vo. Pages iv + 365. 163 Figures. 8s. 6d. net.

—— **INFINITESIMALS AND LIMITS.** Sm. 12mo, paper. 22 pp. 6 Figures. 1s. net.

HARNACK (AXEL). INTRODUCTION TO THE ELEMENTS OF THE DIFFERENTIAL AND INTEGRAL CALCULUS. From the German. Royal 8vo, cloth. 10s. 6d.

HART (EDWARD, Ph.D.). CHEMISTRY FOR BEGINNERS. Small 12mo.
   Vol. I. Inorganic. Pages viii + 188. 55 Illustrations and 2 Plates. Fourth Edition. 4s. 6d. net.
   Vol. II. Organic. Pages iv + 98. 11 Illustrations. 2s. net.
   Vol. III. Experiments. Separately. 60 pages. 1s. net.

—— **SECOND YEAR CHEMISTRY.** Small 12mo. 165 pages. 31 Illustrations. 5s. net.

14 Henrietta Street, Covent Garden, London, W.C.

CATALOGUE OF PUBLICATIONS. 45

HOFF (J. H. VAN'T). STUDIES IN CHEMICAL DYNAMICS. Revised and enlarged by Dr. Ernst Cohen, Assistant in the Chemical Laboratory of the University of Amsterdam. Translated by Thomas Ewan, M.Sc., Ph.D., Demonstrator of Chemistry in the Yorkshire College, Leeds. Royal 8vo, cloth. 10s. 6d.

HORNELL (JAMES, F.L.S.). REPORT TO THE GOVERNMENT OF BARODA ON THE MARINE ZOOLOGY OF OKHAMANDAL IN KATTIAWAR. With Supplementary Reports on Special Groups by other Zoologists. Demy 4to, cloth, with full-page Plates. Part I. 15s. net.

HOWE (J. L.). INORGANIC CHEMISTRY FOR SCHOOLS AND COLLEGES. By Jas. Lewis Howe, Washington and Lee University. Being a Second Edition of "Inorganic Chemistry according to the Periodic Law." By F. P. Venable and J. L. Howe. Demy 8vo, cloth. 12s. 6d. net.

JOHNSTONE (J.). BRITISH FISHERIES: Their Administration and their Problems. A short account of the Origin and Growth of British Sea Fishery Authorities and Regulations. 10s. 6d. net.

JONES (J. T. SHARE-). SURGICAL ANATOMY OF THE HORSE. To be completed in 4 Parts. With above 100 Illustrations, a number being in colour. Part I. Head and Neck. Part II. Fore Limb. Part III. Hind Limb. Price per part, 15s. net, sewed; cloth, 16s. 6d. net.

—— **LIFE-SIZE MODELS**, Illustrating the Superficial Anatomy of the Limbs of the Horse. Price per set of four models, £21; or separately—Fore Limb, Inner and Outer Aspects, £6, 16s. 6d. each; Hind Limb, Inner and Outer Aspects, £6, 6s. each.

JONES. THE FREEZING POINT, BOILING POINT, AND CONDUCTIVITY METHODS. 12mo. Pages vii+64. 14 Illustrations. 3s. net.

JOURNAL OF THE LINNEAN SOCIETY. Botany. At various prices. Index to Journal (Botany), 20s. **Zoology.** At various prices. General Index to the first 20 vols. of the Journal (Zoology) and the Zoological portion of the Proceedings, 20s.

JOURNAL OF THE ROYAL MICROSCOPICAL SOCIETY, containing its transactions and Proceedings, with other Microscopical information. Bi-monthly. Previous to 1893 at various prices; after that date bi-monthly, each 6s. net.

JOURNAL OF THE QUEKETT MICROSCOPICAL CLUB. Nos. 1-26, 1s. net; Nos. 27-31, 2s. 6d. net. 1893, No. 32, and following Nos., half-yearly, 3s. 6d. net.

---

14 Henrietta Street, Covent Garden, London, W.C.

LANDOLT (Dr. HANS). THE OPTICAL ROTATING POWER OF ORGANIC SUBSTANCES AND ITS PRACTICAL APPLICATIONS. 8vo. Pp. xxi+751. 83 Illustrations. 31s. 6d. net.

LEAVENWORTH (Prof. W. S., M.Sc.). INORGANIC QUALITATIVE CHEMICAL ANALYSIS FOR ADVANCED SCHOOLS AND COLLEGES. 8vo. Pages vi+154. 6s. 6d. net.

LEBLANC (Dr. MAX). THE PRODUCTION OF CHROMIUM AND ITS COMPOUNDS BY THE AID OF THE ELECTRIC CURRENT. 8vo. 122 pages. 5s. net.

LIVERPOOL MARINE BIOLOGY COMMITTEE. MEMOIRS ON TYPICAL BRITISH MARINE PLANTS AND ANIMALS. Edited by W. A. Herdman, D.Sc., F.R.S. All demy 8vo, stiff boards.

1. **Ascidia.** By W. A. Herdman. With 5 Plates. Price 2s. net.
2. **Cardium.** By J. Johnstone, Fisheries Assistant, University College, Liverpool. With 7 Plates. Price 2s. 6d. net.
3. **Echinus.** By Herbert Clifton Chadwick, Curator of the Port Erin Biological Station. With 5 Plates. Price 2s. net.
4. **Codium.** By R. J. Harvey Gibson, M.A., F.L.S., Professor of Botany in University College, Liverpool, and Helen P. Auld, B.Sc., With 3 Plates. Price 1s. 6d. net.
5. **Alcyonium.** By Sydney J. Hickson, M.A., D.Sc., F.R.S., Beyer Professor of Zoology in Owens College, Manchester. With 3 Plates. Price 1s. 6d. net.
6. **Lepeophtheirus and Lernea.** By Andrew Scott, Resident Fisheries Assistant at the Peel Hatchery. With 5 Plates. 2s. net.
7. **Lineus.** By R. C. Punnett, B.A., with 4 Plates. 2s. net.
8. **Pleuronectes.** By Frank J. Cole, Jesus College, Oxford, Lecturer in the Victoria University, Demonstrator of Zoology, University, Liverpool, and James Johnstone, B.Sc. Lond., Fisheries Assistant, University, Liverpool. With 11 Plates. 7s. net.
9. **Chondrus.** By Otto V. Darbishire, Owens College, Manchester. With 7 Plates. 2s. 6d. net.
10. **Patella** (the Common Limpet). By J. R. Ainsworth Davis, M.A., Professor of Zoology in the University College of Wales, Aberystwyth, and H. J. Fleure, B.Sc., Fellow of the University of Wales. With 4 Plates. 2s. 6d. net.
11. **Arenicola** (the Lug-Worm). By J. H. Ashworth, D.Sc., Lecturer in Invertebrate Zoology in the University of Edinburgh. With 8 Plates. Price 4s. 6d. net.
12. **Gammarus.** By Margaret Cussans, B.Sc., Zoological Department, University of Liverpool. With 4 Plates. 2s. net.
13. **Anurida.** By A. D. Imms, B.Sc. (Lond.). With 7 Plates. Price 4s. net.
14. **Ligia.** By C. Gordon Hewitt, B.Sc., Demonstrator in Zoology, University of Manchester. With 4 Plates. 2s. net.

LIVERPOOL MARINE BIOLOGY COMMITTEE MEMOIRS—Contd.

    15. **Antedon.** By Herbert Clifton Chadwick. With 7 Plates. 2s. 6d. net.
    16. **Cancer.** By Joseph Pearson, M.Sc., Demonstrator in Zoology, University of Liverpool. With 13 Plates. 6s. 6d. net.
    17. **Pecton.** By W. J. Dakin, M.Sc. With 9 plates. 4s. 6d. net.
    18. **Eledone.** By Annie Isgrove, M.Sc. With 10 plates. 4s. 6d. net.
    19. **Polychael Larvae.** By F. H. Gravely, M.Sc. With 4 plates. 2s. 6d. net.

LONG (J. H.). A TEXT-BOOK OF URINE ANALYSIS. Small 8vo. Pages v+249. 31 Illustrations. 6s. 6d. net.

MACFIE (RONALD C., M.A., M.B.). SCIENCE, MATTER, AND IMMORTALITY. Crown 8vo, cloth. 5s. net.

MARRINER (GEORGE R., F.R.M.S.). THE KEA: A New Zealand Problem. With Illustrations. Demy 8vo, cloth. 7s. 6d. net.

MASON (W. P., Prof. of Chem.). NOTES ON QUALITATIVE ANALYSIS. Sm. 12mo. 56 pp. 3s. 6d. net.

MEADE (RICHARD K., B.Sc.) CHEMIST'S POCKET MANUAL. 16mo. Leather. Pocket Edition. Pages vii+204. Out of Print. 8s. 6d. net.

—— **PORTLAND CEMENT: ITS COMPOSITION, RAW MATERIALS, MANUFACTURE, TESTING, AND ANALYSIS.** Second Edition. With 100 Illustrations. 14s. 6d. net.

MOISSON (HENRI). THE ELECTRIC FURNACE. 8vo. Pages x+305. 41 Illustrations. 10s. 6d. net.

NISSENSON. THE ARRANGEMENTS OF ELECTROLYTIC LABORATORIES. 8vo. 81 pages. 52 Illustrations. 5s. net

NOYES (ARTHUR A., Ph.D.) ORGANIC CHEMISTRY FOR THE LABORATORY. Small 12mo. Pages xii+257. 22 Illustrations. 6s. 6d. net.

—— **and MULLIKEN (SAMUEL P., Ph.D.). LABORATORY EXPERIMENTS ON CLASS REACTIONS AND IDENTIFICATION OF ORGANIC SUBSTANCES.** 8vo. 81 pp. 2s. net.

OTTO (RUDOLF). NATURALISM AND RELIGION. See Crown Theological Library, p. 11.

PFANHAUSER (Dr. W.). PRODUCTION OF METALLIC OBJECTS ELECTROLYTICALLY. 5s. net.

PHILLIPS (FRANCIS C.). METHODS FOR THE ANALYSIS OF ORES, PIG IRON AND STEEL. Second Edition. 8vo. Pages viii + 170. 3 Illustrations. 4s. 6d. net.

PIDDINGTON (HENRY). THE SAILORS' HORN-BOOK FOR THE LAW OF STORMS. Being a Practical Exposition of the Theory of the Law of Storms, and its uses to Mariners of all Classes in all Parts of the World. Shown by transparent Storm Cards and useful Lessons. 7th Ed. Demy 8vo, cloth. 10s. 6d.

PRAY (Dr.). ASTIGMATIC LETTERS. Printed on Millboard, size 22 by 14 inches. 1s.

PROCEEDINGS OF THE OPTICAL CONVENTION, No. 1, 1905. Crown 4to, cloth. 10s. net.

RANSOM (W. H., M.D., F.R.S., F.R.C.P.). THE INFLAMMATION IDEA IN GENERAL PATHOLOGY. Demy 8vo, cloth. 7s. 6d.

RAY (Prof. P. C.). A HISTORY OF HINDU CHEMISTRY FROM THE EARLIEST TIMES TO THE MIDDLE OF THE SIXTEENTH CENTURY A.D. With Sanskrit Texts, Variants, Translation, and Illustrations. Vol. I. Second Edition, Revised and Enlarged. Crown 8vo. 10s. 6d. net. Vol. II. Cloth. 10s. 6d. net.

SANG'S LOGARITHMS. A new Table of Seven-place Logarithms of all Numbers continuously up to 200,000. 2nd Edition. Royal 8vo, cloth. 21s.

SCHREBER (D. G. M.). MEDICAL INDOOR GYMNASTICS, or a System of Hygienic Exercises for Home Use, to be practised anywhere, without apparatus or assistance, by young and old of either sex, for the preservation of health and general activity. Revised and Supplemented by Rudolf Graefe, M.D. With a large plate and 45 illustrations in the text. Royal 8vo, cloth. 3s. net.

"The exercises described, when efficiently used, will undoubtedly be of value in strengthening and developing the muscular system. The descriptions of the exercises and the figures in the text are excellent."—*Physician and Surgeon.*
"Well worthy of the attention of those who go in for regular physical training as a means for the preservation of health."—*Scotsman.*
"A very sensible little treatise."—*Glasgow Herald.*

SCHROEN (L.). SEVEN-FIGURE LOGARITHMS OF NUMBERS from 1 to 108,000, and of Sines, Cosines, Tangents, Cotangents to every 10 Seconds of the Quadrant. With a Table of Proportional Parts. By Dr. Ludwig Schroen, Director of the Observatory of Jena, etc., etc. 5th Edition, corrected and stereotyped. With a description of the Tables by A. De Morgan, Professor of Mathematics in University College, London. Imp. 8vo, cloth, printed on light green paper. 9s.

---

14 Henrietta Street, Covent Garden, London, W.C.

CATALOGUE OF PUBLICATIONS. 49

SEGER. COLLECTED WRITINGS OF HERMAN AUGUST SEGER. (Papers on Manufacture of Pottery.) 2 vols. Large 8vo. £3, 3s. net per set; per volume, 31s. 6d. net.

SNELLEN'S OPHTHALMIC TEST TYPES. Best Types for the Determination of the Acuteness of Vision. 14th Edition, considerably augmented and improved. 8vo, sewed. 4s. Single Sheets: E T B, M O V, B D E, ш ш ш, and Large Clock Sheet. 8d. each. Small Clock Sheet and R T V Z. 4d. each.

SNYDER (HARRY, B.Sc.). SOILS AND FERTILISERS. Second Edition. 8vo. Pages x + 294. 1 Plate. 40 Illustrations. 6s. 6d. net.

SONNTAG (C. O.). A POCKET FLORA OF EDINBURGH AND THE SURROUNDING DISTRICT. A Collection and full Description of all Phanerogamic and the principal Cryptogamic Plants, classified after the Natural System, with an artificial Key and a Glossary of Botanical Terms. By the late C. O. Sonntag, the Royal High School, Edinburgh; formerly Secretary of the Microscopical Society of Glasgow, etc. Fcap. 8vo, limp cloth, round corners, with Map of the Environs of Edinburgh. 3s. 6d. net.

STILLMAN (THOS. B., M.Sc., Ph.D.). ENGINEERING CHEMISTRY. Third Edition. 8vo. Pages x + 597. 139 Illustrations. 19s. net.

TOWER (O. F., Ph.D.). THE CONDUCTIVITY OF LIQUIDS. 8vo. Pages iv + 190. 20 Illustrations. 6s. 6d. net.

TRANSACTIONS OF THE ROYAL SOCIETY OF EDINBURGH. Vol. XXXVIII. Part 1, 40s. Part 2, 25s. Part 3, 30s. Part 4, 7s. 6d. Vol. XXXIX. Part 1, 30s. Part 2, 19s. Part 3, 43s. Part 4, 9s. Vol. XL. Part 1, 25s. Part 2, 32s. 6d. Part 3, 26s. Part 4, 20s. Vol. XLI. Part 1, 20s. Part 2, 29s. 6d. Part 3, 45s. Vol. XLII. 42s. Vol. XLIII. 42s. Vol. XLV. Part 1, 29s. Part 2, 27s. Part 3, 33s. 9d. Part 4, 4s. 6d. Vol. XLVI. Part 1, 21s. 10d. Part 2, 25s. 8d. Part 3, 27s. 3d. General Index to First Thirty-four Volumes (1783-1888), with History of the Institution. 4to, cloth. 21s.

TRANSACTIONS OF THE ROYAL IRISH ACADEMY, DUBLIN. Vols. I.-XX. 4to. £22, 5s. 6d. Vols. XXI.-XXXI. Various prices.

TRANSACTIONS OF THE ROYAL DUBLIN SOCIETY. Various volumes at various prices.

---

14 Henrietta Street, Covent Garden, London, W.C.

VEGA. LOGARITHMIC TABLES OF NUMBERS AND TRIGONOMETRICAL FUNCTIONS. Translated from the 40th, or Dr. Bremiker's Edition, thoroughly revised and enlarged, by W. L. F. Fischer, M.A., F.R.S., Fellow of Clare College, Cambridge; Professor of Natural Philosophy in the University of St. Andrews. 75th Stereotyped Edition. Royal 8vo, cloth. 7s.

VENABLE (T. C., Ph.D.). THE DEVELOPMENT OF THE PERIODIC LAW. Small 12mo. Pages viii + 321. Illustrated. 10s. 6d. net.

—— **THE STUDY OF THE ATOM.** 12mo. Pages vi + 290. 8s. 6d. net.

—— and HOWE. **INORGANIC CHEMISTRY ACCORDING TO THE PERIODIC LAW.** Second Edition. *See under* Howe, p. 45.

WILEY (HARVEY W., A.M., Ph.D.). PRINCIPLES AND PRACTICE OF AGRICULTURAL CHEMICAL ANALYSIS. 3 vols. 8vo. New Edition in preparation. Vol. I. Soils. Ready. 18s. net. Vol. II. Fertilizers.

WYSOR (HENRY, B.S., Assistant Professor of Analytical Chemistry, Lafayette College). METALLURGY. A Condensed Treatise. Demy 8vo, cloth. 12s. 6d. net.

14 Henrietta Street, Covent Garden, London, W.C.

VI. Miscellaneous.

ANTHROPOLOGY—SOCIOLOGY—MYTHOLOGY—BIBLIOGRAPHY—BIOGRAPHY, ETC.

AVEBURY (Lord, D.C.L., F.R.S., etc.) (Sir John Lubbock). PREHISTORIC TIMES, as Illustrated by Ancient Remains and the Manners and Customs of Modern Savages. 6th Edition, revised, with 239 Illustrations, a large number of which are specially prepared for this Edition. Demy 8vo, cloth, gilt tops. 18s.

"To anyone who wishes to obtain a succinct conspectus of the present state of knowledge on the subject of early man, we recommend the perusal of this comprehensive volume."—*Jour. Brit. Archæolog. Assoc.*

"The fact that this well-known standard work has reached a sixth edition is evidence of its value to ethnologists and archæologists. The many and beautiful illustrations are most helpful in better understanding the plain but accurate letterpress. Lord Avebury is to be congratulated on the new edition, which is sure to further popularise a fascinating subject for investigation by cultured people."—*Science Gossip.*

"It is necessary to compare the present volume with the fifth edition in order to see how much it has been improved. The illustrations to this sixth edition are immeasurably superior to the fifth."—*Knowledge.*

BLACKBURN (HELEN). WOMEN'S SUFFRAGE. A Record of the Women's Suffrage Movement in the British Isles, with a Biographical Sketch of Miss Becker. Portraits. Crown 8vo, cloth. 6s.

—— *See also* Vynne, Nora, and Blackburn, "Women under the Factory Acts."

CATALOGUE OF THE LONDON LIBRARY, St James's Square. By C. T. Hagberg Wright, LL.D., etc. xiv + 1626 pp. 4to, cloth. 42s. net. Supplement I., 1902-3. Buckram, 1 vol., 196 pp. 5s. net. Supplement II. 198 pp. 1903-4. Buckram. 5s. net. Supplement IV. 1905-6. 5s. net.

"The present catalogue is essentially a working catalogue. . . . The general level of accuracy in the printing and editing of the work appears to us to be an unusually high one. . . . We heartily applaud the work, both as a landmark in library land, and as a monument standing upon a firm foundation of its own."—*The Times.*

14 Henrietta Street, Covent Garden, London, W.C.

ENGELHARDT (C.). DENMARK IN THE EARLY IRON AGE. Illustrated by recent Discoveries in the Peat-Mosses of Slesvig. 33 Plates (giving representations of upwards of a thousand objects), Maps, and numerous other Illustrations on wood. 1866. 4to, cloth. 31s. 6d.

GOLDAMMER (H.). THE KINDERGARTEN. A Guide to Fröbel's Method of Education. 2 vols. in 1. 120 pp. of Illustrations. 8vo, cloth. 10s. 6d.

GRIEBEN'S ENGLISH GUIDES. Practical and handy; size, suitable for the pocket, $6\frac{1}{4} \times 4\frac{1}{4}$, and bound in cloth.

    Switzerland. A practical guide with seven maps. Cloth. 3s. net. Ready.

    Norway and Copenhagen. With six maps. Cloth. 3s. net. Ready.

    Ostend and other Belgium Watering Places. With two maps. Cloth. 1s. 6d. net. Ready.

    Lakes of Northern Italy. With maps. Cloth. 3s. net. Ready.

    The Rhine. With maps. Cloth. 3s. net. In the press.

    North Sea Watering Places. Cloth. 3s. net. In the press.

    Belgium. With maps. Cloth. 3s. net. In the press.

    Brussels and the Universal Exhibition 1910. With maps. Cloth. 1s. 6d. net. In the press.

    Holland. With maps. Cloth. 3s. net. In the press.

    The Riviera. With maps. Cloth. 3s. net. In the press.

    Dresden and Environs. With maps. Cloth. 1s. 6d. net. In the press.

HENRY (JAMES). ÆNEIDEA; or, Critical, Exegetical and Æsthetical Remarks on the Æneis. With a personal collation of all the first-class MSS., and upwards of 100 second-class MSS., and all the principal editions. Vol. I. (3 Parts), Vol. II. (3 Parts), Vol. III. (3 Parts), Vol. IV. (1 Part). Royal 8vo, sewed. £2, 2s. net.

HERBERT (Hon. A.). THE SACRIFICE OF EDUCATION TO EXAMINATION. Letters from "All Sorts and Conditions of Men." Edited by Auberon Herbert. Half-cloth boards. 2s.

—— **and WAGER (HAROLD). BAD AIR AND BAD HEALTH.** Dedicated to Professor Clifford Allbutt. Reprinted from the "Contemporary Review." 8vo, cloth, 1s. 6d.; sewed, 1s.

CATALOGUE OF PUBLICATIONS. 53

JOHNSON (E.). THE RISE OF ENGLISH CULTURE. With a brief account of the Author's Life and Writings. Demy 8vo, cloth. 15s. net.

KIEPERT'S NEW ATLAS ANTIQUUS. Twelve Maps of the Ancient World, for Schools and Colleges. Third hundred thousand. 12th Edition, with a complete Geographical Index. Folio, boards. 6s. Strongly bound in cloth. 7s. 6d.

—— **WALL-MAPS OF THE ANCIENT WORLD—**

Wall-map of Ancient Italy. Italia antiqua. For the study of Livy, Sallust, Cicero, Dionysius, etc. Scale 1 : 800,000. Mounted on rollers, varnished. 20s.

General Wall-map of the Old World. Tabula orbis terrarum antiqui ad illustrandam potissimum antiquissimi ævi usque ad Alexandrum M. historiam. For the study of ancient history, especially the history of the Oriental peoples : the Indians, Medes, Persians, Babylonians, Assyrians, Egyptians, Phœnicians, etc. Scale 1 : 5,400,000. Mounted on rollers, varnished, 20s.

General Wall-map of the Roman Empire. Imperii Romani tabula geographica. For the study of the development of the Roman Empire. Scale 1 : 300,000. Mounted on rollers, varnished. 24s.

Wall-map of Ancient Latium. Latii Veteris et finitimarum regionum tabula. For the study of Livy, Dionysius, etc. Scale 1 : 125,000. With supplement: Environs of Rome. Scale 1 : 25,000. Mounted on rollers, varnished. 18s.

Wall-map of Ancient Greece. Græciæ Antiquæ tabula. For the study of Herodotus, Thucydides, Xenophon, Strabo, Cornelius Nepos, etc. Scale 1 : 500,000. Mounted on rollers, varnished. 24s.

Wall-Map of the Empires of the Persians and of Alexander the Great. Imperia Persarum et Macedonum. For the study of Herodotus, Xenophon, Justinian, Arian, Curtius. Scale 1 : 300,000. Mounted on rollers and varnished. 20s.

Wall-Map of Gaul, with portions of Ancient Britain and Ancient Germany. Galliæ Cisalpinæ et Transalpinæ cum partibus Britanniæ et Germaniæ tabula. For the study of Cæsar, Justinian, Livy, Tacitus, etc. Scale 1 : 1,000,000. Mounted on rollers and varnished. 24s.

Wall-Map of Ancient Asia Minor. Asiæ Minoris Antiquæ Tabula. For the study of Herodotus, Xenophon, Justinian, Arian, Curtius, etc. Scale 1 : 800,000. Mounted on rollers and varnished. 20s.

---

14 Henrietta Street, Covent Garden, London, W.C.

WILLIAMS & NORGATE'S

LONDON LIBRARY SUBJECT INDEX. To be issued about the end of November. A quarto volume of about 1200 pages in three columns, bound in buckram. 31s. 6d. net.

Opinions of some of those who have read through the proof-sheets:

". . . My admiration for the Index increases daily. . . ."—Professor BURY, Regius Professor of Modern History, Cambridge.

". . . I feel certain that this Index will become a standard book of reference, and will be a *vade mecum* to every man of letters. . . ."—FREDERIC HARRISON.

". . . This Index will have a signal educational value. There never was a piece of work better worth doing, or, I think, better done. . . ."—Dr WARD, Master of Peterhouse, Cambridge.

". . . As far as I have seen the proof-sheets I am satisfied that the new Subject Index will be one of the best Catalogues of the kind ever produced. . . ."—H. R. TEDDER.

". . . The specimen page is exceedingly neat. A good Catalogue is one of the few human works that can do no harm. . . ."—Sir FREDERICK POLLOCK, Bart.

". . . I am more than surprised at its accuracy and fulness. . . ."—Sir FRANK MARZIALS, C.B.

MARCKS (ERICH, Professor of Modern History at the University of Leipzig). **ENGLAND AND GERMANY: Their Relations in the Great Crises of European History, 1500-1900.** Demy 8vo, stiff wrapper. 1s.

PEDDIE (R. A.). PRINTING AT BRESCIA IN THE FIFTEENTH CENTURY. A List of the Issues. 5s. net.

RING OF POPE XYSTUS, THE. A Collection of Aphorisms and Short Sayings in use among the Christian Communities as early as the Second Century of our Era. There is no question but that it was widely read, for Latin, Syriac, and Coptic versions are known besides in the original Greek. The original Greek was discovered at the end of last century, and is now translated into English for the first time. Beautifully printed on hand-made paper, and bound suitable for presentation.

SCHLOSS (DAVID F.). METHODS OF INDUSTRIAL REMUNERATION. 3rd Edition, revised and enlarged. Crown 8vo, cloth. 7s. 6d. Popular Edition, 3s. 6d.

"In its new as in its old form the book is well nigh indispensable to the student who desires to get some insight into the actual facts about the various methods of industrial remuneration, and the degree of success with which they have been applied in the various trades."—*Manchester Guardian.*
"More useful than ever to the students of the labour problem."—*Political Science Quarterly.*

SPENCER (HERBERT). AN AUTOBIOGRAPHY. See p. 30.

14 Henrietta Street, Covent Garden, London, W.C.

CATALOGUE OF PUBLICATIONS. 55

SPENCER (HERBERT). PRINCIPLES OF SOCIOLOGY. See p. 30.

—— **STUDY OF SOCIOLOGY.** See p. 31.

—— **DESCRIPTIVE SOCIOLOGY.** See p. 31.

STEPHENS (GEORGE). PROFESSOR BUGGE'S STUDIES ON NORTHERN MYTHOLOGY EXAMINED. Illustrations. 8vo, cloth. 8s.

—— **THE RUNES, WHENCE CAME THEY?** 4to, sewed. 6s.

—— **OLD NORTHERN RUNIC MONUMENTS.** Vol. IV. Folio. 20s. net.

VEILED FIGURE (THE), and Other Poems. Large post 8vo, buckram, gilt, cover designed by Mr. T. Blake Wirgman. 2s. 6d.

VYNNE (NORA) and HELEN BLACKBURN, and with the Assistance of H. W. ALLASON. WOMEN UNDER THE FACTORY ACTS. Part 1. Position of the Employer. Part 2. Position of the Employed. Crown 8vo, cloth. 1s. net.

WELD (A. G.). GLIMPSES OF TENNYSON AND OF SOME OF HIS FRIENDS. With an Appendix by the late Bertram Tennyson. Illustrated with Portraits in photogravure and colour, and with a facsimile of a MS. poem. Fcap. 8vo, art linen. 4s. 6d. net.

"This is a delightful little book, written by one who has all the qualifications for the task—the opportunities of observation, the interest of relationship, and the sympathetic and appreciative temper. . . . We do not attempt to criticise, but only to give such a description as will send our readers to it."—*Spectator*.

"Everyone who reads the book will understand Tennyson a little better, and many will view him in a new aspect for the first time."—*Daily Chronicle*.

"It is quite worthy of a place side by side with the larger 'Life.'"—*Glasgow Herald*.

14 Henrietta Street, Covent Garden, London, W.C.

LIST OF PERIODICALS, REVIEWS, AND TRANSACTIONS AND PROCEEDINGS OF LEARNED SOCIETIES

PUBLISHED BY WILLIAMS & NORGATE.

THE HIBBERT JOURNAL: A Quarterly Review of Religion, Theology, and Philosophy. Single numbers, 2s. 6d. net. Subscription, 10s. per annum, post free.

JOURNAL OF THE FEDERATED MALAY STATES MUSEUMS. Issued quarterly. Single numbers, 1s. 6d. net. Subscription, 5s. per annum.

JOURNAL OF THE ROYAL MICROSCOPICAL SOCIETY, containing its Transactions and Proceedings, with other Microscopical Information. Bi-monthly. 6s. net. Yearly subscriptions, 37s. 6d., post free.

JOURNAL OF THE QUEKETT MICROSCOPICAL CLUB. Issued half-yearly, April and November. Price 3s. 6d. net. 7s. 6d. per annum, post free.

LINNEAN SOCIETY OF LONDON. Journal of Botany and Journal of Zoology. Published irregularly at various prices. Also Transactions, published irregularly.

ROYAL SOCIETY OF EDINBURGH. Transactions. Issued irregularly at various prices.

LIVERPOOL MARINE BIOLOGY COMMITTEE. Memoirs. I.–XIX. already published at various prices. Fauna of Liverpool Bay. Fifth Report written by Members of the Committee and other Naturalists. Cloth. 8s. 6d. net. *See* p. 47.

ROYAL ASTRONOMICAL SOCIETY. Memoirs and Monthly Notices. Yearly volumes at various prices.

ROYAL IRISH ACADEMY. Transactions and Proceedings issued irregularly; prices vary. Cunningham Memoirs. Vols. I.–XI. already issued at various prices. *Vide* pp. 43–44.

ROYAL DUBLIN SOCIETY. Transactions and Proceedings. Issued irregularly at various prices.

14 Henrietta Street, Covent Garden, London, W.C.

INDEX UNDER AUTHORS & TITLES

Abhidhanaratnamala. Aufrecht, 33.
Acland, Sir C. T. D. Anglican Liberalism, 12.
Acts of the Apostles. Adolf Harnack, 12.
Addis, W. E. Hebrew Religion, 11.
Æneidea. James Henry, 52.
Agricultural Chemical Analysis. Wiley, 50.
Alcyonium. *Vide* L.M.B.C. Memoirs, 46.
Allin, Rev. Thos. Universalism Asserted, 14.
Alton, E. H. Romans, 32.
Alviella, Count Goblet D'. Contemporary Evolution of Religious Thought, 14.
Alviella, Count Goblet D'. Idea of God, 13.
Americans, The. Hugo Münsterberg, 29.
Analysis of Ores. F. C. Phillips, 48.
Analysis of Theology. E. G. Figg 17.
Ancient Assyria, Religion of. Sayce, 14.
Ancient Egyptians, 32.
Ancient World, Wall Maps of the, 53.
Anglican Liberalism, 12.
Annotated Texts. Goethe, 39.
Antedon. *Vide* L.M.B.C. Memoirs, 46.
Anthems. Rev. R. Crompton Jones, 20.
Antiqua Mater. Edwin Johnson, 20.
Anurida. *Vide* L.M.B.C. Memoirs, 46.
Apocalypse. Bleek, 7.
Apocalypse of St John, 37.
Apologetic of the New Test. E. F. Scott, 12.
Apostle Paul, the, Lectures on. Pfleiderer, 13.
Apostolic Age, The. Carl von Weizsäcker, 6.
Arabian Poetry, Ancient, 34.
Arenicola. *Vide* L.M.B.C. Memoirs, 46.
Argument of Adaptation. Rev. G. Henslow, 18.
Aristotelian Society, Proceedings of, 29.
Army Series of French and German Novels, 38.
Ascidia. Johnstone, L.M.B.C. Memoirs, 46.
Ashworth, J. H. Arenicola, 46.
Assyrian Dictionary. Norris, 35.
Assyrian Language, A Concise Dictionary of. W. Muss-Arnolt, 35.
Assyriology, Essay on. George Evans, 34.
Astigmatic Letters. Dr. Pray, 48.
Athanasius of Alexandria, Canons of, 37.
Atlas Antiquus, Kiepert's, 53.
Atonement, Doctrine of the. Sabatier, 10.
At-one-ment, The. Rev. G. Henslow, 18.
Aufrecht, Dr. T. Abhidhanaratnamala, 33.
Auf Verlornem Posten. Dewall, 38.
Autobiography. Herbert Spencer, 30.
Avebury, Lord. Prehistoric Times, 51.
Avesti, Pahlavi. Persian Studies, 33.

Babel and Bible. Friedrich Delitzsch, 9.
Bacon, Roger, The "Opus Majus" of, 28.
Bad Air and Bad Health. Herbert and Wager, 56.
Ball, Sir Robert S. Cunningham Memoir, 45.
Bases of Religious Belief. C. B. Upton, 14, 26.
Bastian, H. C. Studies in Heterogenesis, 43.
Baur. Church History, 7; Paul, 7.
Bayldon, Rev. G. Icelandic Grammar, 38.
Beard, Rev. Dr. C. Universal Christ, 15; Reformation of the Sixteenth Century, 13.
Beeby, Rev. C. E. Doctrine and Principles, 15.
Beet, Prof. J. A. Child and Religion, 10.
Beginnings of Christianity. Paul Wernle, 4.

Beliefs about the Bible. M. J. Savage, 24.
Benedict, F. E. Organic Analysis, 43.
Bergey, D. G. Practical Hygiene, 43.
Bernstein and Kirsch. Syriac Chrestomathy, 33.
Bevan, Rev. J. O. Genesis and Evolution of the Individual Soul, 15.
Bible. Translated by Samuel Sharpe, 15.
Bible, Beliefs about, Savage, 24; Bible Plants, Henslow, 18; Bible Problems, Prof. T. K. Cheyne, 9; How to Teach the, Rev. A. F. Mitchell, 22; Remnants of Later Syriac Versions of, 37.
Biblical Hebrew, Introduction to. Rev. Jas. Kennedy, 20, 34.
Biltz, Henry. Methods of Determining Molecular Weights, 43.
Biology, Principles of. Herbert Spencer, 30.
Blackburn, Helen. Women's Suffrage, 51.
Bleek. Apocalypse, 7.
Boielle, Jas. French Composition, 39; Hugo, Les Misérables, 39; Notre Dame, 39.
Bolton. History of the Thermometer, 43.
Book of Prayer. Crompton Jones, 20.
Books of the New Testament. Von Soden, 10.
Bousset, Wilhelm. Jesus, 10.
Bremond, Henri. Mystery of Newman, 15.
Brewster, H. B. The Prison, 28; The Statuette and the Background, 28; Anarchy and Law, 28.
British Fisheries. J. Johnstone, 45.
Bruce, Alex. Topographical Atlas of the Spinal Cord, 43.
Buddha. Prof. H. Oldenberg, 35.
Burkitt, Prof. F. C. Anglican Liberalism, 12.

Calculus, Differential and Integral. Harnack, 44.
Caldecott, Dr. A. Anglican Liberalism, 12.
Campbell, Rev. Canon Colin. First Three Gospels in Greek, 15.
Campbell, Rev. R. J. New Theology Sermons, 15.
Cancer. *Vide* L.M.B.C. Memoirs, 46.
Cancer and other Tumours. Chas. Creighton, 43.
Canonical Books of the Old Testament, 3.
Cape Dutch. J. F. Van Oordt, 41.
Cape Dutch, Werner's Elementary Lessons in, 42.
Cardium. *Vide* L.M.B.C. Memoirs, 46.
Carlyle, Rev. A. J. Anglican Liberalism, 12.
Casey, John. Cunningham Memoirs, 43.
Catalogue of the London Library, 51.
Celtic Heathendom. Prof. J. Rhys, 14.
Celtic Studies. Sullivan, 41.
Centenary History of South Place Society. Moncure D. Conway, 16.
Chadwick, Antedon, 47; Echinus, 46.
Chaldee Language, Manual of. Turpie, 37.
Channing's Complete Works, 15.
Chants and Anthems, 20; Chants, Psalms and Canticles. Crompton Jones, 20.
Character of the Fourth Gospel. Rev. John James Tayler, 25.
Chemical Dynamics, Studies in. J. H. Van't Hoff, 45.

INDEX—Continued.

Hill, Rev. Dr. G. Child and Religion, 10.
Hindu Chemistry. Prof. P. C. Ray, 48.
Hirsch, Dr. S. A., and W. Aldis Wright, edited by. Commentary on Job, 27.
History of the Church. Hans von Schubert, 3.
History of Dogma. Adolf Harnack, 4.
History of Jesus of Nazara. Keim, 7.
History of the Hebrews. R. Kittel, 5.
History of the Literature of the O.T. Kautzsch, 20.
History of the New Test. Times. Hausrath, 7.
Hodgson, S. H. Philosophy and Experience, 28; Reorganisation of Philosophy, 28.
Hoerning, Dr. R. The Karaite MSS., 19.
Höfer, E. Erzählungen, 38.
Hoff, J. H. Van't. Chemical Dynamics, 45.
Hornell, J. Marine Zoology of Okhamandal, 45.
Horner, G. Statutes, The, of the Apostles, 36.
Horse, Life-Size Models of. J. T. Share Jones, 45; the, Surgical Anatomy of, 45.
Horton, Dr. R. Child and Religion, 10.
Howe, J. L. Inorganic Chemistry, 45.
How to Teach the Bible. Mitchell, 22.
Hugo, Victor. Les Misérables, 39; Notre Dame, 39.
Hunter, Dr. John. De Profundis Clamavi, 20; The Coming Church, 20.
Hygiene, Handbook of. Bergey, 43.
Hymns of Duty and Faith. Jones, 20.

Icelandic Grammar. Rev. G. Bayldon, 38.
Idea of God. Alviella, Count Goblet D', 13.
Imms, A. D. Anurida, 26.
Incarnate Purpose, The. Percival, 22.
Indian Buddhism. Rhys Davids, 13.
Individual Soul, Genesis and Evolution of. Bevan, 15.
Individualism and Collectivism. Dr. C. W. Saleeby, 29.
Indoor Gymnastics, Medical, 48.
Industrial Remuneration, Methods of. D. F. Schloss, 54.
Infinitesimals and Limits. Hardy, 44.
Inflammation Idea. W. H. Ransom, 48.
Influence of Rome on Christianity. Renan, 13.
Inorganic Chemistry. J. L. Howe, 45.
Inorganic Qualitative Chemical Analysis. Leavenworth, 46.
Introduction to the Greek New Test. Nestle, 6.
Introduction to the Old Test. Cornill, 3.
Introduction to the Preparation of Organic Compounds. Fischer, 44.
Isaiah, Hebrew Text, 34.

Jeremias, Prof. A. Old Testament in the Light of the East, 2.
Jesus of Nazara. Keim, 7.
Jesus or Christ? The Hibbert Journal Supplement for 1909, 19.
Jesus. Wilhelm Bousset, 10.
Jesus, Sayings of. Harnack, 12.
Job, Book of. G. H. Bateson Wright, 27.
Job, Book of. Rabbinic Commentary on, 37.
Job. Hebrew Text, 34.

Johnson, Edwin, M.A. Antiqua Mater, 20; English Culture, 20; Rise of Christendom, 20.
Johnstone, J. British Fisheries, 45.
Jones, Prof. Henry. Child and Religion, 10.
Jones, Rev. J. C. Child and Religion, 10.
Jones, Rev. R. Crompton. Hymns of Duty and Faith, 20; Chants, Psalms and Canticles, 20; Anthems, 20; The Chants and Anthems, 20; A Book of Prayer, 20.
Jones, J. T. Share. Life-Size Models of the Horse, 45; Surgical Anatomy of the Horse, 45.
Jones. The Freezing Point, 45.
Jordan, H. R. Blaise Pascal, 28.
Journal of the Federated Malay States, 56.
Journal of the Linnean Society. Botany and Zoology, 45, 56.
Journal of the Quekett Microscopical Club, 45, 56.
Journal of the Royal Microscopical Society, 45, 56.
Justice. Herbert Spencer, 31.

Kantian Ethics. J. G. Schurman, 29.
Karaite MSS. Dr. R. Hoerning, 19.
Kautzsch, E. History of the Literature of the Old Testament, 20.
Kea, the. G. R. Marriner, 47.
Keim. History of Jesus of Nazara, 7.
Kennedy, Rev. Jas. Introduction to Biblical Hebrew, 34; Hebrew Synonyms, 34.
Kiepert's New Atlas Antiquus, 53.
Kiepert's Wall-Maps of the Ancient World, 53.
Kindergarten, The. H. Goldammer, 52.
Kittel, R. History of the Hebrews, 5.
Knight, edited by. Essays on Spinoza, 32.
Knowledge, Evolution of. Perrin, 22.
Kuenen, Dr. A. National Religions and Universal Religion, 13; Religion of Israel, 8.
Kyriakides, A. Modern Greek-English Dictionary, 39.

Laboratory Experiments. Noyes and Mulliken, 47.
Ladd, Prof. G. T. Child and Religion, 10.
Lake, Kirsopp. Resurrection, 11.
Landolt, Hans. Optical Rotating Power, 46.
Laurie, Prof. Simon. Ethics, 29; Metaphysica Nova et Vetusta, 29.
Lea, Henry Chas. Sacerdotal Celibacy, 21.
Leabhar Breac, 40.
Leabbar Na H-Uidhri, 40.
Leavenworth, Prof. W. S. Inorganic Qualitative Chemical Analysis, 46.
Leblanc, Dr. Max. The Production of Chromium, 46.
Le Coup de Pistolet. Merimée, 38.
Lepeophtheirus and Lernea. Vide L.M.B.C. Memoirs, 46.
Letter to the "Preussische Jahrbucher." Adolf Harnack, 18.
Lettsom, W. N., trans. by. Nibelungenlied, 40.
Liberal Christianity. Jean Réville, 9.
Life and Matter. Sir O. Lodge, 21.
Life of the Spirit, The. Eucken, 12.

INDEX—Continued.

Lilja. Edited by E. Magnusson, 40.
Lilley, Rev. A. L. Anglican Liberalism, 12.
Lineus. *Vide* L.M.B.C. Memoirs, 46.
Linnean Society of London, Journals of, 56.
Liverpool Marine Biology Committee Memoirs, I.—XIX., 46, 47.
Lobstein, Paul. Virgin Birth of Christ, 9.
Lodge, Sir O. Life and Matter, 21; School Teaching and School Reform, 40.
Logarithmic Tables. Sang, 48; Schroen, 48.
London Library, Catalogue of, 51.
London Library Subject Index, 54.
Long, J. H. A Text-book of Urine Analysis, 47.
Luke the Physician. Adolf Harnack, 11.
Lyall, C. J., M.A. Ancient Arabian Poetry, 34.

Macan, R. W. The Resurrection of Jesus Christ, 21.
MacColl, Hugh. Man's Origin, Destiny, and Duty, 29.
Macfie, R. C. Science, Matter, and Immortality, 21.
Machberoth Ithiel. Thos. Chenery, 35.
Mackay, R. W. Rise and Progress of Christianity, 21.
Magnusson, edited by. Lilja, 40.
Mahabharata, Index to. S. Sorensen, 36.
Mahaffy, J. P., D.D. Flinders Petrie Papyri. Cunningham Memoirs, 44; Hellenic Studies, 32.
Man and the Bible. J. A. Picton, 23.
Man's Origin, Destiny, and Duty. MacColl, 29.
Man *versus* the State. Herbert Spencer, 31.
Maori, Lessons in. Right Rev. W. L. Williams, 42.
Maori, New and Complete Manual of, 40.
Marchant, James. Theories of the Resurrection, 21.
Marcks, Erich. England and Germany, 54.
Marine Zoology of Okhamandal, 45.
Markham, Sir Clements, K.C.B. Vocabularies of the Incas of Peru, 40.
Marriner, G. R. The Kea, 47.
Martineau, Rev. Dr. James. Modern Materialism, 21; Relation between Ethics and Religion, 21.
Mason, Prof. W. P. Notes on Qualitative Analysis, 47.
Massoretic Text. Rev. Dr. J. Taylor, 26.
Masterman, C. F. G. Child and Religion, 10.
Meade, R. K., Portland Cement, 47.
Mediæval Thought, History of. R. Lane Poole, 23.
Ménégoz, E. Religion and Theology, 21.
Mercer, Right Rev. J. Edward, D.D. Soul of Progress, 21.
Merimée, Prosper. Le Coup de Pistolet, 38.
Metallic Objects, Production of. Dr. W. Pfanhauser, 47.
Metallurgy. Wysor, 50.
Metaphysica Nova et Vetusta. Prof. Simon Laurie, 29.

Midrash, Christianity in. Herford, 19.
Milanda Panho, The. Edited by V. Trenckner, 35.
Mission and Expansion of Christianity. Adolf Harnack, 3.
Mitchell, Rev. A. F. How to Teach the Bible, 22.
Mitchell, Rev. C. W. Refutation of Mani, Marcion, etc., 37.
Modern Greek - English Dictionary. Kyriakides, 39.
Modernity and the Churches. Percy Gardner, 12.
Modern Materialism. Rev. Dr. James Martineau, 21.
Moisson, Henri. Electric Furnace, 47.
Molecular Weights, Methods of Determining. Henry Biltz, 43.
Monasticism. Adolf Harnack, 12.
Montefiore, C. G. Religion of the Ancient Hebrews, 13.
Moorhouse Lectures. *Vide* Mercer's Soul of Progress, 21; Stephen, Democracy and Character, 25.
Morrison, Dr. W. D. Anglican Liberalism, 12.
Mosheh ben Shesheth. S. R. Driver. Edited by, 22.
Moslem Present. Faizullah-Bhai, Shaikh, B.D., 34.
Münsterberg, Hugo. The Americans, 22.
Muss-Arnolt, W. A Concise Dictionary of the Assyrian Language, 35.
My Struggle for Light. R. Wimmer, 9.
Mystery of Newman. Henri Bremond, 15.

National Idealism and State Church, 16; and the Book of Common Prayer, 16.
National Religions and Universal Religion. Dr. A. Kuenen, 13.
Native Religions of Mexico and Peru. Dr. A. Réville, 14.
Naturalism and Religion. Dr. Rudolf Otto, 22.
Nautical Terms. L. Delbos, 39.
Naville, Prof. E. The Old Egyptian Faith, 12.
Nestle. Introduction to the Greek New Test., 6.
New Hebrew School of Poets. Edited by H. Brody and K. Albrecht, 35.
New Theology Sermons. Rev. R. J. Campbell, 15.
New Zealand Language, Dictionary of. Rt. Rev. W. L. Williams, 42.
Nibelungenlied. Trans. W. L. Lettsom, 40.
Nissenson. Arrangements of Electrolytic Laboratories, 50.
Nöldeke, Theodor. Delectus Veterum, 35; Syriac Grammar, 35.
Norris, E. Assyrian Dictionary, 35.
Noyes, A. A. Organic Chemistry, 47.
Noyes, A. A., and Milliken, Samuel. Laboratory Experiments, 47.

O'Grady, Standish, H. Silva Gadelica, 41.
Old and New Certainty of the Gospel. Alex. Robinson, 24.

INDEX—Continued.

Oldenberg, Dr. H., edited by. Dipavamsa, The, 33; Vinaya Pitakam, 37.
Old French, Introduction to. F. F. Roget, 41.
Old Testament in the Light of the East. Jeremias, 2.
Oordt, J. F. Van, B.A. Cape Dutch, 41.
Ophthalmic Test Types. Snellen's, 49.
Optical Rotating Power. Hans Landolt, 46.
"Opus Majus" of Roger Bacon, 28.
Organic Chemistry. A. A. Noyes, 47.
Otto, Rudolf. Naturalism and Religion, 11.
Outlines of Church History. Von Schubert, 3.
Outlines of Psychology. Wilhelm Wundt, 32.

Pali, Handbook of. Dr. O. Frankfürter, 34.
Pali Miscellany. V. Trenckner, 35.
Parker, W. K., F.R.S. Morphology of the Duck Tribe and the Auk Tribe, 44.
Pascal, Blaise. H. R. Jordan, 28.
Patella. *Vide* L.M.B.C. Memoirs, 46.
Paul. Baur, 7; Pfleiderer, 13; Weinel, 3.
Paulinism. Pfleiderer, 8.
Pearson, Joseph. Cancer, 47.
Pecton. *Vide* L.M.B.C. Memoirs, 47.
Peddie, R. A. Printing at Brescia, 54.
Percival, G. H. The Incarnate Purpose, 22.
Perrin, R. S. Evolution of Knowledge, 22.
Persian Language, A Grammar of. J. T. Platts, 36.
Peters, Dr. John P. Early Hebrew Story, 9.
Pfanhauser, Dr. W. Production of Metallic Objects, 47.
Pfleiderer, Otto. Early Christian Conception, 10; Lectures on Apostle Paul, 13; Paulinism, 8; Philosophy of Religion, 8; Primitive Christianity, 2.
Phillips, F. C. Analysis of Ores, 48.
Phillipps, V., B.A. Short Sketch of German Literature, 41.
Philo Judæus. Dr. Drummond, 16.
Philosophy and Experience. Hodgson, 28.
Philosophy of Religion. Pfleiderer, 8.
Picton, J. Allanson. Man and the Bible, 23.
Piddington, H. Sailors' Horn Book, 48.
Pikler, Jul. Psychology of the Belief in Objective Existence, 29.
Platts, J. T. A Grammar of the Persian Language, 36.
Pleuronectes. *Vide* L.M.B.C. Memoirs, 46.
Pocket Flora of Edinburgh. C. O. Sonntag, 49.
Polychael Larvae. *Vide* L.M.B.C. Memoirs, 47.
Poole, Reg. Lane. History of Mediæval Thought, 23.
Portland Cement. Meade, 47.
Pray, Dr. Astigmatic Letters, 48.
Prayers for Christian Worship. Sadler, 24.
Prehistoric Times. Lord Avebury, 51.
Pre-Islamitic Arabic Poetry. Shaikh Faizul-lah-Bhai, B.D., 34.
Primitive Christianity. Otto Pfleiderer, 2.
Printing at Brescia. R. A. Peddie, 58.
Prison, The. H. B. Brewster, 28.
Proceedings of the Aristotelian Society, 29.
Proceedings of the Optical Convention, 48.
Prolegomena. Réville, 8.

Protestant Commentary on the New Testament, 8, 23.
Psalms, Hebrew Text, 34.
Psychology of the Belief in Objective Existence. Jul. Pikler, 29.
Psychology, Principles of, Spencer, 30; Outlines of, Wundt, 32.
Punnett, R. C. Lineus, 46.

Qualitative Analysis, Notes on. Prof. W. P. Mason, 47.

Ransom, W. H. The Inflammation Idea, 48.
Rashdall, Dr. Hastings. Anglican Liberalism, 12.
Ray, Prof. P. C. Hindu Chemistry, 48.
Reasons for Dissenting from the Philosophy of M. Comte. Herbert Spencer, 32.
Re-Creation. Rev. C. W. Formby, 17.
Reform in Primary Education. J. G. Hagmann, 39.
Reformation of the Sixteenth Century. Rev. Dr. C. Beard, 15.
Refutation of Mani, Marcion, etc., 37.
Reinforced Concrete in Europe. Colby, 43.
Rejoinder to Prof. Weismann, 31.
Relation between Ethics and Religion. Rev. Dr. James Martineau, 21.
Religion and Modern Culture. Sabatier, 10.
Religion and Theology. E. Ménégoz, 21.
Religion of Ancient Egypt. Renouf, 14.
Religion of the Ancient Hebrews. C. G. Montefiore, 13.
Religion of Israel. Kuenen, 8.
Religions of Ancient Babylonia and Assyria. Prof. A. H. Sayce, 14.
Religions of Authority and the Spirit. Auguste Sabatier, 3.
Renan, E. Influence of Rome on Christianity, 13.
Renouf, P. L. Religion of Ancient Egypt, 14.
Reorganisation of Philosophy. Hodgson, 28.
Resurrection of Jesus Christ. Lake, 21; R. W. Macan, 21; Marchant, 21.
Réville, Dr. A. Native Religions of Mexico and Peru, 14.
Réville. Prolegomena, 8.
Réville, Jean. Liberal Christianity, 9.
Rhys, Prof. J. Celtic Heathendom, 14.
Ring of Pope Xystus, 54.
Rise and Progress of Christianity. R. W. Mackay, 21.
Rise of Christendom. Edwin Johnson, 20.
Rise of English Culture. Edwin Johnson, 20.
Rix, Herbert. Dawning Faith, 24; Tent and Testament, 23.
Robinson, Alex. Old and New Certainty of the Gospel, 24; Study of the Saviour, 24.
Roget, F. F. First Steps in French History, 41; Introduction to Old French, 41.
Romans. Alton and Goligher, 32.
Rosing, S. English-Danish Dictionary, 41.
Royal Astronomical Society. Memoirs and Monthly Notices, 56.
Royal Dublin Society. Transactions and Proceedings, 49.

INDEX—Continued.

Royal Irish Academy. Transactions and Proceedings, 49.
Royal Society of Edinburgh. Transactions of, 49.
Runes, The. Geo. Stephens, 55.
Runic Monuments, Old Northern. Geo. Stephens, 55.
Ruth, Book of, in Hebrew Text. Rev. C. H. H. Wright, 27.

Sabatier, Auguste. Doctrine of the Atonement, 10; Religions of Authority and the Spirit, 3.
Sacerdotal Celibacy. Henry Chas. Lea, 21.
Sacrifice of Education. Hon. A. Herbert, 52.
Sadi. The Gulistan (Rose Garden) of Shaik Sadi of Shiraz, 36.
Sadler, Rev. Dr. Closet Prayers, 24; Prayers for Christian Worship, 24.
Sailors' Horn Book. H. Piddington, 48.
Saleeby, C. W. Individualism and Collectivism, 29.
Sang's Logarithms, 48.
Saunders, T. B. Harnack and his Critics, 24.
Savage, M. J. Beliefs about the Bible, 24.
Sayce, Prof. A. H. Religion of Ancient Assyria, 14.
Sayings of Jesus, The. Adolf Harnack, 12.
Schloss, D. F. Methods of Industrial Remuneration, 54.
School Teaching and School Reform. Sir O. Lodge, 40.
Schrader. The Cuneiform Inscriptions, 24.
Schreber, D. G. M. Medical Indoor Gymnastics, 48.
Schroen, L. Seven-Figure Logarithms, 48.
Schubert, Hans von. History of the Church, 3.
Schurman, J. Gould. Ethical Import of Darwinism, 29; Kantian Ethics, 29.
Science, Matter, and Immortality. R. C. Macfie, 21.
Scott, Andrew. Lepeophtheirus and Lernea, 46.
Scott, E. F. Apologetic of the New Test., 11.
Scripture, Edward W., Ph.D. Studies from the Yale Psychological Laboratory, 30.
Second Year Chemistry. Edward Hart, 44.
Seeberg, R. Fundamental Truths of the Christian Religion, 12.
Seger. Collected Writings, 49.
Seven-Figure Logarithms. L. Schroen, 48.
Severus, Patriarch of Antioch. Letters of, 25.
Sharpe, Samuel. Bible, translated by, 15.
Shearman, A. T. Symbolic Logic, 30.
Shihab Al Din. Futuh Al-Habashah. Ed. by S. Strong, 36.
Short History of the Hebrew Text. T. H. Weir, 26.
Silva Gadelica. Standish H. O'Grady, 41.
Snellen's Ophthalmic Test Types, 49.
Snyder, Harry. Soils and Fertilisers, 49.
Social Gospel, Essays on the, 11.
Social Statics. Herbert Spencer, 31.
Sociology, Principles of. Herbert Spencer, 30.
Sociology, Study of. Herbert Spencer, 31.
Soden, H. von, D.D. Books of the New Testament, 10.

Soils and Fertilisers. Snyder, 49.
Soils. *Vide* Wiley's Agricultural Analysis, 50.
Sonntag, C. O. A Pocket Flora of Edinburgh, 49.
Sörensen, S. Index to the Mahabharata, 36.
Soul of Progress. Bishop Mercer, 21.
Spanish Dictionary, Larger. Velasquez, 41.
Spencer, Herbert. An Autobiography, 30; A System of Synthetic Philosophy, 30; Descriptive Sociology, Nos. 1-8, 31; Works by, 30-32.
Spinal Cord, Topographical Atlas of. Alex. Bruce, M.A., etc., 43.
Spinoza. Edited by Prof. Knight, 32.
Spiritual Teaching of Christ's Life, Henslow, 18.
Statuette, The, and the Background. H. B. Brewster, 28.
Statutes, The, of the Apostles. G. Horner, 25, 36.
Stephen, Canon. Democracy and Character, 25.
Stephens, Geo. Bugge's Studies on Northern Mythology Examined, 55; Old Northern Runic Monuments, 55; The Runes, 55.
Stephens, Thos., B.A., Editor. The Child and Religion, 10.
Stereochemistry, Elements of. Hantzsch, 44.
Stewart, Rev. C. R. S. Anglican Liberalism, 12.
Stillman, T. B. Engineering Chemistry, 49.
Storms. Piddington, 48.
Strong, S. Arthur, ed. by. Shihab Al Din, 36.
Study of the Saviour. Alex. Robinson, 24.
Studies on Northern Mythology. Geo. Stephens, 55.
Studies from the Yale Psychological Laboratory. Edward W. Scripture, Ph.D., 29.
Sullivan, W. K. Celtic Studies, 41.
Surgical Anatomy of the Horse. J. T. Share Jones, 45.
Symbolic Logic. A. T. Shearman, 29.
Synthetic Philosophy, Epitome of. F. H. Collins, 32.
Syriac Chrestomathy. Bernstein and Kirsch, 37.
Syriac Grammar. Theodor Nöldeke, 35.
System of Synthetic Philosophy. Herbert Spencer, 30.

Tayler, Rev. John James. Character of the Fourth Gospel, 25.
Taylor, Rev. C. Dirge of Coheleth, The, 25.
Taylor, Rev. Dr. J. Massoretic Text, 26.
Ten Services and Psalms and Canticles, 26.
Ten Services of Public Prayer, 26.
Tennant, Rev. F. R. Child and Religion, 10.
Tent and Testament. Herbert Rix, 23.
Testament, Old. Canonical Books of, 3; Religions of, 11; Cuneiform Inscriptions, 24; Hebrew Text, Weir, 26; Literature, 20.
Testament, The New, Critical Notes on. C. Tischendorf, 26, 27.
Testament Times, New. Acts of the Apostles, 12; Apologetic of, 11; Books of the, 10; Commentary, Protestant, 8; History of, 7; Luke the Physician, 11; Textual Criticism, 6;
Test Types. Pray, 48; Snellen, 49.
Text and Translation Society, Works by, 37.

CPSIA information can be obtained
at www.ICGtesting.com
Printed in the USA
LVHW041235080622
720787LV00003B/12